Transforming Local Political Leadership

By the same author (Nirmala Rao)

GOVERNING LONDON (*with Ben Pimlott*)

LOCAL GOVERNMENT SINCE 1945 (*with Ken Young*)

THE MAKING AND UNMAKING OF LOCAL SELF GOVERNMENT

REPRESENTATION AND COMMUNITY IN WESTERN DEMOCRACIES (*edited*)

REVIVING LOCAL DEMOCRACY?

TOWARDS WELFARE PLURALISM: Public Services in a Time of Change

Transforming Local Political Leadership

Edited by

Rikke Berg and Nirmala Rao

First published in 2005 by
PALGRAVE MACMILLAN
Houndmills, Basingstoke, Hampshire RG21 6XS and
175 Fifth Avenue, New York, N.Y. 10010
Companies and representatives throughout the world.

PALGRAVE MACMILLAN is the global academic imprint of the Palgrave Macmillan division of St. Martin's Press, LLC and of Palgrave Macmillan Ltd. Macmillan® is a registered trademark in the United States, United Kingdom and other countries. Palgrave is a registered trademark in the European Union and other countries.

ISBN-13: 978–1–4039–9283–3 hardback
ISBN-10: 1–4039–9283–5   hardback

This book is printed on paper suitable for recycling and made from fully managed and sustained forest sources.

A catalogue record for this book is available from the British Library.

Library of Congress Cataloging-in-Publication Data

Transforming local political leadership / edited by Rikke Berg
and Nirmala Rao.
    p. cm.
Includes bibliographical references and index.
ISBN 1–4039–9283–5
    1. Local government—Western countries—Case studies. 2. Political leadership—Western countries. 3. Comparative government—Western countries. I. Berg, Rikke, 1968– II. Rao, Nirmala, 1959–

JS78.T73 2005
320.8′5′091821—dc22   2005051280

10 9 8 7 6 5 4 3 2 1
14 13 12 11 10 09 08 07 06 05

Printed and bound in Great Britain by
Antony Rowe Ltd, Chippenham and Eastbourne

Contents

List of Tables

List of Figures

Acknowledgements

This edited volume originated in a conference on *The Political Executive* held at the University of Odense, Southern Denmark, in the autumn of 2003. The editors would like to thank the Danish Municipal VAT Fund which generously funded the event and the City of Odense which generously hosted part of the conference, attended by a number of Danish practitioners. In particular, we as editors are grateful to Professor Poul Erik Mouritzen, who inspired the conference and gave many valuable comments on the manuscript, to Professor Ken Young who provided advice and support throughout the editorial process beyond all reasonable expectations, helping us to bring it speedily to fruition and to Professor James H. Svara, who gave the book its title. Finally, we would like to thank all our contributors for their co-operation and for responding so patiently to our sometimes intemperate demands.

Rikke Berg
Nirmala Rao

1
Institutional Reforms in Local Government
A Comparative Framework

Rikke Berg and Nirmala Rao

This book addresses key issues in the reform of local government worldwide. What new concerns have given rise to such reforms? What happens when established institutions are transformed? Will reform bring about the desired effects on political leadership and the democratic process, or do unintended consequences follow? Are these effects influenced by local and national political cultures? By finding answers to these questions, we hope to broaden our understanding of local government institutions and political leadership in particular. To date, with the exception of Mouritzen and Svara (2002), there have been few studies of local government institutions in the West. By comparing local government forms and the democratic concerns embedded in them – political leadership, political accountability, the involvement of lay politicians, recruitment and professionalism – this book exposes some of the similarities and differences in institutional impact across 11 selected Western countries.

The primary focus of the book is on formal institutions of local democracy, that is, the 'constitutions' of local governments, and we take our theoretical point of departure to be *constitutional institutionalism*.[1] This approach is one of many branches of the new institutionalism, which developed in political science during the last decade (Hall and Taylor, 1996; Peters, 1999). It defines institutions as formal structures, including rules and regulations reflected in the legislative framework, that provide the frames for the behaviour of individuals operating within these structures. By exploring whether institutions matter and examining the consequences of alternative institution forms, our approach attempts to determine the extent to which political and policy outcomes differ with the formal structures (Wolman, 1995: 135; Peters, 1999).

Although our emphasis is on the formal structures of local governments, we acknowledge that the democratic concerns inherent in these structures may also be influenced by local and national political contexts, including national historical traditions and political cultures, local political heritage and the characteristics of particular municipalities. Change often comes about through the complex interactions of both formal and informal structures (Leach and Lowndes, 2004: 561). Therefore constitutional institutionalism must be complemented by what we term the *sociological institutionalism*.[2] This enables us to analyse institutions in terms of the cultural rules which define meaning and identity for individuals and the patterns of appropriate activities in which individuals engage (March and Olsen, 1989). In this perspective, local government forms set basic guidelines for behaviour within these structures, although these guidelines will be subject to further interpretation by local politicians, professionals and citizens. By approaching the research questions from this broad institutional perspective, both constitutional and sociological, the book assesses the extent to which the transformation of political leadership comes about as an explicit object of local government reform, as an unintended consequence of institutional design or a product of the local and national political context.

Political leadership at the heart of institutional reforms

Political leadership lies at the heart of many of the recent institutional reforms of local government. Since Weber (1971) first formulated the classical model of bureaucracy in the nineteenth century, basing political leadership on legal-rational authority, there has been a general recognition that institutions have formative influence on political leaders (Peters, 1999; Elcock, 2001). In the wake of the new ideals of public management, interest in the relations between institutions and political leadership has, however, increased. In many countries, it is generally held that changes in structures and processes could give political leader(s) in local government a more clear-cut role – a role with specific focus on its strategic and visionary aspects, thus making political leadership key to the transformation of local democracy (Rao, 1993; Stewart, 1993; Leach and Barnett, 1998; Stoker, 1999; Bäck, 2000; Berg, 2000; Larsen, 2002; Montin, 2002).

In assessing the significance of local government form for political leadership, a central question pertains to where power lies: who has it and who decides what (Mouritzen and Svara, 2002: 49)? Much will depend on the specific institutional arrangements, as the formal authority of the political leader will differ from one government form to another, encouraging or restricting different types of leadership behaviour (Stone, 1995: 96). In some systems, political leadership is vested in a single person, such as the mayor. Here the leader can use political power to force through his or her ideas, goals and visions in the council, in the administration and to the citizens (John and Cole, 2000: 88). In other systems, power lies in the hands of a collective, with the mayor and the CEO acting together, or with a political cabinet appointed exclusively from the majority party, or reflecting the proportional strength of the party. Instead of focusing on the personal formal power and impact, the political leader(s) has to gain the support of other actors in order to accumulate influence. This particular form of political leadership, sometimes labelled 'facilitative leadership', will to a much greater extent be oriented towards coordination, communication and cooperation between the central actors of the local government (Svara, 1994: xxviii; Hambleton and Sweeting, 2004: 481).

The functions of political leadership will also vary across different forms of local government. Its fundamental objective is to infuse political life with power and energy and to give direction to the political-administrative system (Mouritzen and Svara, 2002: 52). In practice, however, political leadership also has to fulfil a range of other different functions. These include agenda setting, where the political leader(s) must formulate and promote visions and priorities; implementation, calling for oversight of the production of local services and network building and maintenance, requiring them to generate resources, make compromises and gain the support of the population (Leach and Wilson, 2000). However, the relative importance attached to the three functions will depend on various aspects of the electoral and executive systems.

First, the priorities of the political leader will depend on the form of election. If the leader is directly elected, his or her mandate will be more secure and will reduce the need to make broad compromises within the council. If, on the other hand, the leader is appointed by the council, he or she will be obliged to attend to network building and maintenance. Second, the priorities of the leader will depend on his or her powers vis-à-vis a cabinet. If the leader is able to choose the cabinet members, he or she will be less inclined to give attention to network building and maintenance. Third, the relative importance attached to agenda setting, implementation and networking will depend on the length of the election period; the longer the time frame, the greater the freedom to focus on programme implementation.

A comparative framework for the study of institutional reforms

Political leadership cannot be isolated from other democratic dimensions of local government form. When political leadership is transformed by institutional change, other aspects of local democracy are likely to be altered too. It is our proposition that this interrelationship is particularly apposite to political accountability, to the involvement of laymen politicians, to political recruitment and to professionalism. They are inherent features of any local government system. Together with political leadership, these four aspects form the basis of the comparative framework adopted in this book.

Political accountability

The ability of citizens to call policymakers to account – and of policymakers to hold bureaucrats to account – are standard premises of democratic government. The greater the accumulation of power, the greater the need to establish accountability (March and Olsen, 1995: 152). It follows, then, that altering local political leadership by increasing or reducing the formal powers of the political leader(s) will have implications for political accountability. While accountability is a universal tenet of democratic theory, there is little agreement as to how it should be achieved (March and Olsen, 1995: 162; Roberts, 2002: 658). Most theories of accountability emphasise mechanisms for providing information and communication and for imposing sanctions (March and Olsen, 1995; Sims and Vrooman, 1998: 52–3; Roberts, 2002: 658 ff.). Information and communication are vital to accountability between elections. An open and transparent policy process will promote responsiveness to citizen preferences, as citizens will be able to monitor and control results and express their opinions to their elected representatives (Beetham, 1996: 43). Regular, open and competitive elections, a free press and public meetings can all be regarded as important preconditions for accountability. So too can the capacity of voters to exert direct influence on their representatives between elections, as the politician, who will be held to account in some future contest has an incentive to respond to demands in order to secure re-election (Eulau and Prewitt, 1973: 446; Heywood, 2004: 226). A clear location of political leadership will send a clear signal to the voters as to whom to hold responsible when things go wrong.

Accountability in local government can be improved through changes to institutional arrangements. Such changes pertain not just to the electoral arrangements, but also to the internal decision-making process including new mechanisms for citizens' participation and scrutiny. The introduction of directly elected mayors provides one example of how citizens' influence on political leadership might be advanced by institutional means, while the introduction of public meetings and open agendas is yet others.

The involvement of lay politicians

Most theories of representative democracy involve elected laymen in both the representation of citizens and in the decision-making process. For the purposes of this discussion, we reserve the term 'laymen politicians' for those in non-leadership positions. The lay politician acts as the connecting link between the citizens and the municipal administration. However, the extent and type of their involvement will depend on the design of the local government institutions in a number of ways.

First, rules of election determine the size of the council. Some local government forms, emphasise a broad representation of various interests in the council and, consequently, the number of council members is relatively high. In other local government forms, this aspect of representation is downplayed in favour of other aspects, such as professionalism; here, the number of council members is likely to be small. Second, the political organisation of the executive functions will influence the kinds of decisions and functions in which laymen are involved. If the executive functions are located within political leadership, the responsibilities of the lay politicians will often be limited to broad steering and control. Instead if executive functions are divided among various committees, the tasks of the lay politicians will range from steering to administration, and may include a wide range of tasks, such as policy formulation, physical planning, decisions on budget, preparation of council business, decision-making within a sector specific area adjudication on individual cases and so on. Reforms of formal processes and tasks will thus be likely to affect both political leadership and involvement of laymen politicians.

Recruitment

Clearly, many of the changes to formal institutions, such as the rules of election, the structures of power and the nature of the political tasks to be undertaken can both restrain and encourage individual candidates to run for election and, consequently, affect the actual composition of the councils (Young, 2000: 195).

The recruitment of local politicians may be directly affected by the rules of election (Prewitt, 1981). The direct election of mayors may, for instance, attract a particular type of political leader at the expense of other candidates who would be more attracted by indirect election. Likewise, the duration of the election cycle may have an indirect impact on the pattern of representation, as the period of tenure may bear upon potential candidates' motivation to run for election, while the arrangements for selecting the candidates may influence the recruitment of politicians. At the selection meeting, the parties themselves may bring their influence to bear on the composition of the party list in respect of gender, age or geographic affiliation (Kjær, 2000: 131). This process may prove daunting, and deter some others candidates from seeking elective office. Another example of the influence of formal structures on the selection of candidates is the rules specifying who is allowed to run for election. In some countries, municipal employees are not allowed to contest elections, whereas in others there are no restrictions on potential candidates.

The arrangements for the election of political leaders and councils are not the only matters affecting recruitment to local office (Przeworski *et al.*, 1999: 19). The scope and the content of the political tasks they are called upon to undertake may also be of importance for potential candidates to the political leadership. Whether holding office is a full-time or a part-time commitment may, for instance, influence the gender distribution in the political leadership (Goldsmith, 2000: 15; Young, 2000: 194).

Professionalism

A fourth – and last – democratic feature inherent in local government forms is the role of professional bureaucrats that comprises both the ability to analyse and make strategies for the future development of the municipality, and the ability to utilise resources efficiently and provide stability for day-to-day administration. The organisation of the executive, patterns of political leadership and the electoral system have an impact upon the administrators' autonomy, their interaction with the elected officials and the style of decision-making. In particular, the organisation of the executive has direct consequences for the degree of independence accorded to the professionals. Where some local government forms explicitly emphasise professionalism by assigning executive decisions to the administrative organisation, others do not attribute any special competence to it. In the latter case, the professionals' autonomy will depend on the informal day-to-day delegation of decisions from the political leaders to the professionals. The control of the administration will tend to be stronger if the executive decisions are located with a well-defined political leader, such as a mayor or a cabinet, rather than shared among several political organs, such as standing committees (Jacobsen, 1997: 97).

The form of the local government system may also have indirect consequences for the professionals. This can be seen from the type of electoral arrangements in operation. First, if the council is elected on the basis of proportionality, there may be pressures to form alliances and make political compromises. Compromises tend to produce vague political decisions, leaving an extensive degree of interpretation to the professionals, and increasing administrative autonomy (Jacobsen, 1997: 95). If all the seats are distributed by the principle of majority and local government is stable for an electoral cycle, political decisions will tend to be clearer and more detailed and the autonomy of the administration is reduced (Jacobsen, 1997: 95; Mouritzen and Svara, 2002: 207–8).

Further, the rules concerning the election of the political leader may also influence the autonomy accorded to the professionals, as the incentive to take political control is partly a function of the mandate given to the political leader. If the political leader is directly elected, he will be more inclined to exercise a strong political control in order to achieve the visible results that might increase his chances of re-election. A political leader who is appointed from within the council, rather than directly elected, may, on the contrary be less inclined to limit the autonomy of the professionals, as his re-election will be less dependent on personal support from the voters (Kammerer, 1964: 426).

Up to this point, our discussion has followed the conventional distinction between (elected) politicians – both leaders and laymen – and (appointed) professional staff. However, as will become clear in the following chapters, the emergence of strong local executives has blurred this distinction, for the phenomenon of the full-time executive leader amounts to nothing less than the professionalisation of politics. In terms of the actual pattern of decision-making, the professionalism of appointed officials and the professionalisation of political leaders create an area of overlapping responsibility in which their actual influence becomes difficult to discern.

A web of democratic concerns

These four aspects of local democracy are obviously interdependent. First, the role attributed to lay politicians has direct implications for political accountability. In those local government forms where the political and executive functions are clearly separated, one of the most important functions of the lay politicians is to control the implementation of the decisions of the council. An example of this might be a committee appointed to control and scrutinise the political leadership of the local authority. Such a committee has the competence to organise hearings, collect information and carry out analyses in order to enhance control by the laymen and, by these means, improve the ability of the citizens to hold the political leaders accountable for their policies (Leach and Copus, 2004: 334–5). In other systems, the lack of institutional arrangements to support laymen politicians can inhibit them from fulfilling this role and consequently restrict the citizens' ability to hold the political leaders to account (Montondon, 1995: 66–7).

The involvement of lay politicians also relates to the dimension of political recruitment, for representation may be broader based if the lay politicians are only involved in a limited number of tasks that are not too time-consuming (Rao, 2003: 10). The content of those tasks may also bear upon the recruitment of laymen politicians, with some systems attracting candidates who seek to influence the decision-making process and others candidates who are more interested in solving citizens' problems (Goldsmith, 2000: 18–19). Empowering professional politicians equally bears upon the process of political recruitment, as increasing their autonomy inescapably weakens the position of the lay politician, reducing the incentives that drive recruitment to these first rungs of elective office.

Finally, the professionalisation of politics and political accountability are interrelated too. Those reforms that increase the autonomy of professional politicians may also affect political accountability, as representatives need to be held accountable both at election time and between elections. And when institutional changes relocate executive decisions at the administrative level, they will impede the responsiveness of the elected officials, cutting them off from implementation and preventing them from responding quickly to the day-to-day concerns of their constituents.

One way of understanding these five democratic dimensions is to regard them as a web within which their mutual influences can be observed (Figure 1.1). Whenever one of the dimensions is transformed by the institutional reform of local government, the others are likely to be transformed too. If we regard political leadership as the central core of this web, the interactions between the changing conditions of leadership and the other four dimensions will be readily understood.

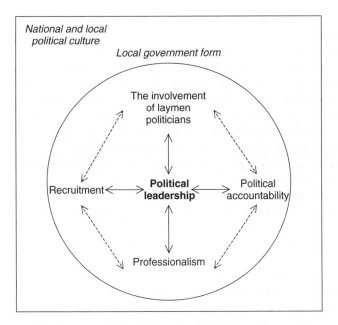

Figure 1.1 The structure and the context of local government forms.

Comparing local government forms

In order to assess the significance of different local institutional arrangements, it is necessary to examine the complex relations between actors within a particular local government form and the local and national context in which it is embedded. Approached in this way, comparative case studies can provide rich contextual insight. The national case studies of this volume, deal with these common issues, yet from different perspectives. Some of them draw on case studies of particular municipalities within the nation under consideration, others on national survey data. The book draws upon experiences from 11 countries. Not all are undergoing transformation of their political leadership structures; some are making adaptations to well-established systems. Among those that have introduced radical change are the Netherlands, Germany and Britain. In the case of these countries, there have been moves away from 'parliamentary' to more presidential models of government, or towards the concentration of powers in smaller executives. In other countries, structural changes have been restricted to some few municipalities, typically the largest cities. Among these are Norway, Spain and Denmark, although in Denmark the reversion has not been towards executive dominance but rather towards a more diffuse decision-making system. Finally, some of the systems under consideration have been relatively immune to this international trend towards institutional reforms: Switzerland, Sweden, the United States, France and Belgium, although in the case of the last, there is an ongoing intense debate on the proposals to introduce directly elected mayor. The chapters presented in this book are organised to reflect these three broad groupings.

Within the first group, Netherlands has called for proposals to strengthen the democratic accountability of local government. Denters and colleagues' contribution to the reform of the political executive in Dutch local government describes the background of the 2002 reforms and shows how these changes have altered the traditional model of governance, bringing about a separation between the legislature and executive through a reallocation of power from the council to the Council of Mayor and Aldermen.

Wollman traces the development of Germany's strong mayoral system before going on to assess its significance. Between 1945 and 1990, German local government was remarkable for maintaining a great variety of arrangements in the different Länder, reflecting both pre-Nazi traditions and the influence of the occupying powers. In the early 1990s, however, German local government was transformed. In the East, the Länder opted for direct election of mayors as the most visible expression of democratic empowerment and as a tribute to the norms of peaceful revolution. In the West, the directly elected mayoral form hitherto practiced only in the southern Länder was adopted on grounds of its apparent superiority in terms of governability and effectiveness. This became the uniform model across the newly reunified nation.

The replacement of the traditional committee-based system in Britain has important implications for political accountability and the representative process. Rao shows the prevalence of the cabinet system under the local government legislation of 2000. She considers the limited extent to which localities opted for the directly elected mayor and assesses the problems and prospects of the cabinet system. She locates this resistance to change in the light of the deep-rooted traditions of backbench political activism.

Among the second group of countries which have restricted the reforms to a limited number of municipalities is Norway. In 1986, the capital, Oslo, reformed its executive structures to introduce a ministerial model of decision-making, a move that represented a significant break with two dominant traditions of local government organisation in Norway: the alderman model of political governance and the directorate model of administrative organisation. The alderman system failed to provide adequate lines of accountability, while the lack of a clearly defined head of administration under the directorate model rendered it impossible to hold individuals to account. A cabinet system of decision-making was seen as the answer to the first, while the introduction of a city manager model was to provide a solution to the second. Baldersheim charts the process of reform in the city of Oslo and explores the tensions in bringing about political and managerial co-ordination.

Political practice in Spain has been such that the dominance of local party structure and its independence from the national parties have given the mayor a presidential profile. However, the recent reforms to modernising local government aim to break with this presidential trend and propose, in the case of large cities, for a strong executive body to take on most of the management functions from the mayor. In their chapter on Spanish municipal presidentialism and democratic consolidation, Ferran and Horta analyse the organisation of the political executive, distinguishing the form of government of 'common regime' municipalities from the institutional organisation of large cities.

The resistance to executive dominance led three of the largest municipalities in Denmark to move in the opposite direction, reverting to the more collective forms of decision-making embodied in the committee system. Berg illustrates this trend through a case study of Copenhagen, Aalborg and Odense, and assesses the implications for accountability and the roles of non-executive councillors. Such a reversal is not without its problems and Berg asks just how easy it is to hold the elected representatives to account, a problem that is compounded when a single party has political control.

Among those countries which have been largely unaffected by international moves for reform is Switzerland. The distinctive feature of the Swiss political executive is their multiparty composition and the extent to which the lay public are engaged in decision-making. Ladner examines the constraints on executives emerging from a lack of legislative backing and illuminates the ways in which power sharing between lay politicians, the public and professional bureaucrats work to deliver effective political changes.

Local government in Sweden has long been characterised by the involvement of elected politicians at all levels of decision from policy-making to implementation. In this, the cadre of full-time politicians work closely with the appointed officials on a day-to-day basis, while the unsalaried politicians generally relate to more junior officers. Montin traces the developments leading to the recent changes, which include the provision for extensive delegation to committees, select committees, individual representatives or officials, and a striking reduction in the number of elected representatives from 70,000 in 1980 to 44,500 in 1999. One effect of this reduction has been the concentration of power in a smaller number of leading councillors, a development that has produced a reaction among unsalaried elected representatives.

Svara reviews the structures and processes of US urban governance, focusing on the relations between appointed and elected officials in mayor-council and council manager systems. City size as well as formal arrangements bears upon the ways in which issues of leadership, accountability and the political control of the bureaucracy operate. Regardless of the system, the performance of political and administrative functions in US cities is complementary, with interdependence and mutual influence exercised within a broad framework of shared values. The challenges facing US cities are promoting change in these configurations, with an increasingly professionalised body of managers facing greater activism and assertiveness on the part of elected officials.

Local government in France is characterised by two distinctive features. The first is the wish to maintain local governments, most of which are very small and the second is the persistence and popularity of the French mayor. Kerrouche shows the mayor to be the cornerstone of French territorial administration, being both the focal point of the local representative process and the embodiment of the State. Mayors have become more active and entrepreneurial since the decentralisation of 1992, as development of the French municipalities became the key issue in French local politics. During this period, mayors have become significantly younger. Further reforms in 1999 have promoted widespread co-operation and joint action between municipalities in which some mayors have risen to new prominence, with formal powers derived from the larger community of municipalities. Kerrouche shows that the corollary of the role of the super mayors has been a further reduction in the role of the citizen, raising issues about the health of local democracy in France.

Belgium followed 2001 proposals for greater devolution to the regions, with the Federal government retaining control of key services, such as police and fire brigade. Ackaert's chapter shows how the latest reforms, without proposing any fundamental changes to the roles of the existing mayors, their duties and competences, are aimed at strengthening the mayoral role through greater transparency in the selection of mayors and board members, and enhancing voter turnout.

With the specific aim to examine the complex interaction between the local government forms and the local and national context, Stone examines the contrasting cities of Atlanta, Hampton, Boston and New Haven. He makes the point that US city government depends crucially on complex networks of formal and informal relationships to mobilise resources. The mayor is an important player, but works alongside issue-specific networks of other public and voluntary organisations. Thus, it is the promotion of civic co-operation, rather than the exercise of executive authority, on which the effectiveness of city policies depends.

Following these national studies, Larsen examines the international trend in the emergence of directly elected mayors and identifies the common institutional, social and political factors driving this change process worldwide. Larsen's *tour d'horizon* of local government reforms, in a range of countries including England, Germany and Italy, locates the problem in low electoral participation and the need for a more visible, accountable and transparent decision-making systems. The specific study of Norway – the first Nordic country to introduce experiments on directly elected mayors in 1999 – that is characterised by the professionalisation of the mayoral position, sheds light on the likely future developments in the growth of the new political executives elsewhere in the United States and Europe.

Overall, two important conclusions could be drawn from the various case studies presented in this volume: first that the significance of local government form is not always direct, intended and uniform, and second, that specific forms of local government cannot maximise all the important concerns of local democracy at the same time. Rather, each local government form carries certain risks and opportunities which need to be taken into consideration when designing and reforming local democracy. The debate on local government institutions must surely acknowledge this point if the risks and opportunities are to be appropriately weighed and balanced to achieve, as nearly as possible, the preferred outcomes of a local democratic system.

Notes

1. There are a variety of different approaches to the study of constitutional institutions (see for instance Weaver and Rockman (1993) and Lijphart (1994)). Guy Peters summarises many of these approaches by the collected term: 'Empirical Institutionalism' (Peters, 1999). However, as we find this term too general and somehow misleading, we have for want of a better term chosen 'Constitutional Institutionalism'.

2. Sociological institutionalism has been labelled differently by different scholars. DiMaggio and Powell label the approach: 'New Institutionalisms' (DiMaggio and Powell, 1991: 1), and Peters (1999) label the approach 'Normative Institutionalism'. However, we have chosen the label of Hall and Taylor (1996) in order to make clear that this particular approach has its roots within the sociological branch of organisation theory.

2

The Reform of the Political Executive in Dutch Local Government

Bas Denters, Pieter-Jan Klok and Henk van der Kolk

Following the Local Government Act of 1851 in the Netherlands, the legislative and executive primacy in the local political arena rested with the municipal council, an elected body that represented the local citizenship. In 2002, however, the then newly elected municipal councils were confronted with a radically revised legal setting. This paper assesses the implications of the 2002 reform for the role of the political executive in Dutch local government.

In addressing this question, the AID-framework developed by Elinor Ostrom *et al.*, is used to describe the changes in the positions of various relevant actors in the local political process (Ostrom *et al.*, 1994). The discussion begins with a description of the traditional model of Dutch municipal government (pre-2002) and the problems that arose within it in terms of the involvement of laymen and professionals in local administration; co-ordination; political accountability; political leadership and political recruitment. It then gives an account of the new model of Dutch municipal government (post-2002) and considers the implications of the recent reforms.

The pre-2002 institutional structure

All Dutch municipalities have the same basic structure. The most relevant positions are those of enfranchised citizen, council-member, alderman, mayor and local civil servant. All EU citizens over 18 and all non-EU living for at least 5 years in a municipality are eligible to vote. Every four years, council-members are elected. The number of councillors increases with the population size of the municipality. The allocation of seats on the council to the political parties is determined by a system of proportional representation. Prior to 2002, aldermen were elected by the council from among its members. This method of selection implied that under the traditional model all aldermen were indirectly elected by the local citizenry (since only members of the directly elected council were eligible as aldermen). Moreover, after their election, the aldermen retained their membership and voting rights in the municipal council. The aldermen were conceived of as representatives of the council in a special council committee (the Board of Mayor and Aldermen, or BMA) that was given the responsibility for executing the council's decisions. Rather than as two separate bodies, council and board were seen as parts of one organic whole. The number of aldermen should not be higher than 20 per cent of the number of council-members. Like all decisions taken by the council, the allocation of aldermanic seats was determined by majority vote, although most boards were based on a grand coalition in which all the major parties on the council were represented in proportion to their size.

The mayor is appointed by central government. Since the 1970s, central government has sought the advice of the council while deciding upon mayoral appointments. In about 70 per cent of the cases central government heeds local advice. Both the selection of the Mayor by the central government and, his or her chairmanship of the council, are based on constitutional articles, which makes any significant change in the position of the mayor a rather cumbersome endeavour. Finally, civil servants are a special class of local position holders. Most civil servants are (formally) appointed by the BMA. Before 2002, the most notable exception to this rule was the 'municipal secretary' – the local Chief-Executive-Officer (CEO) – who was the highest-ranking local civil servant and the most senior assistant of the BMA. In the pre-2002 era, the council appointed this functionary.

The tasks and powers of specific actors are mainly determined by the context in which they are executed. In Dutch local government we can distinguish between at least five different contexts or 'arenas'. An arena is defined as an institutionally defined space where a set of actors interact in making a particular set of political decisions, and in this instance they include: the board of Mayor and Aldermen, the politico-administrative arena, party group meetings, committee meetings and the council (Denters *et al.*, 2000; Denters and Klok, 2003a). Each of these five arenas can be described by the positions or actors which are in membership ('boundary rules'), the precise tasks set for this specific arena ('scope rules'), the distribution of powers of each actor within the arena ('authority rules'), the rules used to aggregate the preferences of the members of the arena ('aggregation rules') and the rules describing the flow of information to and from the arena and its members ('information rules').

The first arena to be distinguished is the board of mayor and aldermen. This body has the power to deal with the daily routines of local government, the preparation and execution of council decisions, and the organisation of local administration. This means that the board's scope rules are rather broad. Nevertheless, in a formal sense, both in terms of legislation and in terms of executive responsibilities the primacy in local government ultimately resides with the directly elected council. This ultimate sovereignty in both legislative and executive affairs was one of the major dogmas of the traditional model of municipal government.

Another traditional dogma is the doctrine of collegiality of decision-making in the BMA. The principle of collegiality is a legal doctrine that implies that all decisions of the BMA require the consent of a majority of the board. The decisions of the BMA are to be made in secret meetings of this body. From a legal perspective, the members of the board are collectively responsible for decisions of the BMA; aldermen therefore do not have individual responsibilities. The position and the responsibilities of the mayor are somewhat special. On the one hand, the mayor is a member of the BMA and also subject to the collegiality doctrine, although as the chairman of the BMA he has some special prerogatives (e.g. having a casting vote in the BMA). On the other hand, under Dutch law, the mayor also has some specific individual responsibilities. These individual responsibilities – which do not fall under the operation of the collegiality principle, and for which the mayor is individually accountable to the council, pertain to his or her chairmanship of the municipal council and for his or her responsibility for matters of public safety and the command of the police, the fire brigade and other security forces in the case of fires, disasters and turmoil.

The legal doctrine of collegiality, however, should not obscure the 'departmentalisation' of local administration. In actual fact within the board, especially in the medium-size and large municipalities, individual aldermen are more or less 'autonomous' rulers in a specific policy domain, for which they bear primary responsibility and for which they are held to account by the council. This departmentalisation is supported by a rather strong social norm of non-interference amongst the members of the board. Because of this norm of non-interference, the preparation and execution of policy-decisions is mainly done in a second arena consisting of an alderman with his or her administrative staff. The informal rule of departmentalisation implies that it is this second arena where policy proposals are prepared and where major decisions regarding the implementation of policies are made (scope rules).

Before policy proposals prepared by the board are publicly discussed in plenary council meetings, specialised council committees prepare the public debate. Before 2002, the boundary rules of these specialised committees stated that both the alderman (or mayor) responsible for the policy field at hand and some (specialised) council-members of different parties were members of this committee. The scope of this committee was to discuss policy proposals and prepare recommendations for plenary council meeting (scope rule). As no final decisions were taken, there was no voting in committees. Still, normally it was rather easy to infer the political fate of proposals in the plenary debate based on the prevailing mood of the committee spokesmen from the major party groups in the council. Within the committee, a strong position was given to the alderman. He or she chaired the meeting and as such, he/she was also responsible for the committee agenda.

Since Dutch local democracy is essentially a party democracy, councillors try to co-ordinate their activities in the meetings of their party group. These party group meetings constitute another important local set of political arenas. In the pre-2002 era, it was customary for both councillors and aldermen to attend such meetings. In a legal sense, the scope of these meetings is undefined and largely left to the discretion of the party groups. In the period before the reforms, aldermen typically played a key role in the party group meeting. As member of the board, they were typically well informed about policy issues and could rely on the expertise of their officers. Moreover, in political terms an alderman was also a figurehead if not the leader of his political party. The conclusions of the discussions in these party groups were normally considered as binding upon the party members' voting behaviour in the plenary council meeting ('scope rule').

The fifth and final arena is the council meeting itself. Before 2002, the boundary rules specified that all council-members (including the aldermen) and the mayor were members of the council. The scope of the council meetings was to decide on all policy proposals, and since the council was seen as the head of the administration, its scope was only restricted by national legislation. Within the council, the mayor played an important role because he chaired the meetings and, strongly influenced the agenda of the council. The mayor and aldermen dominated the council meeting. They were the experts, supported by a large contingent of specialised officers. They were the political leaders of the council's majority coalition, and the aldermen also had full voting rights in the council. Finally, the information rights of the council under the traditional model were not well developed, partly because the model was based on the notion that the council and the BMA were not two separate branches of government, but rather two parts of an organic whole.

The main characteristic of the pre-2002 institutional structure of Dutch municipalities was the legislative and executive primacy of the council. The role of the board was merely derivative. In constitutional theory, aldermen are primarily normal members of the council, who on behalf of the council bear the responsibility of preparing this body's decisions and taking care of the implementation of its decisions. This model is based on a concentration of the executive and legislative powers in one body, the council.

Problems of the traditional structure

After 1851 the basic system of local government remained largely unchanged. This institutional stability is remarkable in the light of the social and economic changes that completely reshaped the Dutch municipal landscape in the past 150 years (Denters, 2000). Against this background, the call for a modernisation of local government became ever louder.

The increasing scale of municipalities is one of the most significant changes in Dutch local government. This development was the combined result of an increasing population and a decreasing number of municipalities. The Dutch population grew from somewhat more than 3 million in 1851 to around 16 million in 2002. In the same period, the number of municipalities was reduced from more than 1200 to less than 500. As a consequence of both developments, the average population size of municipalities increased from around 2500 in 1851, to more than 32,000 in 2002. This change in the size of municipalities was accompanied and partly legitimised by the increasing local government responsibilities. In 1851, the main tasks of local government were related to the direct living environment: infrastructure, safety and public hygiene. Industrialisation, population growth and the urgent social problems induced councils to experiment with new policy initiatives in such areas as education, health care and public housing. At a later stage of the development of the Dutch welfare state, many of these local initiatives provided the basis for national policies implemented by central government. But even these central policies were often characterised by local involvement in policy implementation. As such, Dutch local government, as in most other Northern- and Middle-European countries, gained responsibility for a large share of personal, client-oriented welfare state functions (Hesse and Sharpe, 1991: 607).

At the end of the twentieth century the number of municipal tasks was extensive. But the rise of the welfare state also implied considerable restrictions on municipal autonomy. In many areas local government's role is restricted to the implementation of national programmes, even though local government at times enjoys considerable discretion in setting concrete goals and in choosing appropriate means. For many years national government delegated the local responsibility for the implementation of such programmes to the board rather than to the council, thereby eroding the primacy of the council in executive matters. This state of affairs was also reflected in the structure of local revenues. Up to 1929, local taxes were the main source of local revenue. This, however, implied a strong burden on relatively poor municipalities. Therefore, in 1929 the national government restricted the municipal privileges to raise taxes and started financing municipalities using nationally raised taxes, at the same time constraining the opportunity to spend the money in the way the council deemed necessary. Due to these developments, there was an increasing mismatch between the formally dominant role of the municipal council in both legislative and executive matters and its actual role in day-to-day local politics.

The ever-broader range of municipal responsibilities, the increasing size of local government organisations and the growing complexity of policy interventions in an increasingly complex society, made the prime role in the policy process of amateur part-time councillors both in policy development and in policy implementation largely illusory. This was further accentuated by the national government's inclination to bypass the council in favour of the BMA when delegating responsibility for the implementation of national policies to local government. Such trends were observed as early as 1910 – even before the big changes in the scale of local government and the expansion of the welfare state – but these developments did not lead to major institutional reforms in that period (Staatscommissie, 2000).

In addition to such changes within municipal government, recent years have also witnessed important changes in the political behaviour among the public. Most people were politically inactive until the early 1960s (Lijphart, 1979; Daalder, 1995 [1964]). Since then improved communication and education generated the rise of more critical citizens, who were prepared to challenge under-performance of the political system, and particularly the core institutions of representative democracy (Klingemann and Fuchs, 1995; Norris, 1999: 269). The growth of critical citizens 'fuelled pressure for major institutional reforms designed to strengthen representative and direct democracy' (Norris, 1999: 270).

Partly due to these institutional and societal changes, local government was seen as an institution having problems. As a result of changes in its scale and responsibilities, the overwhelming trend in the last century was the professionalisation of municipal government. The most spectacular illustration of this is the enormous growth of the local civil service. Between 1899 and 1986 the number of local civil servants rose almost tenfold from 24,700 to 237,300 (Van der Meer and Roborgh, 1993: 77). After that year, cutbacks and privatisations led to a reduction of these numbers. In 1999 the number of civil servants at the local level was 175,000 (BZK, 2002). This growth was associated with a substantial increase in the size of municipal bureaucracies. At the beginning of the twentieth century the average municipality employed about 22 officers. One century later (in 1999), the mean size of the local bureaucracy had gone up to 325 employees.

Bureaucratisation was matched at the political level by a decreasing involvement of part-time 'amateur' lay politicians in local administration. The BMAs in an ever-larger number of municipalities came to be composed of only full-time aldermen. Initially, in both large- and small municipalities, aldermen had been part-time officials and mere aids to the only genuine full-time local 'political' official, the mayor. In the small municipalities aldermen were still part-timers, combining this public office with other pursuits. Since 1994, however, all municipalities with more than 18,000 inhabitants have been able to employ full-time aldermen. The average workload of a contemporary alderman was 47 hours per week according to a recent survey (Bakker *et al.*, 2000: 45), indicating that in most cases aldermen devoted a full working week to their public duties. The professionalisation at the bureaucratic and board level also put pressure on the traditional notion of the council as an assembly of amateur-politicians, who made up a cross-section of local society. The increasing responsibilities of local government and the growing complexity of public policymaking made the job of a councillor much more demanding both in time needed and the skills. In 2000 the average councillor spent 13.8 hours per week on his public duties. In large municipalities this workload will be typically much heavier.

Against this background, it is clear that the political control of the local bureaucracy heavily depended on the relations between the professional politicians in the BMA and the local civil service. This relation tended to differ between large- and small municipalities. In the small municipalities where the mayor was still the only full-time 'political' official the relation between the political executive and the bureaucracy depended upon the personal abilities of the mayor. In medium-size and large municipalities the typical pattern was one in which an alderman, together with the officers in 'his' sector of the local bureaucracy, dominated political decision-making (Derksen, 1985: 90; Berveling, 1994: 290).

The advance of semi-professionalism in the councils tended to erode the political accountability of the councillors to their constituents. In terms of political recruitment, semi-professionalism made it increasingly difficult to combine the role of a councillor with a full-time job. This resulted in a situation where councillors, in terms of background characteristics like gender, education and employment status are far from a cross-section of local society: highly educated males in their forties and fifties, working in the public sector were typical (Denters and Van der Kolk, 1998: 224). At the same time, the continuous, voluminous stream of policy documents, statutes, reports, white papers and other types of information that councillors receive from the local bureaucracy absorbed most of their time, resulting in a rather inward-looking reactive orientation of councillors. Thus, the council was not only far from being representative, but councillors, because of their heavy workload, were dragged into a rather reactive inward-looking approach.

Since the 1960s, the traditional closeness between councillors and the political parties they represent has been loosened because of secularisation and the declining salience of class differences. Alongside these developments, the electoral accountability of the council was also weakening (e.g. Van der Kolk, 1997). Local election results have been largely determined by national trends, while turnout has been declining since the 1980s, with local branches of political parties complaining about the low level of involvement of citizens in political affairs. The legitimacy of the council as an institution of representative democracy at the local level came to be challenged, a tendency that has been further strengthened by the demands for direct-democratic changes urged by the rise of an increasingly critical citizenry.

The combined effects of these developments exacerbated other problems of the council in terms of its dealings with the BMA and the local bureaucracy. Fundamentally, the professionalisation of local politics fundamentally challenged the traditional model of unified political leadership with the primacy of the council in both legislative and executive matters. De facto executive leadership shifted from the council to the BMA. This shift was especially problematic because the exercise of these executive powers by the BMA was largely unchecked, as councillors were unwilling and unable to scrutinise the BMA due to the lack of legal means to control and scrutinise.

Changes in the institutional structure after 2002

In September 1998 a Royal Commission on Local Government Reform was established. The commission was asked to advise the government on a new model for municipal government that would be based on a clear separation of powers between the council and the BMA. The main recommendations of the commission's report – published on 17 January 2000 – were accepted by Dutch Parliament on 26 February 2002.

The task of describing the post-reform institutional structure of local government is again facilitated by the fact that the basic post-reform model of local government is the same for all municipalities. Although the reforms were radical, they did not revolutionise the entire cast on the local political stage. The five mayor offices – citizen, councillor, aldermen, mayor and civil servant – and arenas – BMA, the politico-administrative arena, party group meetings, committee meetings and the council – identified and discussed in the pre-2002 period were retained. As a consequence of the new Act, however, new actors have been added, boundary rules for existing positions have been changed and the relations between various actors in the arenas have been altered.

With regard to the position rules and the related boundary rules four major changes can be identified: the institution of a 'Council Clerk', the establishment of a 'Court of Audit' and a substantial change in the position and boundary rules of the aldermen. The roles of several position holders within the different arenas (their 'authority rules') have also changed.

One of the major objectives of the reforms was to strengthen the position of the elected municipal council through creating the position of a Council Clerk whose task is to support the council and its committees. This official is to be appointed by the council. In small municipalities the Council Clerk will typically be on his own (as a full-time employee or as a part-timer) with some secretarial facilities; in larger municipalities a small staff will support him. The supportive activities of the Council Clerk and his/her staff may take various forms: secretarial (arranging meetings or taking minutes), procedural (process management; advice on legal matters; helping councillors by securing support and information from municipal administrators) and substantive (helping individual members, party groups or the council as a whole in preparing amendments, council initiatives, motions, questions, interpellations and inquiries).

Another new position is the Court of Audit, which is also to be appointed by the council. In the original bill the Court of Audit was to be a genuinely independent position, set up to support the council. A majority in parliament, however, decided that the audit function might also be assigned to a commission (partly) consisting of councillors. The Court has the power (on its own initiative or at the council's request) to inquire into the effectiveness, the efficiency and the rightfulness of all acts of municipal administration. The Court's inquiries should provide the council with ammunition to perform its scrutiny and control functions vis-à-vis the municipal administration.

The reforms implied fundamental changes to the position of the aldermen. The new Local Government Act rules that, after their appointment, aldermen can no longer be council-members. In addition to this, aldermen no longer need to be recruited from inside the council. New aldermen do not even have to be residents when they are recruited. In 2002 recruitment from outside the council occurred in a quarter of the Dutch municipalities (BZK, 2002: 16–18). From a democratic perspective this implies that on average one out of every four aldermen are no longer (indirectly) elected by the citizens.

Finally, if we ignore some short-lived changes, the main rules for the appointment of the mayor remained essentially unaltered. Meanwhile, the discussion about the introduction of a directly elected mayor continues. The present government has recently proposed a new bill that aims at introducing directly elected mayor by 2006. Whether or not this bill will be accepted and enacted remains to be seen. Four of the five major arenas in local government have changed as a consequence of the new Local Government Act. The only arena that was left largely untouched by the legal reform was the largely informal politico-administrative arena. The most important changes in the board of mayor and aldermen is with regard to the scope of this arena and with some changes in the authority of the mayor. A crucial change pertained to the scope of the BMA's powers. Whereas prior to 2002, the primacy in all executive matters rested with the council, the New Act reallocated a number of executive powers to the board. Moreover, in a second law, currently under parliamentary consideration, a further extension of the executive prerogatives of the BMA is scheduled. Under the new regime the council will concentrate on its legislative functions and on the formulation of general principles and guidelines to steer and control the political executive. Within the limits set by local ordinances and guidelines, the BMA will henceforth be allowed to take final decisions on all administrative matters. In order to stimulate the collegiality and co-ordination of municipal policies, the new Local Government Act granted some specific powers to the mayor vis-à-vis the aldermen. The mayor is authorised to add items to the agenda of the board and to present alternative policy proposals for items on the agenda. This, at least, formally strengthens the position of the mayor within the board.

The changes in the appointment are also likely to have brought about indirect changes in the role of aldermen in party groups meetings. Since the aldermen are no longer members of the council, and may even be recruited from outside the council, their attendance at party group meetings is no longer to be taken for granted. In many municipalities it has been agreed that aldermen will only attend party group meetings when explicitly invited by the party group (Begeleidingscommissie Vernieuwingsimpuls, 2003: 23). Even if party groups invite politically sympathetic aldermen to their meetings, the new roles for the BMA and the council may very well have changed the position of the aldermen in the party group meetings. To begin with, aldermen will no longer be able to cast a vote when the group decides on proposals. Moreover, their status as 'guests' in party group meetings is also likely to make their role less dominant than before. Finally, under the new legal regime, aldermen themselves may no longer feel under pressure from fellow-aldermen to impose party discipline on their party group to secure support for BMA proposals.

The committee meetings have also changed. New boundary rules do no longer allow the aldermen to be committee members, nor to chair commissions. This is a significant change. Before 2002, an alderman played a very substantial role in committees and largely set the commission agendas. Under the new law, the council determines its own agenda and aldermen are only present when invited to answer committee members' questions. The effects of these changes on the former predominance of the aldermen will probably be similar to those discussed for the role of aldermen in party group meetings.

The new legislation also has important repercussions for the council. The separation of the legislative and the executive branch implied more than a disconnection of the membership of these bodies. Henceforth, a presidium of councillors is under a legal obligation to set the council's agenda (rather than the mayor). Moreover, the scope and authority rules of the council arena have changed. As indicated before, executive powers of the council have been (or will be) transferred to the BMA. On the other hand, the national legislator has tried to strengthen the ability of the council and its members to steer and control municipal policies by setting general rules and policy guidelines and to better equip the council-members to scrutinise the board with respect to the observance of these rules and the implementation of plans. Under the new law, individual council members are now authorised to amend policy proposals and to initiate new policies. The Council Clerk and the Court of Audit are to provide the councillors with adequate information and professional advice to fulfil these new roles. For much the same reasons, the information rules have also been changed. Under the new Act, the BMA is under an obligation to actively inform the council in order to enable the council to efficiently perform its scrutiny function. Moreover, councillors have a right to ask all necessary information and to conduct inquiries. In doing this, individual council members, party groups and the council as a whole are supported by the Council Clerk.

The Local Government Act 2002 has changed the position of the council significantly. The most significant change is the fact that aldermen are not allowed to retain the membership of the council after their aldermanic election. This is the most visible aspect of a series of measures to set up a system based on a separation of powers between the council and the board. The scope of the council's powers has been restricted as the council is no longer responsible for all executive matters. This implies that the BMA will have to be considered, both *de facto* and *de jure*, as the municipal political executive. Despite these changes, the council is still seen as the head of local government. It might even be argued that these changes will *strengthen* the influence of the council in policymaking as it is no longer burdened with administrative affairs, and is better equipped than before to control and scrutinise the board.

Expected consequences of the reforms

Proponents of the new legislation argued that the reforms would alleviate many of the weaknesses of the traditional model. They claimed that the 2002 institutional reforms might have an effect on the involvement of laymen and professionals in local administration, political accountability, political recruitment, political leadership and co-ordination.

With regard to the involvement of lay politicians and professionals, the expected effects of the measures are likely to be mixed. First, the new rules for recruiting aldermen may contribute to a further professionalisation of this office. The possibility of recruiting outsiders might stimulate the growth of a national cadre of professional political managers, who are available for the fulfilment of both aldermanic and mayoral job openings. On the other hand, so far many aldermen have indicated that the new legislation has made the position less attractive. There are fears too that the possible introduction of a directly elected mayor in 2006 will further reduce the interest of qualified professionals in an alder-manic career (Begeleidingscommissie Vernieuwingsimpuls, 2004).

The proponents of these reforms also expect to see the changes coun-teracting the semi-professionalisation of councillors. By transferring the executive powers to the board, and improving the administrative support for the council (especially through the Council Clerk), they envisage that the workload for councillors should be reduced, thus making the job of a councillor more attractive. From the perspective of the role of lay politi-cians in local administration, the new legislation may also result in more effective democratic controls over the local bureaucracy. Not only do the reforms make control and scrutiny an explicit task for the municipal council, but they also provide the council with new powers of control and scrutiny, and the introduction of the Council Clerk and the Court of Audit are conceived of as major instruments to realise this objective. Whether these measures will actually be effective, remains to be seen.

The current reforms are important in several respects, particularly in changing the relations between citizens and local government and enhancing political accountability. As part of the reforms, though not as part of the new Act, national government has encouraged municipali-ties to revitalise local democracy not only by strengthening representa-tive democracy, but also by the introduction of interactive policymaking and policy implementation. In recent years many municipalities have indeed adopted such practices (e.g. Edelenbos and Monnikhof, 2001; Denters and Klok, 2003a; 2005).

One of the expressed aims of the new Act was not only a separation of powers but also a strengthening of the representative function of the council by stimulating a more outward-oriented type of councillorship, in which direct contacts with citizens and societal organisations would provide councillors with the inspiration and information to better represent community interests and to improve democratic control and scrutiny over the local executive branch that would enhance local gov-ernment as an institution for political representation. On the one hand, the reduced workload that would result from these changes would allow councillors to spend more time on contacts with the local community. On the other hand, it was expected that the reforms would make the office of councillor more attractive for a broader group of candidates. This might result in less one-sided patterns of political recruitment and a more balanced representation of the local community on the municipal council.

The main goals of the institutional reforms, however, pertained to the patterns of political leadership in municipal government. Because the council is now freed from its administrative responsibilities, it is stimulated to develop an active role in controlling and scrutinising the board. The role of the council as head of the municipality has been redefined: instead of the traditional primacy in both legislative and executive matters, the council's new role is defined in terms of steering, control and scrutiny. Although the council may have lost ground in terms of its formal powers, advocates of the reforms argue that, with effective use of the new instruments the council, supported by a Council Clerk using information from the Court of Audit, may actually gain in influence. If the reforms should be successful in this respect they will have contributed to removing a major democratic deficit: the lack of effective controls and accountability of the BMA.

In terms of political leadership it was also hoped that the new Act would improve the co-ordination of local policymaking and increase the local capacity to develop a more adequate approach to joined-up problems. In order to realise this, the new Act aimed at strengthening the position of the mayor, who was made responsible for the coherence of policies prepared by the board, and has been given some powers to co-ordinate the BMA's activities and to structure debates in board meetings.

In terms of the professionalisation of local government, reformers hope that the changes would counteract the semi-professionalisation of the councillor, which would result in a stronger role for lay politicians in municipal politics and administration. With regard to the democratic accountability advocates of the reforms have been enthusiastic about the prospect that the reforms, among other things by making the councillor's role more attractive and changing traditional patterns of political recruitment, will improve the representativeness of the council. A particular strength of the reforms lies in their ability to bring about a new regime for local political leadership, with effective democratic control and scrutiny of the political executive and the municipal bureaucracy. Finally, by strengthening the position of the mayor, the reforms seek to reinforce the co-ordination of municipal policies by improving the performance of the BMA as a collegial body. Early evaluations (e.g. Klok *et al.*, 2002; Begeleidingscommissie, 2004; Stuurgroep Evaluatie Dualisering, 2004) so far have shown mixed results. In all likelihood it is still too early to tell whether the reform of the political executive in Dutch local government meets the expectations that gave rise to it.

3
The Directly Elected Executive Mayor in German Local Government

Hellmut Wollmann

Local government in Germany has recently undergone a dramatic change in the institutional design and arrangement of its local political and administrative leadership. Since the early 1990s, in a conspicuous sequence of legislative acts, all federal States (*Länder*) have amended their individual municipal laws to provide for the direct election of an executive mayor, replacing the previous varied pattern of local government with a largely uniform scheme. This chapter explains the extent of the institutional shift and examines its likely impact on local political and administrative structures.

The first section traces the institutional arrangements of local political and administrative leadership as they developed prior to the late 1980s. The discussion then focuses upon the introduction of the directly elected executive mayor form of local government, reviewing the commonalities as well as differences between the *Länder*. Finally, the key question of the impact of this new form of political and administrative leadership on the local political and administrative arenas will be assessed.

Background

The development of modern local self-government in Germany dates back to the enactment of municipal charters in German States (and statelets) at the beginning of the nineteenth century, with the Prussian Municipal Charter (*Preussische Städteordnung*) of 1808 providing a conceptual and institutional lead (Wollmann, 2000b). From the outset, a common feature of the multitude of municipal charters was an underlying dualistic scheme in which two somewhat contradictory institutional logics merged. On the one hand, the elected councils and the councillors were awarded the right and responsibility to decide (and carry out) all local matters on a voluntary, non-paid basis. On the other hand, a local executive, either a council-elected one-man mayor, or a council-elected collegiate body (*Magistrat*) which, while carrying out local government tasks, also had some administrative functions of its own which were not derived from the council. This dualistic structure, reminiscent of the separation of powers principle of modern parliamentary government has become a distinctive feature of the German local government tradition. It contrasts with the monistic concept of government by council (or government by committee), which characterises the English local self-government tradition.

Several factors contributed to the emergence of this dualistic scheme, including the early design of local self-government in Germany, revealingly termed local self-*administration*.[1] Giving the local administrative body executive powers in their own right vis-à-vis the elected council may have also suited the still semi-autocratic political context of early-nineteenth-century Germany. Furthermore, from the outset the local authorities were given the responsibility of carrying out tasks delegated to them by the State. This possession of a dual function became another essential feature of the German-Austrian local government tradition (Wollmann, 2000b: 118).

The local government charters that were enacted in German states in the nineteenth century exhibited two patterns of local executive power. Some municipal charters followed the French *maire* model of a one-man executive. In other municipal charters, the collegiate board (*Magistrat*) was installed, following the prototype of the Prussian Municipal Charter of 1808.

After 1945, the newly established *Länder* in the three Western Occupation Zones (and after 1949 in the Federal Republic) enacted new municipal charters that reflected their specific regional traditions, but also bore the imprint of the respective Occupation Force (Knemeyer, 2001: 175 ff.; Wollmann, 2004: 152 ff.).

Most of the newly established *Länder* continued to follow the traditional dualistic track of juxtaposing the democratically elected local councils, as the supreme local decision-making body, and the council-elected executive, whose powers were not exclusively derived from the council. In some *Länder*, typically situated in the French Occupation Zone, the elected council plus council-elected chief executive mayor form was put in place. In other *Länder* (particularly in *Hesse*) the elected council plus council-elected (collegiate) board, or *Magistrat*, form was revived.

In the two South German *Länder Baden-Württemberg* and *Bavaria*, located in the American Occupation Zone, the new municipal charters introduced a conspicuous innovation in having the (chief executive) mayor elected directly by the local residents instead of the election by the council. In the *Länder* of *Nordrhein-Westfalen* and *Niedersachsen*, situated in the British Occupation Zone, the traditional dualistic track (allegedly fraught with autocratic potential) was abandoned and the monistic scheme of the English local government model (government by council or government by committee) was introduced. Accordingly, the elected council was designed to be the comprehensively and solely responsible (*allzuständig*) local decision-making body and the council-elected mayor was reduced to the function of chairing the local council while the position of a council-appointed city director was installed as the chief executive of local administration operating under the guidance of the local council. These four distinct local government forms showed a remarkable degree of institutional stability well into the late 1980s, with only minor changes and adaptations.

Adopting the directly elected executive mayor

In the early 1990s, legislative changes effected by the *Länder* parliaments led to a more uniform system. The elected council plus directly elected chief executive mayor form, which had been in force in the two South German *Länder* since the 1950s, came to be adopted in all other *Länder*, with the exception of the City States of Berlin, Hamburg and Bremen. Similar arrangements brought about the direct election of the heads of county (*Landrat*) in most of the *Länder* (Knemeyer, 2001: 178 ff.; Kost and Wehling, 2003; Wollmann, 2004).

In the *Land* of *Nordrhein-Westfalen* where the decision-making process had been tailored on the British local government model, the new institutional arrangement began to increasingly reveal frictions and conflicts between the mayor and the city director (or chief executive), as successive mayors built up their own personnel staffs and claimed decision-making and executive powers of their own, whereas the city directors started to become political players in their own right (Bogumil, 2001: 68). The conflicts between the mayor and the city director in what was labelled a double-headed executive (*Doppelspitze*) became a key concern in the protracted legislative debate about adopting the South German directly elected mayor form instead.[2]

Owing to the legislative moves which the *Länder* embarked upon in the early 1990s, their individual local government charters show a considerable degree of uniformity in basically adopting the directly elected mayor (and *Landrat*) form. The elected council plus directly elected mayor form of decision-making continues to revolve around the elected council as the supreme local decision-making and local policy-making body, while the mayor (or *Landrat*), draws political legitimacy from being directly elected.

Notwithstanding these basic similarities, the municipal charters of the individual *Länder* show significant variations as different regional traditions and political constellations continue to exercise influence. For example, there are differences between the *Länder* in the procedure by which the candidates in the mayoral (or *Landrat*) elections are nominated. The electoral provisions range from giving local political parties the exclusive right to nominate the candidates (as in Bavaria) to extending the right of (self-) nomination only to individuals (which applies in *Baden-Württemberg* and *Saxony*). The remaining 10 of the 13 *Länder* have a mixed system of granting the nomination right to political parties and groups as well as to individuals (Holtkamp, 2003: 12 ff.). It is evident that giving the political parties a formal (if not exclusive) role in the nomination process fosters the politicisation of mayoral elections and of local politics at large, whereas limiting the nomination right to individuals is likely to depoliticise the mayoral contest and local politics in general (Wehling, 1982: 236).

As under the new system both the local council and the mayor (or *Landrat*) are directly elected, it is an important political issue whether the balloting takes places on the same day or at different times. In legislating, the *Länder* have chosen between two options. Most of the *Länder* (11 out of 13) have fixed terms of office for the mayor (or the *Landrat*) different from the legislative period of the councils. The councils mainly serve five years, whereas the terms of office of the mayors (and *Landräte*) is longer, and may be six, eight, or as much as nine years. Hence, the terms of office are staggered and the dates of balloting mostly years apart, and only three *Länder* (*Nordrhein-Westfalen*, *Niedersachsen* and *Bavaria*) have synchronised the terms of office so that the balloting is held on the same day.

In the *Land* of *Baden-Württemberg* the practice of having non-synchronised council and mayoral elections has been in place since the 1950s. The purpose of this provision was to decouple the political life cycle of the elected mayor from that of the elected council. This, together with the individual nomination of mayoral candidates, was expected to foster the non-partisan status of the mayor, reflecting the concept of consensus-oriented (or consociational) democracy (*Konkordanzdemokratie*) which characterises the political culture of *Land* of *Baden-Württember* (Bogumil, 2001; Holtkamp, 2003: 19 ff.). One consequence of synchronised elections has been the emergence of political alignments which, borrowing from the French political parlance, have been called the German version of cohabitation, the council majority and the mayor may belong to rival parties and may pursue conflicting goals and beliefs.

By contrast, the *Land* of *Nordrhein-Westfalen*, when enacting the introduction of the directly elected mayor in 1994, opted to synchronise the local elections. This was done with the explicit political and legislative intention to install an institutional design which, by having the elections simultaneously, would make it likely that a political congruence between the council majority and the mayor would ensue. Along with an electoral law which ensures a major say for the political parties in the nomination of the mayoral candidates, the synchronisation of the council election with mayoral election tends towards the party politicisation of the mayoral election. This mirrors and reinforces the pattern of competitive majoritarian democracy (*Konkurrenzdemokratie*) which with its marked political party competiton marks the political culture of *Land* of *Nordrhein-Westfalen*, and where cohabitation – with a council majority and mayor of different political party complexion blocking each other – becomes less likely.

The South German strong mayor concept in force in *Baden-Württemberg* and *Bavaria* has given the mayor an institutionally remarkably strong position vis-à-vis the elected local council on a number of scores. First, the mayor is given the sole responsibility to conduct all routine administrative matters (*Geschäfte der laufenden Verwaltung*) on his/her own without interference by the council and the councillors. Furthermore, in *Baden-Württemberg*, the elected councils have been explicitly denied the right to call in (*zurückholen*) decisions on routine administrative matters for the council's own determination. It is worth emphasising that in the German State and local government tradition, local authorities carry out important public tasks delegated to them by the State; here the mayors (and the heads of counties, *Landräte*) conduct such delegated business in their own right without interference by the councils.

When adopting the directly elected chief executive mayor seven Länder followed the South German model in taking a broad interpretation of those routine administrative matters which are to be carried out solely by the mayor without the councils right to reclaim them. Only in three *Länder*, typically those *Länder* where the monistic British local government model was in force from the late 1940s to the 1990s, can the council call in (*zurückholen*) any matter, including routine business, on the basis of its claim to comprehensive competence (*Allzuständigkeit*) (Schulenburg, 1999: 123; Holtkamp, 2003: 25).

Where the direct election of the mayors (and *Landräte*) was adopted in the 1990s, this innovation was accompanied by a recall provision through which the mayor (and *Landrat*) can be removed from office at any time by means of a local referendum. Such recall referendums can in some cases be initiated only by a qualified majority in the local council.

Only in three *Länder* (*Schleswig-Holstein, Brandenburg* and *Sachsen*) do the local electorate enjoy the right to initiate a recall referendum procedure on its own – with a required number of signatures varying between 15 and 33.3 per cent of the electorate. In both cases, a recall motion is deemed to be passed, if the yes votes find a majority among the voters and reach a certain threshold (between 25 and 50%) of all eligible citizens, in which case the mayor (or *Landrat)* is obliged to resign, and a new mayoral election is held (Schefold and Naumann, 1996: 73).

The impact of the directly elected mayor on local politics and government

In the South German model, the mayor is faced with a number of challenges. As a local politician he is intensely involved in local politics: seeking election and re-election, keeping in contact with local residents and electors, and dealing with the local media. As a local political leader he has to cope with the political parties and interest groups. As chairman of the local council he has to be able to handle council and committee work effectively while, as chief executive, he is responsible for the efficient running of the local administration. Finally, he has to negotiate with would-be investors and with other levels of government.[3] In view of these multiple roles, concerns have been expressed that the direct election of the mayor might prove an invitation to wild populists and mavericks to seek mayoral positions unless some clear-cut qualification requirement were laid down as an entry threshold. In fact, such requirements have not been stipulated in the South German *Länder* nor in the other *Länder* that followed suit in the early 1990s. The underlying premise of the decisions to do without such requirements obviously was that the positions of the mayors (and of the *Landräte*) are essentially political and should therefore be open to anybody.

Meanwhile, half a century of political experience and practice in *Land* of *Baden-Württemberg* suggests that this apprehension is in any event unfounded. Instead, the year-long experience indicates that, in the absence of a pertinent formal requirement, a remarkable process of professionalisation has taken place in the role perception and role performance of the directly elected mayors. Thus, it turns out that in *Baden-Württemberg* about 90 per cent of the elected full-time mayors has an administrative background (Bogumil, 2001: 185 ff.; Wehling, 2002; Bogumil *et al.*, 2003). Many of those seeking and occupying a mayoral position in smaller and middle-sized towns are graduates from administrative colleges (*Fachhochschulen*), while those in cities of more than 50,000 inhabitants are increasingly law school graduates. In most cases, mayors have considerable prior administrative experience in municipal and county administration or *Land* ministries. While some 60 per cent of the mayors have thus a prior administrative career and most come from outside the municipality concerned, only some 15 per cent are former local politicians from the locality in which they are elected to the mayoralty (Holtkamp *et al.*, 2004: 22). In 20 per cent of the larger towns – those with more than 20,000 inhabitants – the mayors are not members of a political party, whereas in the (many) smaller towns over half of the mayors are non-partisan.

This professionalisation of the mayoral positions is most notable in *Baden-Württemberg*. Voters appear to recognise the value of having a professional mayor preferably with an administrative background and this has become crucial credential for mayoral candidates. Typically, ambitious young people seek to be elected as mayor at first in smaller town and then to climb up the ladder to become mayor in a larger city. Once elected for one term (typically of 6 to 8 years), incumbent mayors, particularly in larger cities, often aspire re-election for a second or even third term which, if they are successful, adds up to long-term mayoral career.

The impact of direct election on the role and influence of the local citizens

The right of the local citizens to directly elect the mayor has significantly changed the power relations within the crucial triad of local political actors: the local citizens, the local council and the mayor. While the German local government of representative democracy put the council centre stage in local decision-making, and limits the role of local citizens to electing the council, the traditional rules of the game have been changed by the introduction of the direct election as an important element of direct democracy. Voter turnout in elections to local councils has been around 60 to 70 per cent in the case of non-synchronised local elections, rising to some 80 per cent when the council elections coincided with elections to the Land parliament or to the federal parliament. In the mayoral elections, the local voter turnout has been somewhat lower, between 50 and 60 per cent.

The direct election of the mayor has strengthened the accountability of the mayor to the local electorate. By virtue of direct election, the mayor is being singled out as one local leader whose political responsibility is clearly identifiable and who accordingly can be called to account. This accountability is confirmed and reinforced if and when the incumbent mayor seeks re-election which has often been the case in the South German experience and will, in all likelihood, become a permanent pattern in the other *Länder* under their new local government charters.

Finally, the direct democratic mechanism of recall as a last resort for calling the mayor to account has been introduced in most *Länder*. Although in the majority of the *Länder* which provide for the recall procedure the right to initiate the recall referendum lies solely with the local council (only in two *Länder* does the initiative lie with the local electorate) recall provides a powerful direct democratic weapon in the hands of the citizens, keeping the mayor politically accountable and responsive to local opinion. In the East German *Land* of *Brandenburg* where the recall procedure can be also initiated by the local citizens, a striking number of recall procedures were initiated between 1994 and 1998, and almost 10 per cent of the full-time mayors lost their office as a result of such referendums. This aroused some alarm among local politicians and also in the media which portrayed a new local sport of the citizens to 'play skittles with the mayors' (*Bürgermeisterkegeln*). Once the threshold to initiate a recall referendum was raised, the wave of recall procedures subsided in *Brandenburg* (Wollmann, 2000c: 229).

The impact of direct election on local democracy

In a number of countries fears have been expressed that the directly elected strong mayor may give rise to an excessive concentration of power that would be detrimental to local democracy (Larsen, 2002; Wilson and Game, 2002: 116). The long experience of this practice in *Baden-Württemberg* does not support such misgivings. While *Baden-Württemberg*'s directly elected mayor has risen to the imposing and powerful position of what has been termed a local elective monarch (*Wahlkönigtum*) (Wehling, 1987: 88), at the same time, the mayors have acquired a presidential stature by adopting a non-partisan stance. Once elected, they have typically reduced their party ties. This tendency reflects *Baden-Württemberg*'s characteristic local political culture, of consensual (or consociational) democracy (*Konkordanzdemoratie*). The inclination to detach themselves from party politics is confirmed by survey data according to which almost three quarters of the incumbent mayors believe the political parties should leave local politics alone (see Wehling and Siewert, 1987: 79).

This same non-partisan stance to which the *Baden-Württemberg* mayors aspire has the effect of countervailing and moderating the exercise of their power. To the extent that the mayors have downplayed or even cut the ties with 'their' political party, and even eschew attending party caucuses, they find it difficult to command the votes of their party group in the council and the committees. Instead, they are obliged to build majorities in council on a case-by-case basis, building all-party coalitions and cross-party consensus instead of counting on majority rule.

Nordrhein-Westfalen, whose regional political tradition and culture is characterised by competitive (majoritarian) democracy (*Konkurrenzdemokratie*), provides an example of similar constraints upon mayoral power arrived at by a different route. Here, the powers of the newly introduced strong majors have been moderated by the traditional and still persisting high degree of party-politicisation. As a rule, the mayors remained tied into the decision-making processes (and political control) of 'their' party, which the synchronisation of the local elections works to ensure (Bogumil, 2001: 183 ff., Holtkamp, 2003).

The impact of direct election on the local council arena

Traditionally, German local councils operate through holding plenary sessions and by establishing (sectoral) committees which process the issues and prepare the decisions to be taken by the full council. The councils are elected by the local electorate on proportionate electoral systems which, as a rule, ushers in a plurality of parties and groups in the council. The size of the councils ranges, in the case of Nordrhein-Westfalen, from 30 councillors in smaller towns to some 70 councillors in larger cities (Schulenburg, 1999: 40). It was part and parcel of the early concept of local self-government that all local government activities, including the administrative day-to-day matters, were taken care of by the part-time non-salaried councillors on the traditional voluntary (*ehrenamtlich*) formula. Today, all councillors, including the chairpersons of the committees (where the committees are not chaired by the mayor), work on a part-time, non-salaried basis. Although they receive some financial compensation, the traditional layman principle still remains, and the institution of full-time salaried council members is unknown in the German tradition.

As German local government developed further during the nineteenth century, some differentiation arose between the part-time, non-salaried, voluntary lay councillors, and the local administration with its professionalised, full-time, salaried administrative personnel under the direction of the chief executive (mayor or board). Councillors still cling to the idea of being comprehensively competent in the conduct of local matters, and are eager to get involved in minor local decisions, not least in response to concrete complaints and concerns of individual electors. Yet in formal terms there are no direct links between the council and its committees, on the one hand, and the local government's administrative units and their staff, on the other. With the introduction of the directly elected strong executive mayor, this formal differentiation between the council and the local administration has been even more accentuated. Administrative leadership is concentrated in the person of the politically accountable mayor through whom, formally speaking, the direct contacts and interactions between the councillors and the administration are supposed to be channelled.

In those Länder, which have further strengthened the directly elected mayor by making him the ex officio chairman of the local council and its committees, this arrangement has noticeably enlarged the political sway which the mayor exercises on the council proceedings. Thus, he/she has direct access to the council and committee debates, can set the agenda, bring proposals already elaborated by the administration and its professional staffs, and bring to bear political as well administrative mayoral muscle and might.

The present situation in *Nordrhein-Westfalen* is quite different on a number of scores. First, the position of the elected mayor is more party-politicised, because the terms of office of the council and of the mayor are synchronised and the electoral campaigns and elections for both local institutions, thus coincide. In so far as the mayor can depend on a politically congruent majority party or coalition in the council, his or her position and influence in the council debates is likely to be quite strong. If, however, he or she is confronted with a politically unsympathetic council majority (which can also happen with synchronised elections), then, the council majority may be eager to give the mayor a hard time and may even make use of the council's formal right to reclaim (*Zurückrufen*) responsibilities from the mayor and thus curb his or her powers (Bogumil *et al.*, 2003: 339).

In sum, although the introduction of the directly elected executive mayor, particularly in the South German strong mayor variant, has further dipped the scales of power between the council and the mayor in favour of the latter, Germany's local government system continues to show a power balance in which the councils and committees and the political party groups continue to play an important role. An indication of the persisting political health of the council system can be seen in the frequency of full council sessions. In Nordrhein-Westfalen on the average nine plenary sessions a year are held with, an average duration of four hours each, backed up by intensive deliberations in committees (Schulenburg, 1999: 40). Another indication of the political health of the local councils is the voter turnout in council elections which stands at around 60 to 70 per cent (quite high by international comparative standards) and may be seen as reflecting a recognition, by the local electorate, of the continuing political relevance of their councils.

The impact of direct election on the administration

In accordance with the traditional organisational arrangements, local administration in the larger cities comprises three levels: the top (administrative leadership) level which is the level of the chief executive; the meso level which is the echelon of the so-called directorates (*Dezernate) and* the lower level which is the layer of the operative units of the sections (*Ämter*). While most of the directorates have sectoral responsibilities, such as social matters cultural matters or public utilities, one directorate typically has cross-cutting responsibilities for organisation, personnel or the budget.

Provision was made for the top echelon to have a number of deputy mayors (*Beigeordnete*) who were elected, for the duration of some years, by the local council on a proportionate formula and were meant to introduce an element of collegiate deliberation into the otherwise monocratic mayoral system. The *Beigeordnete* were expected to support the mayor in certain sectors and fields of local government. A closer linkage at the administrative leadership level (executive mayor and *Beigeordnete*) was achieved by the mayor taking responsibility for organisation, personnel and the budget, while some of the *Beigeordneten* were put in charge of sectoral directorates. While in most new local government charters the positions of the deputy mayor (*Beigeordnete*) has been retained as a second (lower) level of political leadership, their responsibilities have been more clearly defined as being supportive to the mayor. Although they continue to be elected by the council on proportionate formula, they are subordinated to the mayor who, in the case of dispute, retains the power to decide (Holtkamp, 2003: 25).

With the introduction of the directly elected chief executive mayor the traditional organisational scheme was largely retained, but with a number of important modifications. First, the *administrative* leadership of the previous chief executive (be it the chief executive mayor or the chief executive city director) was decisively extended by combining it with the *political* leadership of the directly *elected* mayor, and complemented by his/her membership, chairmanship and leadership of the local council. So, the elected mayor is now able to bring to bear his/her *political* muscle and clout also in directing the local *administrative* world.

Conclusion

It may be too early to draw well-grounded conclusions regarding the impact of the introduction of the directly elected mayor. Institutional shifts can be brought about by legislation but the cultural changes and adjustments in the perceptions and attitudes of actors on which the functioning of these changes depend take longer to take effect. Nevertheless, a reasonably confident assessment can be made with regard to mayor–citizen relations. The introduction of the direct election of the mayor, complemented by the recall procedure, has, no doubt, significantly strengthened and enlarged the political empowerment of the citizens. By establishing the directly elected chief executive mayor as a kind of local president, political as well administrative leadership and responsibility is located in one person who can be clearly identified and held politically accountable both by the electorate and the council. Due to his direct linkage with the electorate, the mayor is motivated to exert influence over the administration to make it more responsive and citizen- or client-oriented.

Another fairly safe assessment can be made regarding the mayor–council relations. The direct election of the chief executive mayor has further accentuated the traditional dualistic scheme of German local government by further spelling out a division of functions and powers between the elected council and the elected mayor, who directs the administration and its professional staffs. The council and its councillors, operating in plenary session and through sectoral committees, has moved more and more towards a parliamentary role in which the council and the councillors concentrate on deciding the major issues of local policymaking and on controlling the chief executive and local administration instead of being involved in, and absorbed by the day-to-day operations of local government. This division of functions has recently been reinforced by the NPM-derived distinction between the steering and the rowing functions, the former being geared to the council, the latter to the chief executive and local administration.

As the available empirical evidence indicates, it is less easy to reach well-founded conclusions regarding the impact of the directly elected chief executive mayor on the performance of local government, and on the governibility of the towns (Kunz and Zapf-Schramm, 1989: 181; Winkler and Haupt, 1989: 155–7). Yet, it seems plausible that, by installing the mayor as a democratically legitimated and politically accountable political as well as executive leader increases the capacity of local government for proactive policymaking and co-ordinated action. The directly elected chief executive mayor, possessing a combination of political legitimacy and administrative clout, has the opportunity to become the key local networker and to exercise a pivotal role in horizontal as well as vertical co-ordination of the German cities.

Notes

1. This tradition drew heavily on the municipal legislation in post-revolutionary France where, as early as 1790, the council-elected mayor (*maire*) was introduced in a dualistic local government arrangement.
2. The governing Social Democrats who were not only the majority party in the *Land* parliament but also held majorities in most local councils were opposed to the direct election of the mayors, as they suspected this would provide the opposition Christian Democrats with a political avenue to gain mayoral majorities. It was only when the Christian Democrats threatened to initiate a *Land*-wide referendum on this issue that the Social Democrats finally gave in and the *Land* parliament enacted the new municipal charter with a broad majority.
3. For an impressive list and survey data on mayoral time input and time budgets see Schulenburg (1999).

4

From Committees to Leaders and Cabinets

The British Experience

Nirmala Rao

For many years now the internal workings of local authorities in Britain have been subject to repeated proposals for change. Inefficiency, lack of accountability, the slow and cumbersome nature of the committee system, together with an apparent inability to attract councillors of the right calibre, have all been seen as problems to be tackled through reform (Rao, 1994). Current moves to radically restructure council structures and management may, then, be seen as the culmination of nearly 30 years of discontent with the decision-making process.

The focus of that discontent has been the committee system itself. The British system of local government, rooted in its nineteenth-century tradition, was essentially 'government by committee' (Wheare, 1955). Decisions were made through council committees, and all councillors, including those from the minority parties, were able to participate in decision-making (Chester, 1968). The result, the critics claimed, was a time-consuming process, that generated great volumes of paper. Decisions took a long, circuitous route at a pace more suited to local government's nineteenth-century origins than to today's needs.

This latest attempt by the Blair Government to streamline local authority management brings the debate full circle. The essential points were all made by the Maud Committee in the 1960s, and repeated periodically since then. The argument is predicated on three fundamental assumptions: first, that more effective management of local authority business and speedier decision-making is required; second, that the overall time commitment of councillors should be distributed more efficiently between their representative and executive functions and, finally, that fundamental reform is required to modernise the local democratic structures.

Attempts at reform

Although issues about management and efficiency in local government dominated local government reform for much of the post-war period, it was generally assumed that the system of decision-making should be one in which the authority remains a corporate body with decisions taken openly by the whole council, or on its behalf in committee. The first proposal, however, to change to the role of councillors and the decision-making process of councils came from the Maud Committee established in 1965 to 'consider in the light of modern conditions how local government might best continue to attract and retain people of the calibre necessary to ensure its maximum effectiveness' (Maud, 1967).

The Committee undertook a thorough analysis of the forms of internal organisation adopted by local authorities in England and Wales, and proposed certain basic principles as being important to the internal organisation of any local authority, including effective and efficient management under the direction and control of councillors, clear leadership and responsibility among both members and officers. In seeking to realise these principles, the Committee proposed to concentrate decision-making power in the hands of a few – presumed to be the most able members. It recommended a small management board of five to nine councillors, which would formulate the principal objectives and control and direct all the work. Consequently, council committees would become deliberative and representative bodies only. Maud's proposals were, however, abandoned in favour of retaining the committee system, on the grounds that majority of members would not have the opportunity to play an important role in decision-making. The Widdicombe Committee, established in 1985 to inquire into the conduct of local authority business, re-examined these issues (Widdicombe, 1986). Unlike the Maud inquiry, Widdicombe reaffirmed the traditional model of decision-making as the most appropriate response to the needs of local government in the late twentieth century. Retaining the existing conventions and practices soon came to be seen as inadequate, as new legislative changes imposed different kinds of pressures on councillor roles. The demands for greater accountability, enhanced transparency and political pluralism required local authorities to radically transform the way in which they operated. Following the departure of Mrs Thatcher, the Major Government sought to address these new developments and advocated several options, including the creation of a cabinet system; the creation of a separately elected executive (whether an elected mayor or otherwise); and the establishment of a council-manager system. These proposals represented a complete reversal of the Widdicombe position. Yet, the objective that underlay them was fundamentally that of the Maud Committee: to achieve a more effective and satisfying use of time, talent and resources available. The central claim of the cabinet model of local government, in the government's view, was that it would enhance decision-making, avoid delays and raise public interest in local government, values which could be realised to an even greater extent through an elective mayoral system. Once again, however, councillors expressed widespread reservations about such a reform, with the result that only a handful of local authorities were willing to experiment with the new proposals.

The election of New Labour in 1997 signalled a new beginning for local democracy. The 1998 White Paper *Modern Local Government: In Touch With the People*, set out an overall strategy for the reform of local government (DETR, 1998). Its underlying assumption was that local people are insufficiently interested in their local authorities, know little about how they are run and are poorly informed by them. They lack the knowledge of how decisions are made, who to hold accountable when things go wrong and who to complain to when problems arise. Local government fails to arouse the interest of the public. This is reflected in the low turnouts at local elections, where Britain trails behind most developed nations with an average of just 40 per cent of the electorate casting their vote. Indeed, in the 1998 local elections – the year after New Labour came to power – turnout reached no more than 28 per cent on average, and in the June 1999 European and Leeds by-election, the lowest levels ever recorded at around 20 per cent.

The onus was upon local councils to revive local democracy and demonstrate a capacity for community leadership (Ashworth *et al.*, 2004). But, according to the government, that capacity is lacking today. In its view, councils had failed to keep pace with a changing society; and their decision-making arrangements were cumbersome, inefficient and opaque. The traditional framework of local government was 'inward-looking, inefficient, and has failed to put the interests of the people first'. Councillors and officers alike tend to the paternalistic view that they are the best arbiters of what services should be provided. Meanwhile, secrecy is pervasive, with decisions taken behind closed doors, and with the majority of councillors having little influence over decisions. A 'better deal' for the public was called for.

First among the key proposals in *Modern Local Government* was the reform of political structures to provide for alternative forms of leadership. 'A bigger say for local people' was to be achieved by new political arrangements that would create a clear focus for local leadership and enhance accountability. Most radically, the government's main aim was to remedy the gulf between the people and local government by increasing the visibility of political leaders. Options included a directly elected mayor, with an executive cabinet, a strong leader with a cabinet and a directly elected mayor with a council manager. In addition, a fourth option was also provided for, approximating to the status quo, which was not to be generally available.

New forms of leadership

The first of the three options was that of a directly elected mayor with a cabinet. Chosen by the local electorate, a directly elected mayor would serve as the political leader for that community, supported by a cabinet drawn from among the council members. Depending on local political circumstance, the cabinet would be formed from a single party or from a coalition of parties. Cabinet members, endowed with their own portfolios, would be empowered to take executive decisions.

In the second model, based upon a directly elected mayor and council manager, the mayor's role would be primarily one of influence, guidance and leadership, defining strategic policy and delegating day-to-day decision-making to the council manager. Of all the models, this one is most obviously an import from the political experience of the United States and Germany. A fundamental change of process, it cannot be said to evolve out of the traditional manner of conducting business, unlike the third model, which represents some kind of logical progression.

The third model – a cabinet with a leader – is the closest to existing practice in partisan authorities. Under this model a leader would be elected by the council, while the cabinet would be made up of councillors, either appointed by the leader, or elected by the council. As with a directly elected mayor model, the cabinet could be drawn from a single party or a coalition. This model is similar to the first, except that the leader (who may assume the role of indirectly elected executive mayor) relies on the support of members of the council rather than the electorate for his or her authority and can be replaced by the council. While the leader could have similar executive powers to a directly elected mayor, in practice they are likely to be constrained by the absence of a direct mandate from the electorate. As under the then existing system, a leader would be as powerful as his or his colleagues allowed him to be.

Under the first and second models, the directly elected mayor is intended to be seen as the political leader for the entire community, putting forward policy for approval by the council and steering implementation by council officers. The mayor depends for his authority on the electorate at large, and thus has a mandate separate from that of the council, enjoying thereby an electoral visibility unparalleled in British local government.

Several studies explored the benefits of having a directly elected mayor including a public attitude survey carried out in 1998 and a further survey of councillor opinion carried out in 1999. These revealed strong support for some, but not all, aspects of the plan. While people thought a directly elected mayor would provide a clear 'voice' for the local area and improve local accountability, there was less certainty as to whether such a role would make it easier to get things done – one of the key arguments behind the government's proposal (Rao and Young, 1999). As many as one-third of councillors conceded that having an elected mayor would mean 'it was always clear who was responsible when things go wrong', while almost half of the members of the public who were questioned did so. At the same time, responses to the survey on the more negative aspects of mayoral democracy – that too much power would reside with one person, and that ordinary councillors would be left with too little influence – were mixed. Almost half of the public and the great majority of the councillors agreed that an elected mayor would concentrate too much power in one person. Only one of the claimed strengths of the plan – the provision of a single clear 'voice' for the area – was generally recognised.

The choice of which model to adopt, however, was left to local assessment of the leadership needs and tasks of the council. Many variations around the basic model thus emerged during the transition that ranged from councils developing joint member-officer style executive to the classic 'political' cabinet. A number of authorities used select committee or members' panels to hear evidence in public about which model to adopt. All models, however, were subject to some common basic requirements: an appropriate ethical framework to ensure probity; provisions to ensure access to information and the proper recording of decisions; strong scrutiny arrangements and special provisions for planning and licensing decisions.

The implications for councillor roles

Underlying all three models of new political leadership embodied in the Local Government Act, 2000 is the idea of a clear separation of councillor roles. Indeed, restructuring councillors' roles is the primary means by which the aims of the modernising agenda are to be achieved. A small executive body of councillors will provide for community leadership, while the majority will play only a representative role. Here is to be found a new doctrine of representative government, and it is one on which councillors themselves have decided views.

The government maintains that 'each role can only be fully effective when it is separated from the other'. Such a separation of roles is expected not only to provide a sharper focus for executive responsibility, but also to enable the majority of non-leading members to be freed from the pressures of council business, and so devote more time to representing their constituents. Moreover, bringing about radical change requires 'clear and close relationships' between executive and non-executive councillors, and between both types of councillor and their communities.

While the executive role is to propose the policy framework and implement policies within the agreed framework, the role of non-executive ('backbench') councillors is to represent their constituents. A small executive, in the government's view, will speed up decision-making, enhance responsiveness and enable local authorities to meet community needs. Increased transparency will enable people to measure the executive's actions against the policies on which he was elected, and thus sharpen local political debate and increase interest in local elections. The non-executive councillors will also share in the policy and budget decisions of the full council, suggest policy improvements and scrutinise the executive's policy proposals and their implementation. More specifically, they would play an advisory role on local issues, reviewing decisions of the executive and taking quasi-judicial decisions.

At the same time, the non-executive role will also provide for greater scrutiny of executive action. While the government acknowledges that the formation of a small separate executive will confirm their exclusion, non-executive councillors will, they claim, gain the compensatory power to challenge or scrutinise decisions. To this end, councils are required to establish scrutiny committees composed of non-leading councillors, whose duty would be to review and question the decisions of the executive. These committees will also review broad policy and submit alternative proposals to the executive. The principle of proportionality, introduced in the wake of Widdicombe by the Local Government Act, 1989, will apply to scrutiny committees, which must reflect the political balance on the council.

Apart from scrutinising the executive, non-executive councillors are expected to spend less time in council meetings. Their effort will instead be deployed in the local community, representing their constituents' aspirations, concerns and grievances to the council and bringing to its decision-making processes 'a full knowledge of what their local communities need and want' (Armstrong, 1999: 21). The government aims to persuade councillors that this enhanced role will open up new opportunities to non-executive councillors. It could be less time-consuming but will be high profile, involving real and direct responsibilities for the well-being of their community.

When, in 1991, similar proposals were first floated by Michael Heseltine, the then Secretary of State for Environment, the Joseph Rowntree Foundation funded a national survey of councillors to assess their response to the proposed changes (Young and Rao, 1994). The survey showed majority of councillors to consider such a separation of roles to have predominantly negative consequences. Loss of influence was anticipated by four in five councillors, while three quarters of them believed that such a concentration of power would remove the incentive to serve as a councillor. Not surprisingly, leading members themselves were rather more favourably disposed to a greater concentration of power in their own hands. Differences between members of majority and minority parties might have been expected, but were in actuality very slight. The overall picture was one of broad concurrence on the adverse effects of change.

Why so negative a response? For many councillors an exclusively representative or scrutiny role is not just likely to be unattractive, but could also be politically untenable. The need for councillors to be 'seen to be doing something' and 'achieving something' in the public's eye is equally vital, particularly, in order to sustain electoral advantage. All councillors have to win elections and, given the potential electoral significance of their case and constituency work, few can afford to disregard their constituents' interests. In order to serve their constituents effectively, they must be able to influence decisions – whether to improve schools or to obtain more housing in their area (Rao, 1993). The traditional system of committees and sub-committees provided just such opportunities where influence over decision-taking could be exercised. Against this, it was argued by the proponents of change that a clearer separation of roles would liberate non-executive councillors from tedious decision-making and allow them to attend to their representative function. They could then concentrate their time in committee on the scrutiny role of performance review.

The 1993 survey was repeated in 1999, and a comparison enabled us to judge how far councillor attitudes had changed in the intervening

Table 4.1 Views on effects of concentrating responsibility in the hands of leading members

	1993 (%)	1999 (%)
Agree that concentrating responsibility would		
Enable ordinary members to devote more time to performance review and monitoring	15	42
Enable ordinary members to devote more time to the problems of their constituents	22	43
Deprive ordinary members of influence over strategic policymaking	80	65
Deprive ordinary members of the incentive to remain on the council	76	57
(Base)	1,636	1,226

period. Table 4.1 shows that while in 1999 a large majority of the councillors surveyed – some 65 per cent – felt that the government's changes would 'deprive ordinary members of influence over decision making', this figure represents a marked shift from the 80 per cent agreeing with this statement in 1993. Moreover, while a majority of councillors (57%) still agreed that 'ordinary members would be deprived of the incentive to remain on the council', here too there was a softening of opposition since the 76 per cent level recorded in 1993.

The composition of councils, of course, changed between 1993 and 1999, and a number of them moved to experiment following the encouragement given by the Labour Government. Councillors, nevertheless, remain very much alive to the need to protect their rights and duties as elected members. In any event, there remains the separate issue of whether scrutiny and representation of constituents' interests, together amount to a meaningful role for the non-executive councillor. Councillors still retain their attachment to the traditional committee system as something that allows them to participate effectively. In both 1993 and 1999, a similar proportion – in excess of 70 per cent – agreed that the committee system enabled the generality of members to play an effective role.

A good number of authorities, however, had already experimented with streamlining their committee structures and decision processes within the existing statutory limits. Both surveys asked whether councillors had experienced such changes and, if so, whether they considered the revised structures to have increased their effectiveness as councillors. In 1999, nearly 60 per cent had experience of their authorities streamlining their committee system, but opinion on whether this enabled councillor to play a more effective role was equally divided.

The Local Government Act, 2000 put in train New Labour's intention to modernise local authorities with a broad ranging scheme to promote democratic renewal. Specifically, Part II of the Act provided for new constitutions offering four options for the establishment of executive arrangements including two forms of elected mayors, the cabinet form and a streamlined committee system for smaller authorities. Part II also provided for the establishment of overview and scrutiny committees, while Part III set out provisions for a new ethical framework. The Act made it a requirement to change from a system of council and committee decision-making to a mayoral or cabinet system of local leadership or (if below 85,000 population) to adopt approved alternative arrangements.

As Table 4.2 shows, the vast majority of councils serving populations over 85,000 adopted the leader/cabinet form. Nationally 316, or 81 per cent, of all authorities operate leader/cabinet constitutions. Most of those authorities with populations below 85,000 had opted for 'alternative arrangements', although a third of these smaller authorities also chose the leader cabinet form. In total, there are now ten mayor-cabinet councils and one mayor-council manager system. The mayoral form thus constitutes only a very small proportion of the new political management arrangements adopted by councils. Why, following the political investment the government had made, should this be so? Clearly, adoption of the leader–cabinet model represents the least change from the status quo, which gave the generality of the councillor body a maximum opportunity to participate in and influence decision-making. The prospect of an elected mayor, wielding sole powers, conjures up a

Table 4.2 Local authorities by type of constitution

	No.
England	
Leader and cabinet	316
Mayor and cabinet	10
Mayor and council manager	1
Alternative arrangements	59
Wales	
Leader and cabinet	19
Alternative arrangements	3

deep-seated fear of an 'elective dictatorship'. Very few councillors would wish to surrender their powers, however limited, to such a figure. The figure of the leader, however, is a familiar one, and accountability to councillors, rather than to the electorate, provides reassurance to councillors that some power remains with them. At the end of the day, the legislation permitted councils to make their choice between more and less radical change – and that they did.

The first phase of a study for the Office of the Deputy Prime Minister (ODPM) to evaluate the new council constitutions over the period 2002–7 has already shown that the claimed advantages of the new arrangements have been largely realised, with more efficient, faster, clearer and more accountable decision-making emerging under stronger and more focused political leadership (Stoker *et al.*, 2003). Equally, the drawbacks anticipated by councillors responding to the earlier studies seem also to have materialised, with the disengagement of backbench councillors – the most widely cited disadvantage (Table 4.3). Such disengagement is perhaps more widespread among mayoral authorities where too much power is seen to be concentrated in the directly elected mayor.

Table 4.3 The advantages and disadvantages of the new constitutional arrangements

	No.
Advantages	
Efficient and quicker decision-making	111
Clearer and more accountable decision-making	64
Stronger and more focused leadership	41
Fewer or shorter meetings, fewer committees	25
Improved public involvement	19
Improved corporate action/dealing with cross-cutting issues	18
Innovative or improved scrutiny	17
Greater delegation to officers	14
New role for backbenchers	12
Fully documented constitution	11
Disadvantages	
Backbench members disengaged	109
Confusion over scrutiny role	34
Changes overly bureaucratic	26
No reduction in meetings	19
Changes too costly	13
Difficulty of persuading officers and members of the need for change	17

Limits to lay involvement

The ultimate test of any reform of councillor structures lies in its effect upon the willingness of lay people to continue to serve as councillors and on the willingness of new generations to put themselves forward for election. In Britain, the recruitment and retention of councillors has for many years been a matter of concern. The Maud Committee found that only 8 per cent of the respondents to their 1965 public attitude survey intended to stand in a local election, or might stand if the opportunity arose; that just 6 per cent had considered doing so; and that 2 per cent had actually stood.

The 1972 reforms of local government structures greatly reduced the number of council seats in England and Wales. This contraction had the dual effect of limiting the opportunities for people to serve as councillors and distancing them from their elected representatives. The 1994 *British Social Attitudes* study found that only about 1 per cent (22 of 1945 respondents) had stood for election in the past, and a further 4 per cent had considered standing but had not done so. As many as 93 per cent had never considered seeking election, despite the fact that one justification of the 1972 reforms had been to enhance public interest in local government.

What reasons have been cited for this persistent unwillingness to become involved? In the Maud study, the great majority of respondents who said they would never wish to stand for election to the local council (88%) were asked to state why. Their reasons ranged widely, but the predominant reasons were that they felt insufficiently confident to play the councillor's role (32%), had insufficient time (23%), were too old or in ill-health (13%) or lacked interest (12%). Similar questions were put forth in 1994, finding the most cited reason to be 'it just doesn't occur to [people] to think of standing', while 'they don't feel they have enough time' ranked second, at 38 per cent of those expressing a view. Other studies also pointed to similar factors, including the perceived low standing of councillors and the negative impact of council service on career and family. Excessive hours also deterred people with jobs and family responsibilities.

The government contends that the separation of roles will reduce the time burdens, as fewer councillors will be involved in decision-making, so solving the problem of councillor recruitment. However, the evidence from studies undertaken in the 1990s suggests that those people already serving as councillors feel quite differently. Although they face difficulties in reconciling their private and public lives (work, family, etc.), the majority find ways of coping that enabled them to continue to serve. Few councillors in any survey so far undertaken report that they contemplate standing down on account of these pressures.

The two problems of councillor recruitment and retention need, then, to be separately considered, at least in the short term. It would be premature to judge the impact of the Local Government Act, 2000 on the ability of local government to attract new cohort of councillors into its ranks. However, what can be said with some certainty is that the direct effect on serving councillors has been to induce among the majority of them a sense of disengagement. Evidence from the latest survey, reported in Table 4.3, shows this to be by far the predominant disadvantage cited by chief executives themselves.

The emergence of an entirely new scrutiny role, however, promises new opportunities for those councillors who might otherwise feel marginalised to play a meaningful role on their councils. What sort of difficulties have councillors faced in adapting to this challenge of scrutiny? How fully has the opportunity it presents been realised?

Developing the scrutiny function

In the traditional committee system, the same committee system made decisions, took a strategic overview, planned specific projects, provided the services and monitored the council's performance. But the key aim of New Labour's modernisation agenda, as set out in the White Paper, was to make decision-making more visible and accountable and to provide satisfying roles for all councillors through separating the executive and the scrutiny function. The Deputy Prime Minister himself announced that 'We want councils to move away from their current ways of working which is often obscure and unclear ... all of these new forms will be efficient, transparent and accountable. People will know who to praise, who to blame and who to call to account' (DETR, 1999: foreword).

Developing an effective scrutiny role was thus central to government's plans. The scrutiny committee would hold the executive to account for the efficient exercise of executive functions; assist in the improvement and development of the council's policies; review and make reports on issues which affect the authority's area or its residents and examine whether the systems that the executive has in place to deliver its functions are robust and are being properly observed. The detail of how scrutiny would operate was largely left to local authorities, with very little prescription from central government. The councils were to choose 'forms of local governance allowing their overview and scrutiny committees to request a debate at full council before a particular decision is made or implemented by the executive. It would be for the council's own new constitution to provide for committees to determine what areas of policy they review, in addition to the task of reviewing the executive. Different methods of scrutiny lend themselves to different methods of review. For example, the executive might involve the scrutiny members in a detailed way on budget deliberations, whereas the scrutiny committee itself might decide on a distinct and more independent approach on another aspect of local policy. Research that are being carried out for the ODPM shows considerable differences to have emerged in the type of scrutiny tasks and the balance between policy development and overview of items in the forward plan, post-decisional scrutiny and policy monitoring and performance management. A number of authorities have established scrutiny co-ordinating bodies, to plan and co-ordinate the work of other committees, and to resolve uncertainties about where issues should be directed.

Several studies have thrown light on the difficulties associated with developing the scrutiny process. One obvious obstacle to the development of scrutiny role is the extreme politicisation of British local government. In almost every council all seats are held by representatives of the major political parties, with a handful of other more locally based groupings and a declining number of true Independents. The Widdicombe Committee charted the growth of party influence and the decision-making practices that flowed from it. Recording the decline of cross-party voting and the rise of party group cohesion under conditions of strict discipline the committee characterised the turbulent 1980s as one of political intensification. Political change since that time with the development of the three-party system has perhaps softened some of the rigidity of party discipline. However, New Labour's reforms have once again opened the doors for the re-entry of the whip system to secure compliance with the executive policies. How then do those backbench councillors who are members of a majority party reconcile the demands of party discipline with the requirements of scrutiny role?

Some of the authorities experimenting with scrutiny have claimed exemptions from party discipline for the scrutiny function. This has involved a considerable change in political culture, yet many councillors continue to be reluctant to challenge colleagues on the executive from within the same party. Second, scrutiny raises an important issue of officer advice and neutrality. Officers are required to give impartial advice without fear of damage to their careers or their relationships with their colleagues. It is feared by some that they will be placed under inappropriate pressure. Some authorities are using special advisors from outside the authority to ensure independence. Some scrutiny committees have found difficulties in obtaining the level and quality of detail they require from officers whose traditional loyalty will have been to the service committee chairs and who themselves have found it difficult to adapt to the dual role.

Can scrutiny then work? Scrutiny by committees is now an established part of UK Parliament, providing the closest analogy to the new requirements for local government. There are, however, important differences. While Parliamentary select committees have discretion in relation to topics of investigation, the manner in which they conduct their work and the power to send for persons, papers and records, the Local Government Act provides little clarity on powers and sanctions that might be available to scrutiny committees. Evidence to date suggests that scrutiny function is underdeveloped and poorly understood by the vast majority of members and officers, including the executive members themselves when attending scrutiny committees to give an account of their decisions (Ashworth and Snape, 2004). Parliamentary select committees are generously supported by staff and by expert advisors. Such specialised support is not yet available to local scrutiny committees. There are concerns about the volume of reporting, and some members are reported to have faced opposition in some authorities to the appointment of dedicated scrutiny officers.

One of the most frequent criticisms of Parliamentary accountability is of the dominance of the majority party. This dominance may be expressed in select committee inquiries when committees divide on party lines with the majority supporting rather than censuring the government. Similarly, in local government it may be that select committees are poorly suited to 'investigatory accountability' because they are 'too influenced by party politics' the higher the profile of the enquiry, the greater the force exerted by party politics (Polidano, 2001: 249). There are fears that loyalty to the local party group will impede scrutiny activities (Copus, 1999) and there have been calls for reforms to party whipping arrangements to facilitate effective scrutiny (Filkin *et al.*, 1999).

Scrutiny function in local government, then, faces formidable obstacles. However, in recent research just 15 per cent of councillors reported that the party whip was applied to scrutiny operations, whereas over half of respondents pointed out that non-councillors were appointed to scrutiny committees. Despite these responses, officers and members suggest that party politics has had an important effect on scrutiny. One councillor was reported as saying 'it is a closed shop to all but a secret few. As the majority party holds the chair of all scrutiny committees and the whip is used, any opposing view is a waste of time' (Ashworth and Snape, 2004). The ODPM survey showed that the great majority of scrutiny committees in majority party councils (83%) are chaired by a majority party member. But party control of the scrutiny function cannot be directly inferred from this. In nearly two in five authorities, party pre-meetings are held prior to the scrutiny committee meetings, but in less than one in ten were the decisions of these committees subject to the party whip. Even so, in a number of authorities visited in the subsequent stage of the study it seemed that dissent was more likely to be expressed through informal internal party meetings than through the formal scrutiny function.

Officer–member relations

Implementing the new arrangements has been more than just a matter of reassigning roles and establishing new structures. Adoption of any of the prescribed models requires a willingness to see power and responsibility redistributed. The discussion so far has centred upon the implied relationships between councillors: those in leading positions, and those whose responsibility is primarily to represent and scrutinise. Equally, the relationship between members and officers will also undergo change, although there is no statutory prescription of change in officer roles. Whether officers gain or lose power as a result of these changes depends on how close they are to leadership, and on the characteristics of their local authority.

Some further degree of delegation to council officers will be required if local authorities are to meet the expectations of the new political management regime. Streamlining political management has been portrayed as freeing up council officers to 'devote more of their time to the effective management of the council and successful policy implementation, with clear direction from the political leadership'. This is bound to implicate officers in the policies of the executive, much as civil servants are implicated in those of their ministers. The government foresees that 'backbench [sic] members will scrutinise the actions of the executive – both those of the executive's political leadership and those of officers implementing that leadership's policies'.

On the one hand, then, officers will continue to serve the whole council and support all councillors in their new roles, providing councillors with the information and facilities they need, whether as members of the executive or as the scrutineers of executive actions. On the other hand, some officers will have the specific role of supporting non-executive councillors, others that of supporting the mayor or the leader and cabinet. There will, then, be a division of function – arguably of interest – within the officer body. Meanwhile, the chief executive will continue as the head of the paid service, and to him or her will fall much of the burden of ensuring that officer–member relations, and those between officers, operate in the council's interest. So far, only the new Greater London Authority has had to face up to these dilemmas, and with ambiguous result (Pimlott and Rao, 2002).

At the same time, government continues to press the case for more extensive delegation. Exactly what is implied by delegation under these new circumstances is far from clear for, as we have seen, new arrangements mean new roles for both councillors and officers. The extent of delegation to officers will depend on the precise arrangements a council adopts, but in any event is expected to be greater than is currently the norm. The mayor and council-manager model, in particular, envisages considerably more delegation to officers than might be expected of other models. The advocacy of greater delegation to officers is no new thing. Nor is the reluctance of many councillors to accept it. Councillors are often opposed to delegating any of their powers to officers, and securing greater delegation is often frustrated by this resistance. In the 1993 survey, 87 per cent of councillors did not want to see further delegation to officers; in 1999, the figure was a comparable 82 per cent. Councillor hostility to accepting any further transfer of power from themselves to the council's officers remains overwhelming.

Currently, a major issue of concern to the officers is how best to support councillors in their scrutiny role. Some officers are reportedly nervous and defensive about the prospect of working with and attending scrutiny committees, while others are reported to be uneasy about being scrutinised by those who do not share their professional background. In yet other authorities, there are concerns that officers were resisting scrutiny and at times attempting to frustrate the process.

Conclusion

Any change has direct implications for the role of elected members, be they leading or backbench councillors. The classic committee system of the municipal model provided for a wide *diffusion* of responsibility. It operated in much that way in non-party authorities. Other authorities, with strong leaderships founded on party discipline, managed to achieve a *concentration* of executive responsibility within the confines of the committee system: something of a quasi-cabinet system. The true cabinet system, like the council-manager system, goes further and provides for a *separate*, though not *constitutionally independent*, focus of authority. Only the directly elected mayor system goes further still to provide an executive mandate that is both *separate* and *independent*.

In British local government, the committee system ensured that the generality of members were involved in the process of deciding what should be done, how it should be done and satisfying themselves that it had been done. Arguably, any attempt to entrust the functions of direct-ing and controlling the activities of the authority to a few selected mem-bers had the potential to be challenged by those who fear relegation to second-class status as simple ward representatives. Studies conducted in the early 1990s showed that few councillors would be satisfied with an exclusively representative or non-executive role, feeling that the conse-quences of a move to a cabinet or mayoral model would be highly adverse to the representative process.

The preliminary indications from the latest research for the ODPM are that most councillors are indeed marginalised by the imposition of sep-arate executive and representative roles. What of the remainder? It is apparent that the professionalisation of local politics has been further advanced by the responsibilities and remuneration given to a handful of leading councillors, who will devote themselves on a full-time basis to running local affairs. Many deplore this development yet, at the same time, the primary aims of reform – to sharpen the decision process – may well have been achieved, at least in part.

5
From Aldermen to Ministers: The Oslo Model Revisited

Harald Baldersheim

When the City of Oslo changed its executive organisation in 1986 from an aldermanic to a ministerial format, this was a revolutionary move in the Norwegian context. Experience as well as theories of institutional development predicted an imminent collapse of the experiment, or a gradual return to pre-existing, well-known ways of running the city, if the experiment was ever implemented. Instead, the Oslo model has been in operation for 17 years. Its radical features have become more fully developed over the years, and today it is taken for granted as the natural form of governance for Oslo. The model has not travelled widely, however. It has been adopted only in the county council of Nordland since 1999 and, since 2000, in the city of Bergen (Fimreite, 2003; Røiseland and Stigen, 2003). After a short trial period, a somewhat similar scheme was abandoned by another county council.

Why did Oslo choose this model and what were the objectives the city sought to achieve? To what extent were the objectives actually realised and did the model work? This chapter addresses these questions and assesses the changes over the past ten years. The concluding section asks just how different the current Oslo model is nearly two decades after its introduction and in the final section of this article alternative explanations of the development of the Oslo model are discussed.[1]

Basic features of the Oslo model

The city council in Oslo elects an executive board – a 'cabinet' – on a majority basis unlike in other Norwegian municipalities, where boards and committees are normally composed on a proportional basis. Oslo is distinctive in another sense in that the cabinet assumes all executive functions and responsibilities, while these are normally allocated to an appointed, professional municipal manager, and to some extent also delegated to a number of standing committees. The cabinet remains accountable to the city council through the mechanisms of accountability including votes of no confidence which, if passed, forces resignation of the cabinet. The cabinet may also threaten to resign over important votes although the council will hesitate to reject cabinet policies if it leads to resignation, unless the council is able and prepared to establish a new majority with a new cabinet. A third distinctive feature of Oslo's government is that council committees are confined to scrutiny and recommendation functions, and have no powers of policymaking, implementation and supervision. All standing committees and boards with executive functions have been abolished.

The role of the mayor was largely unaffected by 1986 reforms. His function was and is that of a speaker, presiding over council meetings; the mayor is not a member of the cabinet. Oslo was modelled on the national system of governance, with the role of the mayor fashioned after that of the speaker of the national assembly. Similarly, the position of the cabinet leader is modelled on that of the prime minister.[2] The position of mayor has traditionally been regarded as the highest political office of the municipality, but it is likely that in the eyes of the public, the new and more powerful office of cabinet leader now overshadows that of the mayor.

In short, the City of Oslo has changed from a predominantly administrative type of executive with committees and strong management to a powerful political, majoritarian executive. It was, however, the introduction of the 'parliamentary' mechanisms of accountability that gave the Oslo model its unique flavour. In this too, Oslo looked primarily to the national form of governance, not to other cities for inspiration. Moreover, Oslo's new city charter actually broke with two further traditions in local government organization in Norway: the alderman model of political governance and the directorate model of administrative organisation.

The alderman model (*formannskapsmodellen*) sees local politics as a matter for laymen, sharing a responsibility for community affairs. The model allocates positions of influence between the political parties according to party strength in the local council. The key positions of influence are seats on the board of the council and seats on a local authority's standing committees and these too are allocated between parties. Proportional representation is designed to foster a political climate of consensus, co-operation and reasonableness. In the case of Oslo, what came to be increasingly seen as a problem with this type of decision-making style was that the lines of responsibility and accountability tended to be blurred; under conditions of increasing financial austerity, parties and individuals were tempted to behave irresponsibly. In the corridors of Oslo's City Hall it was commonly remarked that the city council was in the habit of passing budgets with the volume of expenditures favoured by the Social Democrats and the level of taxation favoured by the Conservatives. Moreover, the control of administrative agencies was seen to suffer from a lack of overall co-ordination and a lack of clear political guidelines.

The central premise of the traditional directorate model (*rådmannsstyre*) is that administration is a task to be conducted by professionals, highly trained and specialised in their respective fields. The directorate model draws a sharp distinction between administration and politics. All administrative appointments are to be strictly meritocratic and non-partisan, and the director (or, as in Oslo, directors) is responsible for the preparation of business to be considered by the council and its committees. The directors have tenure, and could only be fired on the basis of proven misconduct. At the time of the change in Oslo, directors even had a right of appeal to the Ministry of Local Government. The directors, therefore, had a powerful influence over the agenda of the political bodies, and over the range of alternatives these bodies were invited to consider.

All this changed when, faced with a severe financial crisis, an accumulated deficit of nearly one billion kroner, a decision was made to change the city charter. A new charter, it was hoped, would result in better and more responsible government. The city charter was launched as a means to promote six goals with a view to enhancing political control over the administration; clarifying the lines of political responsibility and accountability; laying greater emphasis on 'the view of the whole' in decision-making; providing more flexibility in service provision; more scope for employee participation; and delivering better services to the public.

To achieve these goals, the city cabinet took over the powers and functions formerly possessed by the eight directors, whose positions were abolished. The 'parliamentary' relationship to the council meant that the city cabinet had to be backed by a majority of the council. It had to resign if a vote of no confidence was passed, or if it asked for a vote of confidence and failed to get it.

These two structural changes were supplemented by reorganisation at the top and intermediate levels of administration. The essence of these reorganisations was to replace the directorate model of administration with a managerial one. Under the directorate model there was no clearly defined head of administration, the directors were equals under the authority of the council (with the financial director, perhaps, as *primus inter pares*). They were each supposed to provide the council with independent professional advice and to carry out the council's decisions as they thought fit. The foundation of good administration was assumed to be professional competence in specialised fields. The managerial thinking, introduced along with the new city charter, emphasised administration as a skill in its own right, and maintained that this general sort of skill should guide the professionals. Accordingly, a position of general manager, or city manager, was created, to whom the administrative branches under the leadership of the various professionals were to be clearly subordinated. He or she became the exclusive channel of communication between the political and administrative spheres of city government. The cabinet members were to channel all their communications and directives through him or her, and the subordinate departments were also to reach the cabinet and other political bodies solely through the manager. The new arrangement emphasised the city cabinet as the locus of political responsibility. In Oslo, this was a radical move which led to a rapid dissemination of information throughout the organisation, but at the price of fragmented chains of command and responsibility.

At the lower levels of administration, in the service departments, efficiency gains were expected to flow from moving more decision-taking further down the hierarchy. Wider powers were delegated to the service departments, including reorganisation, personnel matters and reallocation of funds up to a certain amount. Furthermore, employee involvement in decision-making was to be enhanced through new bodies of co-determination with trade union representation at the departmental levels, giving Oslo's employees more say in decision-making than in any other Norwegian city. Overall, the city charter sought to establish solutions to two overarching issues: political accountability and administrative co-ordination. The cabinet and the concomitant parliamentary instruments of control were to be the answers to the first problem, the position of the city manager the solution to the second one. It was not clear that these two sets of solutions could coexist, and commentators pointed out that tensions were likely to arise between managerial and political co-ordination.

Political control over the administration

Before the reform, the process of decision-making and also the political agenda used to be structured by the division of work between the city's administrative branches (health, education, transport and so on). Problems, plans and financial requirements of the administrative or service-providing agencies created a steady and heavy stream of issues that was channelled into the political arena for solutions, decisions or just as information about what was going on. Politicians often felt overwhelmed by this stream and found little room or time for their own initiatives or visions. In order to cope with the workload of information and issues, many tried to become 'super-bureaucrats'. This seemed to have been the fate especially of many of the full-time salaried politicians that several cities, including Oslo, introduced in the 1970s. However, having abandoned the role model represented by the layman amateur councillor, they had difficulties developing distinctive, alternative roles for politicians.

The political agenda was still largely structured in the same way as before: the administrative agencies *acted* and the city cabinet *reacted*. The stream of issues from below was such that it was not possible for a few politicians faced with an army of bureaucrats to change that situation fundamentally. However, the city cabinet was more strategically oriented towards the administration. The cabinet tended to be more specific about issues it wanted considered in strategic plans. After the reform, political guidelines, although more clearly specified than before, had become more partisan. Furthermore, all documents presented to the council and to the wider public were now presented as the city cabinet's documents and views, whereas, before, plans, reports and so on were presented in the name of the director whose agency had produced it in the first place. And if the views of the administration were different from those of the political masters, this would be evident in the documents that finally reached the council (and the public). Now, only the cabinet's opinions and preferences would be known. Earlier, an administrative agency would also be able to receive the credit for new initiatives. After the reform, credit went to the cabinet alone. Professionals tended to resent this downgrading of their visibility clinging to the earlier ideas about the proper role of professionals in city government, embedded in the directorate model. This problem had, at the time of the first evaluation study, yet to be tackled by the cabinet in a constructive fashion. Politicians would have to work through professionals whether there was a city cabinet or an aldermanic board, but at this stage the relationship was strained.

A decade on, it becomes possible to assess the changed relations between the city cabinet and the administrative bodies. The later evaluation studies also permit comparisons to be made between Oslo and the other three larger Norwegian cities (Bergen, Trondheim and Stavanger) that had, at the time, retained the traditional model of municipal governance (Hagen *et al.*, 1999). The new studies demonstrated, first, that, in Oslo, the procedures established by the city charter of 1986 had become standard operating procedures widely accepted by all groups of actors. Most city administrators in Oslo felt that they had a clear under-standing of which issues should be sent to the cabinet level for decisions or instructions and which issues they could decide on their own. They did not feel that this line of demarcation presented any difficulty with regard to the operations of their own departments. There was, however, no conspicuous contrast in this regard between Oslo and the other cities. There was variation, however, in the extent to which administra-tive heads tried to anticipate reactions from the political level; here the Oslo managers were more inclined to look for political guidance than their counterparts in the other cities. Moreover, trade unions were felt to be somewhat less influential in Oslo (Hagen *et al.*, 1999) probably as a result of the abolition in 1989 of the special corporative bodies with enhanced employee representation (Lund, 1995).

Clarifying political responsibility

In the city council of 1986, the liberal or non-socialist parties had a majority of one over the socialist parties. Of four parties on the liberal side, the Conservatives were the largest single party; on the other side, the Social Democrats dominated over two other smaller parties. After some rounds of negotiations on the liberal side, the Conservatives formed a city cabinet, but had to rely on the support of two other par-ties (the Progress Party on the far right, and the Christian People's Party more to the centre). This constellation survived several motions of no confidence put forth by the socialist side in the city council. In one case, the majority for the cabinet was achieved with a margin of just one vote. After the local election in 1987, the Conservative cabinet was reinstated in office. The non-socialist majority now had a margin of six council seats.

By 1998, motions of no confidence had been made altogether on 11 occasions by the opposition. After individual ministerial responsibility and accountability was introduced in 1993, motions of no confidence have been exclusively directed at individual cabinet members, leading to resignations in two cases (Hagen *et al.*, 1999: 72–3). The no confi-dence motion is triggered either by the cabinet's (alleged) failure to provide full disclosure of relevant information, procedural slip-ups or disagreement over policies. The extent to which the new city cabinet succeeded in establishing itself as a focus of attention for public opinion was evident in the proposals that were put before the council as 'the city cabinet's proposals'. Such proposals were previously presented in the media as 'the director's proposals'. Interest groups increasingly tried to arrange to see members of the cabinet to present their case, while earlier they would send delegations to the city council's meetings.

Opinions outside City Hall became increasingly polarised, at least as presented by the media. The city cabinet's proposed budget cuts of June 1988 (see below) caused demonstrations to be held in the streets of Oslo by city employees as well as citizens. Some of the demonstrations ended in riots and confrontations with the police on a scale not seen since the Vietnam demonstrations in the 1960s. A growing overall level of conflict was to be expected. However, the proportion of uncontested or unanimous decisions had actually increased when the spring session of 1985 was compared to the spring session of 1987 (29% against 31% of uncontested decisions). The dominant parties among the insiders and outsiders were the Conservatives and the Social Democrats, respectively (Baldersheim and Strand, 1988). There was no tendency for these parties to oppose each other more vigorously than before. The proportion of joint voting (Conservatives and Social Democrats voting for the same alternative) actually increased (81% of all votes in 1985 and 83% in 1987). It was the parties to the left of the Social Democrats that most often voted against the Conservative city cabinet.

At the same time, all the socialist parties were more active than before in producing counter-propositions, while the non-socialists became less active. So it seemed that the opposition chose to express its dissident views through the suggestion of alternative policies and courses of action on a limited number of issues rather than through an indiscriminate 'nay-saying' to all cabinet proposals. This pattern may point to the existence of a highly responsible opposition as well as to the continued existence of the political climate associated with the aldermanic form of government. The growth in supplementary propositions continued in the 1990s as did the number of questions put to the cabinet during the council's question hour while there was no similar surge in the other three cities (Hagen *et al.*, 1999: 59–60). The increase occurred especially after 1995 in the wake of the installation of a minority cabinet.[3]

The reform was expected to affect the roles of all political actors in the city of Oslo, ordinary council members as well as leading political figures, such as the mayor and vice mayor. The mayor was to concentrate on his role as council speaker, while he would have to share the role of political figurehead with the cabinet leader, the chief executive.

The legislation finally adopted retained the option of allocating minor executive functions to the mayor, which was a potential source of confusion. At least in a transition period this might lead to tensions between the two actors. Surprisingly few reports of role clashes have emerged. Role adjustments have worked out quite smoothly, helped by the fact that mayors and cabinet leaders have generally been from the same party. Oslo's mayors have accepted with good grace the new centre of power in city politics, the cabinet leader. Comparative surveys of perceptions of power in city politics demonstrate quite clearly that Oslo's mayor is now seen by other actors as substantially *less* influential than mayors of other Norwegian cities (Hagen *et al.*, 1999: 87–8), which is a logical result of the reform.

The change from committees with delegated powers of decision-making to committees of scrutiny entailed problems of adjustment for some of the ordinary councillors (Baldersheim and Strand, 1988). Many feared the emergence of a two-tier structure within the council, with some members having privileged access to information by virtue of belonging to the majority coalition or as paid full-time committee chairs or vice chairs. Such fears were voiced, in particular, by the smaller parties. Consequently, steps were taken to ensure that members of the opposition would share some paid positions and access to secretarial assistance (this has made the Oslo model a fairly expensive reform). Not much evidence is available regarding the impact of the Oslo model on ordinary members and recruitment to the city council in the 1990s. The feared (further) marginalisation of the smaller parties has not happened, however. In fact, the smaller parties in Oslo feel they have slightly more influence on decisions than smaller parties in other Norwegian cities with traditional structures (Hagen *et al.*, 1999: 109).

Improving co-ordination

The impetus for changing the city charter and introducing the city cabinet was the desperate state of the city finances in 1984–5. During 1986 and 1987, the financial position seemed to improve, partly because of higher revenues than expected, and partly because special measures to manage the burden of deficits had been negotiated with the Ministry of Local Government. However, in May 1988, it became publicly known that the city's finances were in trouble again. A deficit had built up during 1987 which, together with what remained of the former one, meant that the situation was even worse than it had been in 1984. This failure to balance the books may suggest that co-ordination of the city government was no better under the new city charter than it was before.

It is not clear that this was actually the case, since the setback of the city finances was, to a large extent, clearly caused by occurrences outside the city cabinet's control, for example, reductions in city employee working hours negotiated at the national level, increased contributions to the national pensions fund imposed by the central government and growing urban problems requiring higher supplementary social benefits. Also, the other larger Norwegian cities, working under the old order, had run into even greater financial difficulties than Oslo. Bergen, for instance, had a deficit that corresponded to 17 per cent of its current budget for 1987, while the figure was only 6 per cent for Oslo. So, Oslo shared the fate of other cities. But its new city charter had not enabled it to do much better in terms of financial management than other cities, and no better than it did before.

The extent of responsible budgeting under the new regime may be illustrated with a tale about the 1987 budget. The city cabinet's own presentation of the budget showed that they knew they would have problems in financing the level of activity they would like to maintain. When faced with the problem of balancing the budget, a city has three principal options: cutting expenditures, increasing revenues or trying to bridge the gap through measures improving productivity and when faced with these choices, the cabinet opted for the third strategy to bridge the gap through productivity measures. This amounted to giving the nod to the administrative departments to go ahead with their activity plans although the appropriations did not match the plans. The budget might still have been saved had the cabinet pressed on with systematic measures to improve efficiency and cut manpower, hard as that may be in labour-intensive local services. Against this background, the ensuing deficit was not surprising. This seemingly reckless spending should be seen against a political background, however, and had much to do with the cabinet leader's determination to win the upcoming election for his party – which he did.

Oslo's finances improved gradually from 1990 onwards. This was partly due to higher revenues and partly to more astute financial management under a new cabinet leader who took over from 1989. The precise weights of the two factors are hard to ascertain. A central indicator of municipal financial health is the net surplus indicator which is conventionally recommended to be no less than 3 per cent of the current budget. Of the four cities under comparison, only Oslo managed to stay at the recommended level (or above) after 1995 whereas the other cities hovered around zero for the rest of the decade (Hagen, 1999: 180–1).[4]

Relations between ministers and professionals

City cabinet reform provided an opportunity to introduce two further changes in administrative organisation: the introduction of the city manager with overall responsibility for co-ordination and communication with the political bodies, and delegation of authority to service departments in order to enhance their adaptability and flexibility in service provision. A further step of delegation was taken in 1988, with the introduction of neighbourhood councils with responsibility for social services, including primary health, kindergartens and care for the elderly, but not schools.

The city manager's position was increasingly soured by complaints from the service departments over delays in obtaining guidance from the political bodies, the central position of the manager acting as a bottleneck. In reality, delays in the political responses to issues presented by the departments were often caused by the selective attention exercised by the cabinet. The members of the cabinet tended to give priority to issues *they* felt were politically important, sometimes to the neglect of the departments' concerns. This process of selective attention was, of course, not so visible to the departments, while the manager, for his part, was not in a position to disclose the deliberations of the city cabinet to the departments.

Gradually, pressure was building up to circumvent the city manager, both from above and below. Members of the city cabinet felt it increasingly cumbersome to have to go through the city manager every time they wanted information from a department, or some investigation to be carried out. The cabinet members soon started to practise a division of work that largely corresponded to the city's administrative subdivisions, although they had authority and responsibility only as a collegial body, not as individual 'ministers'. The informal division of work at the cabinet level was soon perceived and acted upon by the outside world, which started to ascribe responsibility to individual members, such as 'the cabinet member for health', 'the cabinet member for transport' and so on. Such a development also seemed to be appreciated by the service departments, who had complained that the new city charter had cut them off from contact with the political processes. In 1989, the cabinet applied to the Ministry of Local Government to be allowed to change the city charter so that cabinet members might be given individual authority over departments, that is, the introduction of a full-blown ministerial model. Such a change would clearly affect the position of the city manager, who felt that he would then become more of a financial adviser and less of a general manager and co-ordinator. The issue was not settled until 1992 when legislation was changed to allow Oslo to abolish the office of the city manager and also to grant cabinet members individual authority over city ministries. At the same time, permission was given for Oslo to recruit cabinet members from outside the ranks of the city council. The option to recruit non-elected individuals to cabinet positions has been frequently taken, often in order to enlist the service of experts. How did it come about?

How did all these changes in the city of Oslo come about?

Oslo has managed not only to implement a cabinet, parliamentary-style of governance but also to develop it more fully over time. The system works largely as intended: new rules of the game have been widely accepted and many of the intended consequences have materialised. On the whole, the distinction between 'ins' and 'outs' has become more clear-cut; this has probably contributed to highlight political accountability. However, the contrast to other cities that have retained the traditional aldermanic model of governance is, in many respects, smaller than expected. Whether the quality of policymaking and service provision has improved as a result of the cabinet system is harder to tell since Oslo also has pursued a series of parallel reforms that may have affected services in particular more directly (e.g. the introduction of quasi-autonomous neighbourhood councils and outsourcing and competitive tendering). The central motivation for the switch to cabinet governance was a fiscal crisis of immense proportions. Unlike several other Norwegian cities, Oslo has managed to balance its books during the last decade. If this is the ultimate test, then the system works. How did it come about?

Organisational change does not depend solely on the design and determination of reformers. Many factors may intervene to stall or derail reforms. Perhaps the strange thing about the Oslo reform is that it did not peter out, but that so many components were actually implemented with a good many of the intended results. There is no lack of experience or theory that would predict failure (e.g. old institutionalism as well as new institutionalism; Peters, 1999). Why did the reform succeed to the extent it did? Was it good planning, good politics, happy coincidence or perhaps the reform was not as radical as it seemed?

Are explanations to be sought in theories of strategic planning, organisational politics (the effectiveness of side payments), the 'garbage can' model or the persistence of the past (as suggested by certain varieties of new institutionalism, for example, March and Olsen, 1989)?

The design of the reform was drawn up during the 1984–5 crisis by a small change in coalition (the vice mayor, the financial manager and the leader of the largest trade union, the latter motivated by fears of job losses). In a very short time this trio contracted a series of reports and memoranda that covered the most central issues such a reform would touch upon, which meant they had answers to the most pressing questions that the proposal was likely to provoke. So, good planning may explain the achievements of the first stages of change.

Some of the goals tacked on to the core reform clearly represented side payments to factions that had the power to block or seriously delay the reform. The enhanced employee representation certainly belongs in this category and so does the neighbourhood council scheme, which the conservatives originally were against. However, the latter scheme was much favoured by the left wing of the Social Democrats and probably helped secure the undivided support of the latter for the cabinet model. So the reform was also based on good politics. Tellingly, the conservative cabinet got rid of the employee representation bodies when they felt stronger after the 1987 elections. The neighbourhood councils were kept and their responsibilities expanded, however, as the system turned out to be very helpful in bringing city finances under control.

There were also elements of a 'garbage can' type of process (March and Olsen, 1976) in the chain of events leading up to the reform. There was a serious financial crisis which helped concentrate minds wonderfully on the necessity of reform. There was a vice mayor on the look-out for a more influential position; he was clearly overshadowed by a highly popular mayor and had no chance of ousting him in direct confrontation. As leader of the cabinet the vice mayor would gain a much more prominent position in the eye of the public as well as in real decision-making (the vice mayor became in fact the first leader of the cabinet). The reform depended upon legislative changes that would have to be introduced by the national government of the day. The Minister for Local Government happened to be the former mayor of Stavanger, a fellow Conservative and sympathetic to the idea of trying out a scheme of governance that would enhance political control over city bureaucrats. After some deliberation, he decided to steer the required legislative amendments through Parliament.

However, not all elements of the reform package were totally new to Oslo Town Hall. Several ideas had been floated before, or tried out partially. The search for enhanced political roles in urban governance had a history dating back to the 1950s. Several schemes had been tried before. Neighbourhood councils also had a modest history in Oslo since 1972. And employee consultation schemes were nothing new. The election of committees on a majority basis was a long standing option in local government legislation, although few municipalities made use of this opportunity. So it can also be argued that there was much continuity in Oslo governance even after 1986. Everything was not as new as it seemed. The power of institutional persistence could not be entirely disregarded.

However, one element of change was really revolutionary: the demise of the eight directors, who used to be the backbone of city administration in Oslo, and the take-over of their functions by elected politicians. This decapitation of the city bureaucracy was achieved through golden handshakes rather than the guillotine. And like all real revolutions, this one, too, was predicted by no one.

In the larger picture, there is one feature, in particular, that calls out for an explanation: why has not the Oslo model spread any further in the Norwegian or Scandinavian context? So far, only two other local authorities have fully adopted the core features of parliamentary politics and cabinet accountability although quite a number of authorities have considered its adoption. Why do some reform ideas, like New Public Management, seemingly become fads and fashions spreading everywhere, while others stay put? The Oslo model has certainly not suffered from lack of publicity. Is it too uniquely adapted to the particular circumstances of the Capital City? Or is it simply not perceived as a good solution to pressing problems of the day? A comparative study of reform processes with a contextually aware research design would be required to answer these questions.

Notes

1. The data presented in this paper draws on two evaluative studies: the first carried out by the author two and a half years after its inception, and the second, conducted ten years later by a different team.

   The first evaluation study was summarised in Baldersheim, Harald and Torodd Strand (1988), "Byregjering" i Oslo kommune. Hovedrapport fra et evalueringsprosjekt. Bergen: Norwegian Research Centre in Organization and Management. Report No. 7. The second round of evaluations was reported in Hagen, Terje P., Trine Monica Myrvold, Ståle Opedal, Inger Marie Stigen, Helge

Strand Østtveiten (1999), Parlamentarisme eller formannskapsmodell? Det parlamentariske styringssystemet i Oslo sammenliknet med formanns-kapsmodellene i Bergen, Trondheim og Stavnager. Oslo: Norsk Institutt for by- og regionforskning. Rapport nr. 3.

The present review of Oslo's system of governance updates the analysis presented in Baldersheim, Harald (1992). "'Aldermen into Ministers'. Oslo's Experiment with a City Cabinet", Local Government Studies, 18: 18–30.

2. Formally, under existing legislation, the council may grant the mayor certain minor executive functions (Lund, 1995–2003: 18); in practice, the City Council of Oslo has been reluctant to do so.

3. Questions were also fewer in number in the other cities; however, rather than an effect of the cabinet system this could be a reflection of a lower case load in the smaller cities (unlike the other cities, Oslo also has the functions of a county council).

4. Bergen's financial situation has in fact worsened substantially after 2000 (Fimreite, 2003: 161) and it is now (2003) on the list of cities under extra-ordinary central government supervision because of its financial chaos. Paradoxically, Bergen introduced the Oslo model in 2000.

6
Municipal Presidentialism and Democratic Consolidation in Spain

Jaume Magre Ferran and Xavier Bertrana Horta

Both from the legislative point of view, and from that of political practice, the history of the Spanish local political system is one of the gradual consolidation of municipal presidentialism. If we interpret presidentialism as a system in which the essential part of executive authority is concentrated in the position of mayor (Delcamp, 1994), then this trend began with the Local Government Act that was passed in 1985 (Law 7/1985), further confirmed by a block of legislation in April 1999. Political practice has shaped this tendency: the long stay in office of mayors, their partial or exclusive dedication to political and administrative management and such political factors as the dominance of local party structure or the notable autonomy of local sections from the central bodies of political parties, have all resulted in giving the position of mayor a presidential profile. However, the recently passed Law of Measures for the Modernisation of Local Government (Law 57/2003) breaks with this presidential trend and opts, in the case of large cities, for a strong executive body taking on most of the management functions at the expense of the mayor.

This chapter recounts the organisation of the political executive in Spain, distinguishing the form of government of common regime municipalities from the institutional organisation of large cities. The political executive of common regime municipalities was only modified in 1999, with the aim of overcoming certain institutional weaknesses resulting from the initial local government legislation in 1985. In large cities, the form of government has undergone substantial changes with the passing of the Law of Modernisation in 2003. The chapter also analyses the political and executive structures, offering an interpretive

Table 6.1   Number of municipalities in the population bands

Population range	Number of municipalities
Less than 100	934
From 101 to 250	1,593
From 251 to 1,000	2,417
From 1,001 to 2,000	1,003
From 2,001 to 5,000	1,001
From 5,001 to 10,000	509
From 10,001 to 20,000	332
From 20,001 to 50,000	201
From 50,001 to 100,000	62
More than 100,001	56
Total	8,108

summary of the trend towards the presidentialism of political practice throughout the last 25 years.

The organisation of the political executive in Spain

The Local Government Act 1985 established three forms of local government depending on population size. First, in municipalities with less than 100 inhabitants, the mayor is elected by a pure majority system and a neighbourhood assembly takes the most important decisions. Second, municipalities with between 100 and 250 inhabitants elect 5 councillors by a majority system and the mayor is chosen from amongst them. Third, in the case of bigger municipalities, local councillors are elected by the citizens with a proportional system and the mayor is also chosen from amongst them. The regulation of the Law 57/2003 follows this same pattern.

As we can see in the Table 6.1, in Spain there are 934 municipalities with less than 100 inhabitants and 1593 from 101 to 250 inhabitants. In this sense, more than 30 per cent of Spanish municipalities have less than 250 inhabitants. However, the level of urbanisation is very high: 85 per cent of the population lives in municipalities with more than 5000 inhabitants and 95 per cent in municipalities with more than 250. For that reason, we will focus this chapter on the political executive of municipalities with more than 250 inhabitants.

The political executive of 'common regime' municipalities

Spanish local governments are made up of the political executive and the council. The number of councillors depends on the size of the

Table 6.2 Number of local councillors according to the local population

Local population	Number of local councillors
Up until 250	5
From 251 to 1,000	7
From 1,001 to 2,000	9
From 2,001 to 5,000	11
From 5,001 to 10,000	13
From 10,001 to 20,000	17
From 20,001 to 50,000	21
From 50,001 to 100,000	25
More than 100,001	One councillor for every additional 100,000 inhabitants or fraction, plus one if the number of local councillors is even

population in the municipality (Table 6.2) and the council itself is chaired by the mayor. The political executive consist of the mayor chosen by the council, deputy mayors and local government board. Some councillors also have executive powers delegated by the mayor.

All councillors at the top of the voting list may be candidates for the position of mayor. If one of them obtains an absolute majority of votes from the councillors, s/he is proclaimed mayor. If there is no absolute majority, the councillor at the top of the most voted list in the municipal election is proclaimed mayor. This indirect election system was introduced to limit, as much as possible, the number of cases in which the mayor had to govern in a minority. At the same time, electing mayors from those first on the lists was designed to encourage people with certain prestige and ability to draw votes in a specific municipality to go in for election and give the local community a clear reference point, as well as the chance to indirectly choose their mayor.

A local government board is established in municipalities of over 5000 inhabitants to assist the mayor in carrying out his/her responsibilities, while in smaller municipalities the council itself decides whether to have one. The board is made up of a maximum of one-third of the total number of local councillors. The mayor appoints the members of the local government board and the deputy mayors from the elected local councillors, and has the power to dismiss them. The mayor's power to choose the councillors that will form part of the government in each local authority affords him/her a pre-eminent position in the political executive.

The pragmatism that dictated the legal and institutional design of Spanish local governments passed in 1985 assigned important executive responsibilities to the position of Mayor. The political aim was to

Figure 6.1   The delegation system.

strengthen the mayor's leadership in order to help local bodies operate and implement policies more efficiently on a day-to-day basis (Magre, 1999: 67). This tendency was further confirmed by a block of legislation in April 1999. The main feature of Law 11/1999, which reformed Law 7/1985, was to increase the mayor's executive powers. The new law took away most of the powers previously held by the council relating to economy and finance (e.g. carrying out economic management), certain powers relating to staff management, town planning, contracts and concessions and others (e.g. those relating to the administration and management of patrimony or to granting licences). Thus, since 1999, the mayor has monopolised the daily management of local services, as well as the administration and economic activity of the body. Therefore, functionally speaking, there was a clear trend towards making local government more presidential in nature.

The mayor and the council can delegate some of the powers accorded to them by statute. There are two kinds of delegation. The first is general and indefinite in nature. As a result of the mayor's general delegation, deputy mayors usually take charge of the main sectors of municipal activity. This kind of delegation can be related to certain sectors of municipal activity and include the direction and management of public services and policies. Second, there are special temporary delegations on the part of the mayor in order to manage specific issues or services that can also be attributed to any local councillor. The delegation system is shown in Figure 6.1.

Political accountability

The strengthening of executive authority brought into force by Law 11/1999 involved a functional relocation of the council within the institutional framework of the municipality, partially modifying the way this organ works and is organised. Study, report and consultation (or informative) committees were institutionalised, as were local political groups. Before 1999, informative committees were optional. In that year, they were made compulsory in municipalities of over 5000 inhabitants and optional in smaller municipalities. They are made up of local councillors elected by their political groups according to their weight in the council. Their main aim is to round beforehand all the issues that must be discussed in the council, and the council itself decides the number and thematic specialisation of the committees.

In Spain, the council full assembly has the power to remove the mayor from office. In 1999, the parliamentary elements of the system were improved: a motion of confidence brought by the mayor was introduced, and the motion of no confidence brought by the council was reformed. The regulations governing a vote of no confidence (1985 Organic Law on the General Electoral Regime, modified in 1993 and in 1999) require the motion to be put into practice: it must be signed by at least the absolute majority of councillors and only one can be signed during each mandate; it must be constructive in nature and must include the name of a proposed substitute; and it does not need to be justified.

Organic Law 8/1999 also allowed the mayor to present the town council with a confidence vote. This was a novelty in comparative local law as Spain was the first country in the European Union to initiate such a vote at a local level. A vote of confidence can only be moved under limited circumstances, with the sole aim of guaranteeing governability when the local government is faced with deadlock situations, institutional paralysis, instability or political crisis. It is linked to the approval or modification of subjects relating to yearly budgets and the body's organic regulations. The mayor can also ask for such a vote in relation to tax bylaws and the final approval of general municipal matters. Before calling for a vote of confidence, the council full assembly must have discussed the agreement to be taken and must have failed to approve it. This allows the mayor to bring a vote of confidence linked to the agreement related to this subject.

In the case of 'common regime' municipalities, legislation governing the local regime has not institutionalised an area of professionalised management that is stable and differentiated from the political area in councils. Legislation has favoured the elected body, and especially the mayor, in bestowing executive or management functions. The only public managers acknowledged by legislation are civil servants with national capacities – secretaries, auditors and treasurers. Even here, the legislation restricts them to classic bureaucratic functions: legal advice and authority to attest documents in the case of secretaries, control and internal supervision of economic, financial and budgetary management in the case of auditors, or accounting, treasury and payment collection in the case of treasurers.

The political executive of large cities

In 2003, Law 57/2003 was passed to create a strong executive made up of the mayor and a local government board, whose members are appointed and removed freely by the mayor. The mayor can appoint people who are not councillors as members of the local government board, provided their number does not exceed a third of the total number of members of this body. The Act attributed to the local government board almost all the powers of management. Although occupying a central position in the system, the mayor is no longer the holder of many management powers. Rather he/she is the head of an executive body, with broad powers of delegation to individual members and, to a lesser extent, to the executive staff.

For the first time, the dual nature of the mayor, traditionally both head of the local executive and, at the same time, president of the full assembly, is divided so that the latter function may be delegated to a councillor. In fact, some of the authors discussing the innovations introduced by this law highlight the prominence of the parliamentary characteristics of local government (Jiménez Asensio, 2004). Moreover, in large cities the full assembly has become a chamber of debate, in which the powers of legislation, planning, control and symbolic powers are concentrated, some of these powers being delegated to its committees, if so desired.

In municipalities with large populations, relations between politics and administration have been transformed. The Law divides the organs of the high administration of large cities into two broad groups: higher organs, which are the Mayor and the members of the Government Board; directive organs, among others the General Co-ordinators, General Directors and other similar organs. General Co-ordinators report directly to the members of the Government Board. Their main function, as implied by their name, is to co-ordinate the different General Directorates, be responsible for managing the common or administrative services of these or other similar functions. With some exceptions, the Mayor and Government Board are allowed to delegate their powers, to General Co-ordinators, General Directors or similar organs. Finally, the 2003 Law obliges cities with large populations to adopt some mechanisms of citizen involvement. These include proper consultation, regulations concerning citizen involvement, the creation of a councillor committee for consideration of citizen complaints and suggestions made up of councillors, the division of cites with large populations into districts and the setting up of a social council for the city, in which the local organisations might be represented.

The operation of the political structures

Involvement of lay politicians

Spain's first democratically elected councillors were closely linked to interests in their towns rather than to a general political project. Often they were more closely concerned with executive management than dealing with social demands, and they had a negative view of the professionalisation of political activity while dedicated to local administrative work (Brugué *et al.*, 2001: 221). During the first few years of democracy, political discussion was muted as the bureaucratic structure increased. This was the time of building up the Spanish welfare municipalities, and the process of management partification arose, by which political parties and their elected members were placed in the centre of political activity, not as political agents, but to take on managerial responsibilities (Brugué and Vallès, 1997: 514).

At the beginning of the 1990s, local governments started to undergo significant changes as they overcame the structural deficits inherited from the dictatorship. There was a steady increase in the municipal services in response to growing demands. Local governments could no longer concentrate on internal management and basic services, but had to tackle more complex problems of an increasingly fragmented community. They came to be less closely linked to immediate interests and specific problems and more engaged by medium- and long-term projects. Furthermore, the consolidation of professional administrative structures liberated councillors from their devotion to management and allowed them to increase their community-based activities.

Arising from these changes, these types of councillor can be distinguished: assistance, executive and political. Assistance councillors are characterised by their emphasis on the logic of service to the community, disapproving of sterile party controversies and the sophisticated detachment of technocrats. Executive councillors are those who aim to use their technical background and professional skills to resolve administrative dysfunctions, getting involved in the management of the council. Finally, political councillors believe their work should be related to the promotion, direction and control of public policy (Brugué, 2002: 29–30). From the 1980s to the 1990s the presence of political councillors increased, assistance councillors practically disappeared and the number of executive councillors fell (Brugué, 2002: 31). The attitudes of councillors regarding their role show the shift from traditional local *government* to local *governance*. Councillors have started to adopt new roles in local government that are more open to the outside world looking to collaborate and co-operate with other municipal agents and administrations in defining and implementing their political programmes and in defining future strategies for local communities.

This evolution has had an effect on political-bureaucratic relations. If during the first decade of local democracy we could say there was a clear trend towards politicising management latterly, locally elected representatives have gained the capacity to develop technical and management structures that are more autonomous.

Professionalism

The trend towards the professionalisation of local politics, which began during the process of political transition, has clearly consolidated itself. In those first few years, strong political leadership was essential in order to try to attain the political stability required and to create a cadre of experts in local politics, as well as to bring a personal element into local politics. In reality, we are simply highlighting the intimate relationship that Juan Linz has described between the concepts of legitimacy and efficiency in the processes that consolidated the new regimes (Linz, 1987: 36–52).

This situation was reflected and consolidated by legislation on the local regime. The Local Government Act 7/1985 placed the executive functions relating to management in the hands of local politicians and not in those of the administration, with limited delegation to elected members. For that reason, with the exception of large cities since the passing of Law 57/2003, it may be said that Spanish local administration does not follow a professional model but is governed directly by elected members who are, especially in the case of the mayor, highly active in its day-to-day running. Furthermore, electoral candidates from the larger municipalities currently expect to hold full-time, remunerated, local government posts of responsibility. In smaller municipalities, this prospect is vital due to the difficulty of hiring people with the necessary professional qualifications.

In common regime municipalities, the local political and executive management system revolves around the mayor, but the mayor can delegate some of his/her powers to members of the local government board or carry out special delegations in favour of councillors. Local politicians with governmental responsibilities are the only people who can enable their respective organisations to carry out a professional, managerial function, but this involves limiting their possibilities of occupying the managerial area (Longo, 1999: 34).

In most small- or even medium-sized councils, the municipal public managers are civil servants with national authority, since they are the only bureaucrats with a university qualification. They serve not only as advisors and supervisors but also as managers, albeit often without sufficient recognition of their work and without them having received the necessary training to carry out a managerial role.

The situation in medium and large municipal administrations is different and much more complex. Depending on the organisational model each council has adopted and on the management areas defined, in 'common regime' councils in Spain we can find three kinds of management, present either simultaneously or separately: 'unit' managers, who head the whole administrative structure under the direction of the mayor, 'sector' managers, found in each of the sector areas under the direction of deputy mayors or sector councillors and, finally, managers from public companies or autonomous bodies.

For the first time, Law 57/2003 has defined a professional executive structure for the local governments of large Spanish cities. It also enables the mayor and local government board of cities with large populations to delegate some of their powers to local public managers, formalising a situation that was already taking place in practice in some councils. This is intended to facilitate the appearance of professional public management, although it will probably give rise to highly diverse situations depending on the type of government established by each mayor and government board. Those not elected locally may become members of the government board (i.e. who are not councillors), and there are doubts as to whether this would attract 'politically reliable' public managers into local government.

Political accountability

Spain's agitated political and constitutional history meant that it was advisable to avoid too many experiments that would lead to a feeling of instability or a breakdown in the fragile structure of consensus on which the operational framework of local institutions had to be built. The constitutional text proclaimed political pluralism as one of its fundamental values, endorsing political parties as the expression of this pluralism and as the fundamental instrument for political involvement. This was encouraged by regulations governing the mechanisms of citizen involvement that go beyond party organisations. For example, the possibility for citizen involvement in legislative processes was much less, the electoral system did not permit any kind of opening up of the electoral lists, the regulation of referenda was very cautious and the regulations governing votes of no confidence were meagre and excessively restrictive.

By the middle of the 1990s, two factors helped certain experiences of participatory democracy to proliferate in Spanish municipalities, especially in Catalonia and the Basque Country: an increase in abstention in municipal elections and the awareness that municipalities are the ideal government arena to promote the active involvement of citizens in public affairs. The main instruments in Spanish local government are citizen councils or participatory centres, that is councils made up of citizens chosen at random to discuss a specific, controversial issue or one that has clear importance for the municipality, affecting a broad section of the population, the most definitive example being the Child Councils, based on the experience of Italian pedagogue Francesco Tonucci and applied previously to several Italian cities.

More recently, numerous municipalities have passed their own Citizen Involvement Regulations. These regulations, in addition to governing some of these participatory methods, cover the individual and collective rights of citizens to take part in the political life of the municipalities. Various councils have also established the Ombudsmen. In 2003, the *Law of Measures for the Modernisation of Local Government* finally established that it was obligatory for cities with large populations to have some mechanisms of citizen involvement.

Political leadership

One of the main objectives in the design of the new institutional architecture of Spanish local government and during the period of political transition was to strengthen the political leadership of the mayor. There was widespread fear of political instability. The legislature therefore decided to adopt a mayoral model inspired by the *bourgmestre* of the Länder in southern Germany which gives significant prominence to the figure of the mayor. Strengthening the figure of the mayor was achieved by limiting the vote of no confidence and providing residual clause of authority in favour of the mayor, as well as enabling the mayor to choose the members of the government committee without needing to take into account the political composition of the full assembly.

The legislative construction of the figure of mayor, therefore, is that of a functional presidentialism.

In spite of this, certain authors have pointed out limitations to mayoral hegemony. First, it is argued that the trend towards presidentialism could be impeded by the proportional electoral system, which could produce fragmentation of the local body. However, stability has been one of the most prevalent characteristics of the Spanish local government. Second, it is argued that the provision for delegation implies mayoral weakness. However, the concentration of power in the figure of the mayor and the significant flexibility of his/her powers of delegation allow the mayor to place him/herself in a real position of command. Finally, strong political parties at the local level could lead to tension between the elected elite and the leaders of the party organisation. A practice has also become consolidated in this case which has ended up shaping the presidential nature of the mayor, as the latter tends also to be the president of the local party group of which he/she is a member.

Conclusion

Cities are said to eventually resemble their mayors. Whatever the case, it is evident that, before the advent of democracy, Spanish cities were very much alike because the mayors were handpicked by an authority that ignored the needs and desires of the population. As a result, they simply implemented the plans set out by the central government (Regàs, 1997).

The dictatorship turned municipalities into simple administrative machines, which did not represent their communities and lacked real decision-making powers. In addition, it made local administration neo-feudal and corrupt in nature because the local power apparatus and dominant private economic interests were interdependent, especially in large cities. It also subjected local administrations to a hierarchical relationship with a central power that applied all kinds of control systems/mechanisms – legal, economic and political – and considerably weakened local revenues.

In this chapter we have tried to demonstrate that the working of local government today is, to a large extent, the result of the political transition to democracy. Throughout these years, there was the fear that the local arena would be a perpetual source of political instability. The large number of municipalities and the recent history of despotism on the part of municipal politicians raised doubts as to how well the local political system could work. One of the main objectives of the legislators was to limit strictly local political affairs as much as possible, and considerable authority was given to political parties as the leaders of political activity. Similarly, the mayor was given significant executive powers and an institutional authority in order to ensure that the effectiveness in providing public services would legitimise the incipient process of transition towards democracy. In this respect, legislation and patterns of political activity have converged to establish a clear presidential character in the figure of the mayor.

This institutional structure, together with the moderation in the electoral behaviour of citizens and the role played by the political elite in their work of political direction, have notably achieved the objective set out at the beginning of the transition; namely, the institutional stability of local government. As an example, the electoral lifespan of Spanish mayors is one of longest in the European Union and this fact acquires real significance when we take into account the fact that, in Spain, councillors are elected via proportional representation. The local political system has therefore managed to avoid the expected political fragility. On the other hand, certain institutional weaknesses have been detected. First among these is the fact that locally elected representatives, especially the mayor, has directed and managed in ways more befitting a professional public executive. Second, an excessive party influence pervades the institutional structure, arising from the prominence accorded to political parties and the consequent lack of renewal of the local political elite.

The Law on the modernisation of local government was intended to provide a response to these and other institutional weaknesses. Yet the measures adopted show a lack of reflection about the institutional model to be applied in municipalities with large populations. The presidential nature of the figure of mayor is diminishing as mayors lose a significant part of their executive authority to a new, strengthened executive.

7

From Cabinets to Committees
The Danish Experience

Rikke Berg

Unlike a number of other Western countries which in recent years have changed their local executive structure from committees to cabinets (Pratchet, 1999; Caulfield and Larsen, 2002), Danish municipalities have kept committees as the ruling principle of their executive structure. Indeed, such minor changes as have taken place in the executive structures of the Danish municipalities have been in the opposite direction: from cabinets to committees. Thus, in 1998 three of the largest municipalities in the country, Copenhagen, Odense and Aalborg reformed their executive structure and moved from cabinets to committees. Today, the committee model organises the executive structure of all but one of the 271 Danish municipalities.[1]

In order to understand the dominance of the committee model in Denmark, we have to look beyond the Local Government Act, which formally regulates the political structure of the municipalities. The Act leaves considerable room for experiments with the organisation of the political executives, the reasons for the dominance of the committee model are to be found in historical conditions rather than in formal law.

The Danish committee model

Denmark has a hundred-year-old tradition of involving laymen in local government. As late as 1949, only a minority of the municipalities had employees. In most of the municipalities, the elected officials carried out all tasks, and the politicians were virtually synonymous with the administration (Knudsen, 1995: 374). In 1970, the Danish local governmental system was altered by a major reform. The number of municipalities was drastically reduced, a large number of tasks were decentralised from the central government to the municipalities and a shared political and administrative structure was constructed in every single municipality. Though the reform created large professional administrative organisations, the tradition of engaging laymen in the day-to-day execution of policies continued. Today, laymen politicians are still intensively involved in policymaking and administration in the Danish local governments, what Mouritzen and Svara refer to as 'the laymen rule' (2002: 51).[2]

According to the Local Government Act, decision-making authority is clearly vested in the city council. However, in practice, the organisation of the political executive is much more ambiguous, since it is shared among several political bodies and actors: the city council, the standing committee, the finance committee and the mayor. The city council is elected for a period of four years and typically consists of 11 to 17 members.[3] The city council elects the mayor as well as the members of the standing committees among themselves, the latter typically consisting of five to seven members who are responsible for the 'immediate administration of affairs'.[4] The mayor chairs the finance committee, which supervises all financial and administrative matters and appoints all personnel, except the CEO and the department heads (Ejersbo *et al.*, 1998: 99). The mayor also heads the municipal administration. Thus, the position of the Danish mayor is considered as a full-time job – typically the only full-time job among the elected officials. The mayor can in certain urgent cases decide on behalf of the council, but has no authority to interfere with or block decisions taken by the committees. Thus when it comes to specific, day-to-day administrative matters, the standing committees are fully in charge (Le Maire and Preisler, 2000: 143).

The organisation just described applies to almost all Danish municipalities. It follows that the politicians not only decide on general principles and overall goals but also – and perhaps mostly – are heavily engaged in the day-to-day execution of policies. Thus the executive structures in the Danish municipalities blend the powers of the executive and the assembly and break the doctrine of the separation of powers in government. In other words, the laymen politicians and their involvement in government have been favoured at the expense of independence between the executive and legislative branches of local government.

The influence of the laymen politicians was also the leading motive behind the reform of the executive structure in Copenhagen, Odense and Aalborg. With the cabinet model, the backbenchers experienced only limited influence compared to the political leaders. By transforming the executive structure from cabinets to committees, the advocates of reform hoped to weaken the formal position and influence of the political leaders and increase both the formal and the real power of the backbenchers.

The question is, however, to what extent the executive structures affect the actual influence of the politicians in local government. Do institutions really matter when it comes to real power – in terms of decision-making power and the control of political agendas – of the local politicians (Lukes, 2005: 47–8)? In this chapter, the current situation of the committee model in Denmark will be assessed. Is this particular government form significant to the influence of the laymen politicians or are other factors of greater importance? As councils in Denmark are not allowed to hold a re-election during the election period of four years, the Danish municipalities are particularly strong candidates for institutional analysis. The case studies of Copenhagen, Odense and Aalborg will thus serve as a platform for answering the above questions.[5] By studying the transition from cabinets to committees and, in particular, the relations between political leaders, backbenchers and bureaucrats, both before and after the reform, the chapter aims at evaluating the relative power of the politicians in their particular institutional settings.

The next section of this chapter describes the institutional changes that were implemented in Copenhagen, Odense and Aalborg. The discussion then moves to examine the changes in the relative power of the politicians. Finally, the extent to which the changes might be attributable to the new institutional structures is considered, together with their implications for political accountability.

Institutional change in Copenhagen, Odense and Aalborg

Prior to 1998, the executive structures in Copenhagen, Odense and Aalborg were organised as cabinets. However, the model was very different from cabinet systems found in other countries both in terms of the system of seat allocation and in the nature of responsibility. In the cabinet model of Copenhagen, Odense and Aalborg, the cabinets were made up of a mayor, elected by the council, and four to six deputy mayors (or aldermen) elected among the council members on a proportional basis.[6] In principle, the cabinet could be formed from either a single party or a coalition of parties. However, since the seat allocation system was (and still is) a straightforward d'Hondt proportional representation system, large minority parties were almost guaranteed one of the seats in the cabinet.

The cabinets in the three municipalities had few executive functions, most important of which was preparing the municipal budget and the cases to be presented to the council. However, most of the executive functions were shared between the members of the cabinet. Each of the deputy mayors was endowed with their own portfolios and empowered to make executive decisions concerning the immediate administration of affairs within this area. Consequently, each of the deputy mayors was responsible to the council for their particular policy area.

Each policy area had advisory committees, whose members were elected from within the council.[7] The committees were headed by the deputy mayors, who would normally ask for the opinion of back-benchers before deciding on a case. The deputy mayors in Copenhagen, Odense and Aalborg were also heads of the corresponding administrative departments. For these reasons the position of deputy mayor was considered a full-time job, and paid accordingly. This particular cabinet form gave the cabinet members almost absolute power of the day-to-day decision-making in the three municipalities, leaving only a very modest influence to the backbenchers.

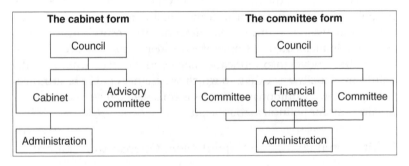

Figure 7.1 The executive structure before and after the reform in Copenhagen, Odense and Aalborg.

In 1994, a new election term started off with a strongly articulated critique coming from a group of young and newly elected politicians. The newcomers were clearly frustrated by their lack of influence in the advisory committees and wanted to reduce the power of the deputy mayors and to create a new and enhanced role for the members of the advisory boards. Their critique found its way not only to the agenda of the press but also to the agenda of the large parties and the councils. However, the reform of the three municipalities was not a reality until the new Local Government Act of 1998, which made it possible to keep the principle of full-time deputy mayor of the committees and to protect the privileged position of the large minority parties in the councils.

The institutional changes in 1998 reduced the formal influence of the deputy mayors in Copenhagen, Odense and Aalborg. They were still administrative leaders of the departments – and employed on a full time basis – but no longer political leaders of the committee. The decision-making power as well as the political responsibility of the executive functions within the particular policy area now rested within the committee as a whole (see fig. 7.1). Though the deputy mayors kept their title and full-time salary, their formal role in the committee was reduced to that of chairman.

Though moving in the direction of the committee model practised elsewhere in the Danish municipalities, the new executive structure of Copenhagen, Odense and Aalborg still varies somewhat from the 'traditional' committee-leader form in Denmark (Mouritzen and Svara, 2002: 60). First, the chairmen of the committees in Copenhagen, Odense and Aalborg are all full-time administrative leaders of the departments – a function they share with a full-time manager appointed by the council. In the 'traditional' Danish committee–leader form, the chairmen are not responsible for the administrative affairs in the corresponding departments and are thus not employed on a full-time basis. Second, the chairmen of the standing committees in Copenhagen, Odense and Aalborg are members of the finance committees, which is not the case in the rest of the Danish municipalities. The executive structure in these three municipalities is thus even more ambiguous than elsewhere.

The next section will elaborate on some of the most important findings from the study of the transition from cabinets to committees in the three municipalities.

The power of the backbenchers

In responses to a survey of the council members, a large majority declared that they have great influence on the cases considered by the committees. It was also the general view among the council members that their increased influence was attributable to the reform (Table 7.1).

The overall and positive impression of the reform and its consequences for the influence of the backbenchers were confirmed by the qualitative interviews with the backbenchers in these cities.

However, some of their answers may be related to the legitimate authority to make decisions that was given to the committee members by the reform, something that should not be confused with the more general question of real influence (Thomsen, 2000: 63). The question is thus to what extent the formal influence is actually being exercised by the backbenchers and further, how is it exercised.[8]

Table 7.1   Perceptions of backbench members' influence

	Copenhagen (%)	Odense (%)	Aalborg (%)
The committee meetings give me great influence on the sector[9]	77	92	90
(Base)	(39)	(25)	(29)
The politicians have increased their influence on the municipal affairs due to the transition from cabinets to committees[10]	78	76	91
(Base)	(25)	(17)	(24)

Source: Berg and Pedersen, 2001.

The study revealed that the actual power of the backbenchers depends on a range of factors that are being only indirectly influenced by the reform. These factors include the backbenchers' knowledge, workload and ability to co-operate and build coalitions in the committees. The actual influence of the backbenchers also seems to depend on other actors and their relative influence, especially the influence of the chairmen of the committees and of the department heads in the administrative organisation.

Knowledge

One of the new bases of power originates in the committee meetings. Under the cabinet model, the usual practice for the department heads was to clarify most of the cases with the deputy mayor before the meeting of the advisory committee. However, with the new executive structure, the committee decides the majority of the cases and neither the chairman of the committee nor the mayor can interfere with or block the decisions. As a consequence of this, the appointed officials not only have to prepare the cases, they also have to ensure that the cases are followed by recommendations when presenting them to the committee. The detailed cases provide the backbenchers with full information that they did not have before. Being well informed, most of the backbenchers feel empowered to exercise their influence in the committee (Berg and Pedersen, 2001: 38). Some of the backbenchers even feel that it is now legitimate to approach the appointed officials in order to get further information regarding a case or to get a new analysis worked out. This was clearly seen as an illegitimate act during the cabinet model, where the appointed officials were perceived as the right arm of the mayor and the deputy mayors and – for that reason – not available to the backbenchers.

For backbencher under the new system, new sources of knowledge provide a new experience – the ability to win arguments on factual grounds. During the cabinet model, the discussions in the advisory committees were, at best, characterised by symbolic arguments. At worst, there was no discussion at all. With the increased knowledge, the backbenchers feel more prepared for the discussions and the majority of the politicians, including the chairmen, also find that the decisions now taken are better informed than before the reform. Research shows that the department heads share this opinion too.

Workload

There is also a downside to the thoroughly prepared cases: the politicians spend much more time preparing for the committee meetings than before the reform. The workload is in fact so heavy that about 40 per cent of the politicians find it impossible to get through all the cases in time for the meetings (Berg and Pedersen, 2001: 43). Consequently, the level of information and knowledge is, in practice, unevenly distributed among the members of the committees. This factor must be viewed in light of the fact that all the politicians except for the mayor and the chairmen have civilian jobs outside the council.

The consequence is that the political task of formulating visions and overall goals is displaced by the urgent business of day-to-day decision-making. In many committees, the initiative to develop new policies is thus left to the department heads.[11] This tendency leaves great opportunities for the department heads to set the political agenda of the committees and to increase their real power at the cost of the laymen politicians.

Coalition building

Yet another base of power that developed in the committee model is the ability to co-operate and build coalitions. By co-operating across the party lines in the committees, even small minorities can make their influence felt and have a say on the decisions (Berg and Pedersen, 2001: 40). During the cabinet model, the political culture was mainly characterised by conflicts, in terms of confrontations and an inability to compromise between the deputy mayor and the rest of the advisory committee members. The cases were only seldom settled in the committees, but rather in the cabinet. Many of the politicians interviewed, particularly in Copenhagen stressed the new culture of dialogue, characterised by sympathetic debates and compromises across the political parties in the committees. It is worth noticing that though the increased consensus may be positive in terms of the political influence of the backbenchers, it may be negative in terms of political accountability. If broad compromises are entered by all the political parties, the citizens may find it very difficult to distinguish between political leaders and opposition and the lines of responsibility risk becoming blurred.

There are, however, certain variations in actual co-operation across party lines. Where a majority of the elected officials in Copenhagen and Odense (57 and 53%, respectively) find that the ability to co-operate has increased, only a minority of the politicians in Aalborg (41%) are of the same opinion (Berg and Pedersen, 2001: 40). The same type of variation counts for the question of conflict. In Aalborg, more than a third of the politicians find the level of conflict between the backbenchers and the chairman of the committee to be high whereas only small minority of the elected officials in Copenhagen and Odense do so (Table 7.2). However, the most dominating culture of consensus is found in Odense. Here more than two-third of the politicians perceive the committee meetings as meetings of consensus (Berg and Pedersen, 2001: 41).

Table 7.2   Perceptions of conflict between backbenchers and chairmen[12]

	Copenhagen (%)	Odense (%)	Aalborg (%)
The debate at the committee meetings is characterised by conflict between the backbenchers and the chairman of the committee	14	4	35
The debate at the committee meetings is characterised by consensus	44	64	59
(Base)	(39)	(25)	(29)

Source: Berg and Pedersen, 2001.

The variations may originate in other structural factors than the executive structures. One of the most obvious factors is the political composition of the council and, hence, of the committees. Unlike the councils in Copenhagen and Odense, the council in Aalborg is dominated by an absolute majority of Social Democrats. Since the party has the decision-making power, the political parties represented in the committees of Aalborg are not forced to collaborate with each other to make decisions. This may well increase the incidence of conflict (Berg and Pedersen, 2001: 41). The variation of conflict among the members of the committee can thus be explained in terms of power struggles between the 'government' and the 'opposition' in the council.

Yet another structural factor that may influence the degree of co-operation and coalition building is the politicians' identification with their fellow committee members. In general, being a member of a particular social group influences the group member's perception of the world and the problems and values at stake (Nisbet and Perrin, 1977: 100). This is also true when it comes to social groups such as political parties and committees, which clearly influence the member's position and political preferences (Serritslew, 2003). In Copenhagen and Aalborg, each of the backbenchers typically sits on several committees whereas the backbenchers in Odense only hold one seat each, and this factor may well explain some of the variations regarding the level of consensus between cities.

In light of the socialisation which takes place in the committees, one can expect a particular committee to gradually develop a specific sector knowledge and a sector-specific loyalty, directing attention away from problems outside their policy area. As a consequence of this, the committee members may even be inclined to discount cross-sector priorities and instead prefer higher spending within their own area of responsibility (Serritslew, 2003).

This tendency was found in the cabinet model, but with the transition to the committee model, it has increased. The explanation is obvious. Having increased their influence on the decisions taken in the standing committees, the backbenchers too have strengthened their ownership vis-à-vis the specific sector, and, hence, their loyalty to the issues considered by the committee. Thus the interests of the sector are no longer just being defended by the chairman of the committee but by all members of the committee. In particular, the expectations and support from the backbenchers, further encourage and empower the chairman to defend the interests of the sector and, hence, the standing committee within the finance committee (Berg and Pedersen, 2001: 84). In this perspective, not only the backbenchers but also the chairman have profited from the reform.

The influence of the chairmen

Besides the new source of influence emanating from 'the sector colleagues' within the standing committee, the executive structure still offers certain advantages to the chairmen. One of the most important sources of real influence left to the chairmen is the responsibility for preparing the committee agenda. In principle, the committee agenda is prepared in close co-operation with the department head, but the chairmen have the power to decide when to bring the cases for the committee and when to initiate new or further analyses. This offers an opportunity to sort out and even withhold important information from the backbenchers in the committee and, hence, to control the political agenda (Morgan, 1986: 167). None of the chairmen in Copenhagen, Odense and Aalborg make a secret of the fact that they exert influence when the agenda is prepared. However, there is a substantial variation in the way this is done.

In Copenhagen and Odense, the influence of the chairmen is mainly exerted indirectly through the daily dialogue between the chairmen and the top officials in the department. From the department heads, the chairmen learn about the cases and in turn give the department heads advice regarding the timing of the case (Berg and Pedersen, 2001: 48). However, there is a clear limit to this power, since the department heads will not accept the chairmen interfering in order to turn the professional recommendation political.[13] In Copenhagen as well as in Odense, the chairmen admit to being tempted to influence the substance of the recommendation, but refrain from doing so because of the risk of losing the confidence of the backbenchers. To lose this confidence would ruin all future opportunities to co-operate and build coalitions within the committee and, hence, in the long run would lead to an erosion in the real power of the chairman.

In Aalborg, such risks are more limited. Here, the majority of chairmen belong to the majority party in the council and consequently do not depend on the goodwill of the backbenchers in the committee. No matter what the committee decides, the chairman can always ask the council to make the final decision in order to support the line of the party. This obvious advantage of the majority chairmen is reflected in the influence exercised by the chairmen in Aalborg. The chairmen do not restrict themselves to strategic influence as in Copenhagen and Odense, but exercise direct influence on the department heads' recommendations to the committees.

Yet another source from which the chairmen draw influence is the media. As a function of their position, most of the chairmen receive calls from the media on a daily basis, in contrast to the majority of backbenchers who only receive calls on a weekly or monthly basis (Berg and Pedersen, 2001: 53). The frequent contact with the media makes it easier for the chairmen to raise their political profile to the public and hence, increase their influence in the role of party politician. However, it is like walking a tightrope, since the chairmen must speak on behalf on the whole committee and not just on behalf of themselves or their party. In cases where the chairman – as the administrative leader of the department – is forced to implement decisions taken in the committee against his or her political opinion, influence as party politician can be put under tremendous pressure.

The variations in the influence of the chairmen revealed in the interviews are also reflected in the data from the survey questionnaire. The majority of the chairmen in Copenhagen and Odense, respectively, report that their influence has actually diminished with the reform, whereas only a minority of the chairmen in Aalborg have the same opinion. This picture is supported by the backbenchers too. Thus in Aalborg, 45 per cent of the politicians feel that the chairmen still exercise too much power over the recommendations made by the department, whereas only 38 and 17 per cent of the politicians in Copenhagen and Odense, respectively, are of the same view (Berg and Pedersen, 2001: 49). Though the reform has empowered the backbenchers, and on some points reduced the influence of the chairmen, the chairmen still have certain structural advantages. And, in Aalborg, these advantages are most often exploited at the expense of the backbenchers.

The influence of the appointed officials

The actual influence of the backbenchers not only depends on the power of the chairmen but also on the power of the appointed officials. Reform has increased the formal influence of the professionals, as they have taken over the responsibility for presenting cases and making recommendations to the committees. However, not all of the chairmen are willing to give up their actual influence on this matter to the officials. In Aalborg, the chairmen tend to ignore the reform and continue, as usual, to exert influence on the recommendations presented to the committees. There is no doubt that in Aalborg, the losers of this trial of strength are the department heads. In all three municipalities, the department heads emphasise the importance of a good relationship between the department and the chairmen, and the department heads are willing to go far in order to keep a positive climate. Indeed, in Aalborg, they will go so far as to alter a professional recommendation, mindful of the risk of getting fired, if they refuse to do so.

Department heads are much less restricted in exerting influence in Copenhagen and Odense. Yet, paradoxically, they restrict themselves from exerting professional influence on the cases decided in the committee. In the early phase of the decision-making process, where the department has not yet presented the case for the committee in the form of a final recommendation, a majority of the department heads choose to discuss the matter informally in one of the committee meetings. Sometimes the department heads even let the case be discussed more than once in order to get a firm grasp of opinion in the committee. They clearly want to ensure that a majority of the committee members will support their recommendation when it is formally presented. However, this procedure is not always appreciated by the politicians. Some of them find that the procedure makes for unnecessary delays in the decision-making process, and a majority of the elected officials even find it wrong that recommendations are made on the basis of the political opinions within the committees. They prefer recommendations to be based on the professional knowledge of the experts in the departments (Berg and Pedersen, 2001: 58). Finally, some of the politicians, especially the backbenchers from small minority parties, find the procedure problematic in light of the private nature of the committee meetings. Since the committee meetings are not public, neither the citizens, nor the media, nor the small minority parties will benefit from the informal discussions going on at the meeting. On the contrary, the possibility of those actors influencing the decision-making process, or even taking part in the discussion is very limited.

A few of the critics, who are all backbenchers, extend the critique to include the control of the appointed officials in general. They argue that their insight into the administration and the daily work of the appointed officials is so modest that they are unable to evaluate the responsiveness of the officials. They claim that there may very well be cases handled in the department which ought to be handled at the political level by the standing committee or the council, but this is out of their control. The few critics are in opposition to the majority of politicians who find that the influence of the appointed officials is balanced by an appropriate amount of political control; the majority of the politicians even find that the political control of the appointed officials has been advanced by the reform.

Both parties may have a point. Due to the backbenchers' increased knowledge and insight into the specific cases regarding the sector, the political control of the appointed officials has in fact been advanced by the transition from cabinets to committees. However, there are certain circumstances limiting the ability of the backbenchers to control the appointed officials. First, the workload may restrain the politicians from requiring more information than already given by the department heads. Second, there are still inequalities in the level of information between the departments and the committees. This inequality gives advantages to the chairmen, and limits the political control carried out by the backbenchers.

However, the influence of the appointed officials not only depends on their ability to make recommendations, but also on their ability to control the political agenda. All three groups of actors – the chairmen, the backbenchers and the department heads – formally have the right to put issues on the agenda. But the backbenchers seldom exercise this right. One explanation is that the politicians are pre-occupied by work and therefore tend to give lower priority to policy formulation. Moreover, the department heads themselves are often astute and perceptive and therefore capable of translating the political opinions within the committee into concrete proposals and recommendations. However, there is no doubt that the professionals have gained new and important influence on the political agenda in the committees.

To conclude, in two out of the three municipalities, the reform has increased the influence of the appointed officials. This is partly due to their ability to make concrete decisions on behalf of the committees and partly due to their ability to control the political agenda of the committees. However, their influence is not unlimited. It is restricted by the political control exercised by the backbenchers in the standing committees and, further, by department heads fearing that the committee will turn down their recommendations.

Do institutions matter?

One of the major reasons for transforming the executive structure from cabinets to committees was to weaken the position and influence of the political leaders and to increase the power of the backbenchers. Generally speaking, the relative power of the politicians has indeed changed during the three-year period of the study.

First of all, the backbenchers have increased their real influence in the committees due to the increased insight and knowledge of the sector-specific cases discussed there. Further, the backbenchers have increased their influence due to the reduced formal influence of the chairmen, who are now much more cautious about controlling the agenda and much more co-operative with the backbenchers in the committees. Finally, the backbenchers have to some extent increase their actual influence due to their improved opportunities to control the appointed officials.

However, there are exceptions to this general picture. Most of the variation in terms of the backbencher's ability to exercise influence is derived from Aalborg. Here the relative power of the politicians almost is, but not entirely, unchanged. Though the backbenchers' insight and knowledge of the specific cases decided in the committees has improved and hence their influence, the chairmen still dominate the officials and the political agenda of the committee too. The general picture of the political executive in Aalborg is that the chairmen are still in power, almost as they were as deputy mayors during the cabinet model period.

To explain why a change in the institutional set-up had a greater effect in Copenhagen and Odense than in Aalborg, some variations between the three municipalities should be considered. One of the major differences between the three municipalities is the composition of the council. In Copenhagen and Odense, none of the parties holds the absolute majority in the council and, hence, the coalition supporting the mayor consists of several parties. In Aalborg, however, one single party, the Social Democrats, holds the absolute majority. Consequently, the Social Democrats do not depend on the support of other parties in appointing the mayor and this independence also applies for the decision-making process in the committees. If the majority chairmen cannot muster support for their policy in the committees, they are always capable of mustering the required support in the council. The option to put a proposal to the vote in the council is only very seldom applied. However, simply possessing the opportunity of doing so gives the party a far-reaching influence on the decision-making process in general – an influence that is almost independent of the executive structure.

What this study shows is that the institutional set-up is not trivial. The committee model certainly offers more opportunities to the backbenchers in terms of participating in and controlling the policy process than did the cabinet model. However, the study also demonstrates that, when it comes to the final decision, a single majority party will always holds the decisive power – even with an institutional set-up favouring the layman rule. Realizing that the executive structure is not superior, but conditioned by the political context, it seems reasonable to conclude, that institutions matter, but so too do political majorities.

There are implications for political accountability. As the study has shown, the chairmen of the committees are capable of acting exactly as they did under the old cabinet model – acting as strong political leaders without paying much attention to one of the most important rules of the new committee model, the layman rule – as long as their single party holds the absolute majority of the council. In institutional settings where the decision-making process is open and transparent to the public, the consequences of having the laymen politicians replaced by strong political leadership are modest and by knowing who to hold accountable for the decisions, voters can voice their dissatisfaction more effectively at the next election (Maravall, 1999: 159).

Elsewhere in Denmark, the consequences for accountability are more far-reaching. First, the voters face problems of monitoring their representatives and their decision-making in the committees where the meetings are not held in public. Second, the executive power and responsibility are ambiguous, as they are shared among the city council, the standing committees and the mayor. From the perspective of the voters, it is unclear whom to blame when things go wrong. Consequently, the citizens may face major difficulties in trying to hold their elected officials accountable for their actions. Though the difficulties regarding accountability apply to the Danish committee model in general, it cannot be ignored that the problem is intensified in municipalities where a single party holds the majority. The risk is an uncontrolled concentration of power.

Notes

1. A new Local Government Act in 1998 made it possible to alter the organisation of the political executive in four of the largest municipalities in Denmark: Copenhagen, Aarhus, Odense and Aalborg. However, Aarhus preferred to retain the existing organisation and is still organised as a cabinet with a leader.
2. The municipalities in Denmark are responsible for a large number of services, all very important to the welfare state: social welfare programmes (e.g. primary schools, day-care institutions and programs for the elderly), cultural activities (e.g. libraries and music schools for children) and technical services (e.g. water supply and refuse collection), just to mention some important services (Ejersbo *et al.*, 1998: 97). The individual municipality decides the level of most services in terms of quality, coverage and spending and also provides the services. The service is managed by a professional administration directed by the city council.
3. Local councils decide themselves (prior to an election) how many seats the next council will have, the minimum and maximum limits now being 9 and 33, respectively. Copenhagen, however, may have a 55-member council. Since the 1970 municipal reform, the three largest cities next to Copenhagen, Aarhus, Aalborg and Odense have had 31, 31 and 29 members, respectively.
4. The seat allocation system is a straightforward d'Hondt proportional representation system among competing lists, which represent either national political parties presenting local lists or local groups of concerned citizens (concerned, obviously, for various reasons).
5. The study of Copenhagen, Odense and Aalborg was conducted over a three-year period in order to study the transition from cabinets to committees, starting in 1997, just few weeks before the reform of the cabinets was initiated,

and ending in 2000 after almost three years of experience with the new committee form. The study was carried out as three single case studies, primarily based on qualitative data. The study included more than 70 interviews of elected officials and bureaucrats, analysis of documents (formal agendas, reports from meetings, articles from local newspapers, etc.), observations of meetings held by the standing committees, questionnaires to all council members in the three municipalities and questionnaires to all chairmen of the local party groups (Berg and Pedersen, 2001).

6. All members of the cabinet were elected to a four-year term.
7. The seat allocation system here was also a straightforward d'Hondt proportional representation system.
8. There are different approaches to empirical studies of power and most of them (if not all) are associated with several methodological problems. In order to avoid some of the problems, the qualitative study of the power in Copenhagen, Odense and Aalborg combines three methods to reveal the actual power of the politicians: the method of position (Mills, 1959), the method of decision (Dahl, 1961) and the method of reputation (Hunter, 1963).
9. The response rates in Copenhagen, Odense and Aalborg, respectively, were 71, 86 and 94 per cent.
10. Only council members who were members during the cabinet model too were asked this question. The response rate in Copenhagen, Odense and Aalborg, respectively, were 77 (N = 25), 94 (N = 17) and 96 (N = 24).
11. It is important to note that the initiative to develop new policies may depend on a range of factors besides time and pressure of work, for instance the leadership role, traditions of administration, the norms of the leading officials, etc. (Berg, 2000).
12. The response rates in Copenhagen, Odense and Aalborg, respectively, were 71, 86 and 94 per cent.
13. In the interviews, the officials validate the statements by examples of cases, where the recommendations from the officials to the committees were in opposition to the political opinion of the chairman.

8
Laymen and Executives in Swiss Local Government

Andreas Ladner

Swiss local government is distinguished by the extent to which laypeople are directly engaged in policymaking. This is made possible in large part by the very small scale of its municipalities, together with the country's constitutional tradition of direct democracy. This chapter identifies the key features of Swiss local decision-making and the nature of public involvement in holding their elected representatives to account. Like other countries, Switzerland has experienced reform movement, albeit modest in scope. The final section of this chapter reviews recent changes and shows their limited aspirations working within the basic assumptions of the Swiss political system.

The characteristics of Swiss local government

Swiss municipalities and their governments are generally very small, with more than half of them having less than 1000 inhabitants. However, the importance of the few big municipalities stems from the fact that about 60 per cent of the population live in municipalities with more than 5000 inhabitants (see Swiss Federal Statistical Office, 2000b).

Despite their small size, the municipalities play an important role in the Swiss political system. According to the principle of subsidiarity, all activities which are not assigned to higher political levels remain within the realm of the municipalities. The activities of the municipalities include issuing the communal code, appointing the executive and the administrative authorities, administration and control of the communal finances, assessing the tax rate, care for elderly people, including constructions of homes for the aged, social security and public health and hospitals, schools, education, waste, sewage, electricity, water and gas supply, local roads, culture, communal citizenship and maintaining municipal property. The fact that their share of public spending is less than 30 per cent, relatively low, is mainly due to the existence of an intermediate layer, called the cantons, which are responsible for rather more than 30 per cent of the overall public spending.

The several features that make Swiss municipalities different from those in many other countries is their far-reaching fiscal autonomy. They not only set up their own budget according to their financial needs, they also fix the tax rate. Transfers from higher political levels are comparatively very low, by pulling less than 20 per cent. Their main sources of funding are local taxes (46%) and fees and charges (24%). The local taxes paid by the citizens amount to about one-third of the total individual taxation and are paid directly to the municipality; taxes differ considerably between municipalities in different cantons and even within a canton.

Due to the small size of most municipalities and to the existence of the cantons, the scale of the municipal administrations is rather small. For the core administration, which covers tasks like registration of the citizens, finances, tax, building and planning and social assistance, the average figures range between less than two full-time jobs in municipalities with fewer than 500 inhabitants and 3800 in the big cities (see Table 8.1).

To this must be added the municipal employees in the different public utilities and services which range up to an average of 3420 employees, excluding teachers. It is in the medium-sized executives

Table 8.1   Size of the administration and size of the municipality

	Administration (limited)			Administration (extended)		
	No. of employees	Employees per 100 inhabitants	N	No. of employees	Employees per 100 inhabitants	N
−500	1.8	1.01	751	0.8	0.36	679
501–1,000	2.4	0.33	380	2.4	0.34	361
1,001–2,000	3.5	0.25	346	4.1	0.29	339
2,001–5,000	8.1	0.26	319	11.0	0.35	313
5,001–10,000	21.1	0.31	119	30.6	0.45	116
10,001–25,000	67.4	0.45	68	90.6	0.62	63
25,001–50,000	219.6	0.65	5	194.0	0.66	5
50,000–	3800.0	1.72	5	3420.0	1.68	5

Source: Local Secretary Survey 1994, in Geser *et al.* (1996)

where economies of scale seem to work whereas in bigger municipalities the administration becomes more complex and covers a range of different tasks.

Swiss municipalities enjoy a remarkable degree of freedom with regard to their organisation. This has led to a number of distinct political systems developing throughout the country (Ladner, 1991). Since the political organisation of a municipality is not governed by national but by cantonal legislation, there are 26 different laws dictating how municipalities should set up and organise their political institutions (Council of Europe, 1998). However, there are quite a few common characteristics as well as the distinctive differences as far as their executives, their administration and their legislative bodies are concerned.

In comparative terms, the Swiss local governments belong to the continental group (Wollmann, 2004). On one hand, there is an elected council – or the assembly of the citizens – as the supreme local decision-making body and on the other hand a local executive in a collegial form, which is also directly elected by the citizens.[1] The most outstanding common features are the direct election of the executives by the citizens and the representation of all important parties in local government. Important differences concern their size and their degree of professionalism. A distinction has to be made between municipalities with a parliament and those with an assembly.

Two different legislative systems: parliament or assembly

There are basically two different ways the Swiss municipalities are organised politically. Some municipalities reflect a division of power in the sense of Montesquieu, at least as far as the executive and the legislative bodies are concerned, and *have a municipal parliament* representing the citizens (see Figure 8.1). Others have a *municipal assembly of the citizens*, which covers at least partly the legislative function (see Figure 8.2), and which represents a form of direct democracy in the tradition of Rousseau and the old Greeks.

The competences of parliament and assembly are very similar. They have both a control and an input function and decide on all important projects and proposals which are not in the realm of the executive or the citizens at the polls. Typical concerns of parliament or assembly are municipal projects of particular importance and with financial consequences above a certain amount of money, minor changes of municipal decrees and regulations, and the acceptance of the municipal account, the budget and the tax rate.

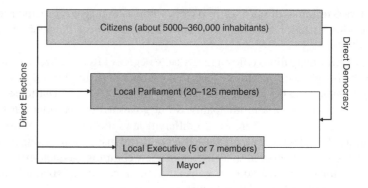

Figure 8.1   Municipalities with a local parliament (about 500 municipalities).
Notes: * The Mayor is a member of the local executive

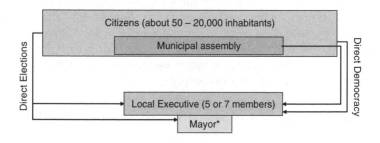

Figure 8.2   Municipalities with a local assembly (about 2300 municipalities).
Notes: * The Mayor is a member of the local executive

Which form a municipality chooses depends on its size and on its cultural background. Bigger municipalities are more likely to have a *parliament*, and parliaments are more widespread in the French-speaking cantons.[2] Given the smallness of the Swiss municipalities and the larger number of municipalities in the German-speaking part, fewer than 20 per cent of the about 2880 municipalities have a local parliament (see Ladner, 1991: 81 ff.). Nevertheless, some municipalities with well above 10,000 inhabitants have a local assembly.[3] The division of power prohibits the mayor and the other members of the executive from being at the same time members of the local parliament. Given the multi-party character of the executive, work within the parliament is based on a commission or committee system, in which all the parties are represented.

The *municipal assembly* is a genuine form of direct democracy. It is a gathering of all citizens entitled to vote in the municipality, taking place three or four times a year. In these gatherings, binding decisions are made on changes of communal rules, on public policies and public spending. Everyone is entitled to have a say, and the decisions are made – unless a secret vote is requested – by a show of hands. Despite the decisional power of the municipal assembly the rate of electoral participation is rather low. The average rate of participation in municipalities with fewer than 250 inhabitants is about 30 per cent of these citizens entitled to vote. This figure steadily falls as the size of the municipality increases. In municipalities in the size bracket 10,000–20,000 inhabitants, the average rate of participation is below 5 per cent (see Ladner, 2002: 823). The main reason for such a low turnout is the demanding character of this form of deliberation.

For the executive it makes quite a difference whether it faces a local parliament or a municipal assembly. The local executive enjoys more freedom when it has to deal with a municipal assembly. The mayor together with the executive and supported by the administration propose political projects for approval by the citizens. Sometimes, the decisions of the citizens may be unpredictable, depending, for example, on the people turning up at the assembly. In municipalities with a local parliament, the executive has to deal with parties and party politics. This means that there is a more open political debate and the positions of the different actors are known in advance. Nevertheless, it would be wrong to believe that the parliament is effectively able to control and steer local politics. The gaps in political knowledge and understanding between the members of parliament and the members of the executive make such a task very difficult.

Regardless of whether they have a parliament or an assembly, all Swiss municipalities also have other forms of direct democracy like referendums and initiatives, which affect the functioning of the local executive and the local parliament (Ladner, 1999, 2002). In municipalities with a parliament, direct democracy is directed against decisions of executive and parliament, in municipalities with an assembly, direct democracy addresses the executive as well as decisions of the assembly.

Electoral systems

In the Swiss municipalities, the executive is *directly elected* by the citizens. The same applies to the Mayor, who is a member of the executive.[4]

Unlike the executive at the national level ('Bundesrat', federal council), the mayor ('Stadt-/Gemeindepräsident') is more than a *primus inter pares* (Geser *et al.*, 1987). He is the one who represents the municipality, and when it comes to a professionalisation of the executive body, it is usually the mayor who is the first to be employed full-time. The mayor chairs the meetings of the executive and of the municipal assembly. Usually, he is also responsible for the local administration. However, in the executive he does not have more formal decisional power than the other members, except for being able to cast his or her own decisive vote when the executive is unable to reach a decision due to deadlock.

In municipalities with an assembly, a number of commissions (finances, schools, social security, construction, etc.) are appointed or elected. Their functions differ considerably, ranging from the control of the executive to the support of the member of the executive in policy-making. Usually the respective member of the executive is a member or even the chair of the commission. If the municipality has a parliament, the parliament is elected by the citizens too, within a separate ballot usually taking place the same day as the election of the executive. The mayor, his colleagues in the executive and the members of parliament are thus all directly and independently legitimatised by the electorate. There are no formal rules forcing parliament and executive to have the same political forces or parties represented as in a system with a governmental party and an opposition. Nevertheless, the balance of power in executive and in the parliament usually corresponds fairly closely. If a municipality has a municipal assembly, it is only the executive and the major which are directly elected by the citizens.

The electoral systems used to elect executive and parliament differ from canton to canton and there might even be differences within a canton. About 70 per cent of the Swiss municipalities elect their *executive* through *majority systems*, compared to 30 per cent using *proportional representation*. Under the former, the voter casts up to as many votes as there are seats. To allocate the seats the majority system takes two different forms: if the candidates winning a plurality of the votes are elected, it is called a 'relative majority' or single-ballot system, because it always produces winners. In the second form, the 'absolute majority system', a candidate needs a minimum percentage of the votes in order to be elected, equivalent to 50 per cent plus 1 of the votes cast per seat. If the first ballot does not fill all the seats, a second ballot based on a relative majority takes place to fill the remaining ones. In proportional elections, the votes do not go to candidates but to political groups (parties) or lists. The seats are allocated to the different groups according to the percentage of the votes obtained. Majority voting favours personalities from the big parties; proportional representation fosters the representation of smaller parties.

The *local parliament* is in general elected in a proportional representation system. Again, there are a few exceptions. About 25 per cent of the municipalities – generally the smaller ones – elect their parliament in a majority system (Ladner, 1991: 88). In municipalities with more than 10,000 inhabitants, there is hardly any majority system to be found. The size of the local executives varies between 3 and 30 members with an average of about 6 seats per municipality. In general, the executives are smaller in municipalities with a parliament than in municipalities with an assembly. The size of the executive increases with the size of the municipalities and reaches its peak in municipalities with between 10,000 and 20,000 inhabitants. In cities with more than 20,000 inhabitants, the size of the executive is smaller again. This effect occurs due to the professionalisation of the executives: in medium-sized municipalities the increasing workload is divided among a larger number of lay executive members, whereas in bigger municipalities their part- or full-time employment allows a reduction of the number of executive seats.

There has been a slight tendency to adapt to smaller executives in recent years. In 1998, about 7 per cent of the municipalities reduced the number of seats for the executives (see Ladner *et al.*, 2000). This trend is more marked in municipalities with an assembly, but there are also municipalities where the number of seats has been increased. The reasons for smaller executives are attempts to make them more efficient and reduce costs as well as the problems encountered in finding enough candidates. In smaller executives it is on the other hand more difficult to meet the demands for an adequate representation of the different groups and parties in the municipalities, the smaller parties find it more difficult to be represented in local government and the workload for each member of the executive increases.

The size of the local parliament varies between 9 elected representatives in some municipalities in the cantons of Geneva and Neuchâtel and 125 (Zürich) or 130 (Basel), the average size of the local parliament increases with the size of the municipalities. A crucial threshold seems to be 100,000 inhabitants, where the size doubles compared to the lower size bracket.

The Swiss political system is strongly reliant upon the principle of power sharing (see Linder, 1994; Lijphart, 1999). This also applies to the local executives. There are hardly any single party executives and the most important parties are usually represented in the local executive.

This might at first sight be surprising, since the majority system is the rule in the majority of the municipalities. In accordance with the principles of *consociational democracy* ('Konkordanzdemokratie'), however, a 'voluntary proportionality' ('freiwilliger Proporz') is practised. The leading party abstains from presenting a full slate of candidates to make room for opposition party candidates. In smaller communities, of course, abstaining from running for all seats is not always voluntary, as it can be difficult to find suitable candidates for each available seat. Running for all seats also carries the danger that some of the same party candidates might take votes away from each other and fall behind the candidates of the other parties. And sometimes the parties present fewer candidates to avoid the risk of possible defeat, especially when running against current office-holders. One common strategy for the leading party is to abstain from running for all seats under certain conditions. The smaller parties are offered a number of seats in accordance to their strength in return for their approved candidates by the stronger parties.

Involvement of laypeople in local government, professionalism and recruitment

Politics in Switzerland are strongly based on laypeople. The so-called *'Milizsystem'* (militia system) is an important pillar of the Swiss political culture. Even the members of the national parliament are not considered to be full-time politicians and are comparatively poorly remunerated.[5] There is no official data available concerning the degree of professionalism in local government as far as the executive is concerned and we have to rely on our survey results. In 1994, the local secretaries provided us with information about the degree of professionalism in their local executives (see Geser *et al.*, 1996). More than 90 per cent of the municipalities have no full-time politicians in their local executive. If the local executives happen to have one it is in most cases the mayor. Only in the big cities, all members of the executives receive a full-time salary. In quite a few municipalities there is an elaborate mixture of honorary, part- and full-time executives.

Full-time local politics in Switzerland means that politicians do not need another job to make a living. It does not mean that they have enjoyed a special training or that they have ever been assessed. The most common pattern for a career as a local politician is to start with a seat in one of the numerous commissions and then get elected for the local executive. Many of the local politicians withdraw from politics after two or three legislatures. In recent years, there have been a few cases of municipalities looking for a mayor by means of an advertisement in the newspapers.

Legally there is no difference between small and big municipalities, as well as between those with an assembly and those with a parliament, as far as their tasks and services are concerned. In practice, of course, the difference between the very small municipalities and the cities is enormous. In a city, each member of the executive heads a department ('Ressortsystem') with an extended administration. The City of Zurich, for example, has an executive with nine members, covering Presidential Department (Mayor), Finances, Police, Health and Environment, Road Construction and Waste Removal, Building, Public Utilities (water, gas, electricity, public transport), School and Sports and Social Services. Each of these departments has several hundred employees. In small municipalities there is hardly any administration apart from a local secretary. Here, the members of the local executive are also engaged in operational routines and everyday policy tasks like, for example, social security benefit claims or decisions on construction permits, since the workload is not big enough to have it done on the basis of employed administrators.

In recent years, there has been a slightly increasing trend towards more professionalised executives. The results from our 1998 local secretary survey (Ladner *et al.*, 2000) reveal that municipalities with a parliament have moved more towards a system with a professionalised mayor than have assembly municipalities. Only very few municipalities undertook reforms in this direction. And even if we look at bigger municipalities (more than 5000 inhabitants), where such reforms make more sense, only one out of ten municipalities has professionalised the function of the mayor in the last ten years.

The Swiss militia system and the smallness of the political units lead to high degree of citizens' involvement in holding public office. Taking the seats in the local executives and parliament together with the various commissions in the different policy fields, an average of about 50 different political functions per municipality have to be fulfilled by the citizens. In small municipalities, one out of eight or ten citizens holds a public office. This can be seen as a form of social capital. In recent years, however, this high demand to fill offices has increasingly encountered problems on the supply side. The municipalities and, more particularly, the local political parties, which are the most important *recruitment* agents for public office holders, find it increasingly difficult to recruit enough qualified candidates. The fact that a municipality has a parliament can, on one hand, make it easier for the parties to recruit candidates among the members of the parliament to run the elections for the local executive. On the other hand, they have to find enough candidates for their seats in the parliament in the first place. According to our survey results, it is most difficult to find enough candidates in the middle-sized municipalities. In the cities, public offices are sufficiently prestigious and, in the case of a seat in the executive, well remunerated. In the very small municipalities these offices are less time-consuming and it is probably more difficult to refuse an invitation, if it becomes obvious that there is nobody else who can do the job.

Relations between laymen and bureaucrats

The most notable feature of the relation between the members of the local executive and the local administration is the paradoxical situation that professional administrators, with expertise in their policy areas, are subordinate to lay people who are responsible for the activities undertaken by the administration. Whereas the civil servants very often remain in their jobs for a lifetime and, at least the younger ones, have enjoyed a specific training, the members of the executives envisage a political career of limited durability and often start their political job with very little relevant preparation. In larger municipalities, and especially in those with a parliament, it is more likely that the newly elected members of the executives can bring to the role some previous political experience in a parliament or in any of the innumerable commissions. This comparative advantage, however, is countered by a bigger and more complex administrative burden. Recent reforms, especially those based on the principles of New Public Management (NPM), attempt to clarify the relation between the members of the executive and the administration, giving the former a stronger strategic orientation and the latter more operative freedom.

The members of the local parliaments are far more distant from the members of the local administration than are the members of the local executives, and the differences between the professional administration and the lay politicians are even more accentuated. Traditionally, the lay politicians interact with the administration through parliamentary instruments (demands, interpellations, postulates), while the members of the executive stand between them and the administration. Personal links between members of parliament and chief bureaucrats, which are known to play an important role at the national level, are considered to be of lesser importance at the local level. This is due to the fact that politics at the local level does not reach the same degree of politicisation, making political considerations of lesser importance when it comes to the selection of local bureaucrats.

In the course of the recent NPM reforms, which have been undertaken in quite a few bigger municipalities, there have also been parliamentary reforms to compensate for shift of competences to the executive and to the administration. The most important features of these reforms were the introduction of standing parliamentary commissions to increase knowledge and continuity among the members of parliament. These commissions prepare the different projects and proposals to be decided in the parliament and exercise a certain control function vis-à-vis the executive. In order to do so, the commissions are given the right to address members of the administration directly or to invite them to report in their meetings. More support was also accorded to lay members of parliament to compensate for their distance from executive matters.

The balance of power between the executive and the parliament, the question what kind of decisions fall in the realm of the parliament and how these decisions can achieve the status of a long-lasting binding character have also been addressed by parliamentary reforms. In general, the members of the local executive are in a much stronger position than the members of the local parliaments, since they are much better informed and have direct access to the administration. But since the local executives are multi-party executives, the possible imbalance of power vis-à-vis the parliament is averted.

Being a member of a multi-party government makes the relation between party fellows with legislative or executive responsibility sometimes rather problematic, especially where, combined with the standard practice, decisions of the executive are taken jointly and controversial positions within the executive are not made public ('Kollegialitätsprinzip'). As soon as a parliamentary group turns against the government it, at least formally, turns also against its party members in the executive. Members of the executive have wider orientation and are expected to put public interests before party interests, whereas members of the legislative are likely to defend the interests of their party.

Political leadership, co-ordination and political accountability

The Swiss political system does not favour strong political leaders. At the local level, however, the direct election of the executive and of the mayor gives them a stronger position vis-à-vis the parliament. Nevertheless, their power is controlled by means of direct democracy. For bigger and more expensive projects they have to consult the citizens. And the fact that the government unites different parties without them having to agree on a joint political programme sets limits on any attempt to take a strong political lead. Their joint and secret decision-making, finally, causes a lack of accountability.

Systemically, Swiss politics is based on *co-ordination and co-operation* among different political actors and across the different policy areas, through the mechanisms of multi-party government, joint decision-making and direct democracy. To promote a political proposal success-fully it requires not only the support of a majority of the members in the executive and in the parliament, but also the approval of the citizens. The elaboration of such proposals is usually very time consuming and the proposals tend to become rather costly, since it is easier to get the necessary support if a majority of those involved see advantage in accepting it.

In the course of recent reforms there have been attempts to bring more continuity and efficiency into local policies by setting up plans and programmes which link political goals for the years to come with the available financial resources. These attempts are usually initiated by the administration or by the executive. However, the more these plans are given a binding character the less the members of the parliament are inclined to tie their hands by accepting them.

Compared with the 1970s and 1980s, when particularly younger and left-wing people complained that the political elite has lost touch with the citizens, an improvement of the responsiveness of the local govern-ments is no longer the most important reform claims. Although there were attempts in the 1990s to increase citizens' involvement in local political decisions, especially by means of information at an earlier stage or by letting the citizens take part in the development of projects, it would probably be misleading to infer that there were serious short-comings in this area. The intensive culture of direct democracy fosters a close contact between the members of the local government and the citizens, and for local politicians to hold office for an extended period has become an exception.

Recent reforms

Swiss local governments, like local governments in other countries (see Wollmann, 2003: 18), have undergone certain reforms in recent years. However, it has not been the relation between the politicians and the citizens which has consulted the core of these reforms. More important than political accountability and responsiveness has been the rethink-ing of the relation between the members of the executive and the professional administration, and between the local parliament and the executive. As a general trend, municipalities have tried to make decision-making easier and more efficient by shifting more powers to other bodies (executive, commissions, administration), by reducing their size, or by reducing the number of commissions. In some cases they extended their administration or transferred services and tasks to the private sector. Reforms of the political system are less common. As far as the electoral system for the local executives is concerned, there is a slight net tendency to replace majority voting by proportional representation (PR) (but there are also shifts from PR to majority voting).[6] Also, municipalities with rather large executive bodies have tended to reduce the number of seats. All these changes can be considered as minor reforms, hardly capable of increasing the overall performance of the municipalities.

Even though there has been a shift in responsibilities and power towards the various parts of local government (executive, commissions, administration), Swiss municipalities are by no means governed by entrepreneurial mayors or city managers. As we have seen above, there are only very few full-time members in local executives, mainly in very large municipalities and cities, and there is no chief administrator assigned to run the municipality. Nevertheless, the concepts and ideas of NPM have influenced the reorganisation of local government considerably, especially in the bigger municipalities. Figure 8.3 shows that about two-thirds of the municipalities with more than 5000 inhabitants stated that they had already undertaken first steps within the area of NPM reforms. A closer look at the different elements of these reforms reveals that the hardcore elements of NPM like product definitions, performance agreements and global budgets are rarer in municipalities with an assembly than in those with a parliament. Among the other NPM reforms, which are less related to a new NPM-like form of political steering, the differences between the two groups of municipalities are of lesser importance. A delegation of power to the administration, the promotion of competition between external providers, a stronger reliance on external experts, the elimination of the civil servant status and the introduction of performance-related pay is even more widespread among municipalities without a parliament.

In Switzerland, there has been little transformation of local decision-making. Inter-municipal co-operation, the amalgamation of municipalities, the division of tasks between the canton and the municipalities and the reform of the administration have been much more important. The reforms aimed directly at the local executive cannot be considered

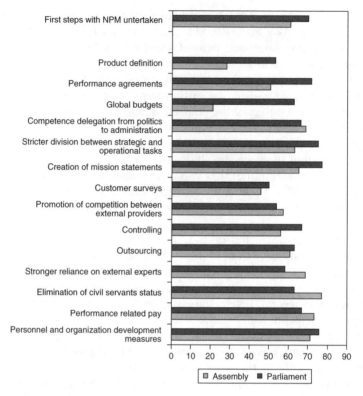

Figure 8.3 NPM-reforms in municipalities with more than 5000 inhabitants (municipalities with an assembly and municipalities with a parliament).

as a fundamental change, and no conclusive judgement can as yet be made as to their likely success.

The way Swiss local government is organised undoubtedly helps in finding policy solutions which are acceptable to a majority of parties and citizens. Compromises or political packages are needed to reach a decision and to take different interests and demands into account. The main problem that local governments actually face is the recruitment and selection of willing and capable citizens to do a time-consuming job on a voluntary basis. To this have to be added the increasing difficulties in keeping the lead vis-à-vis a more professionalised administration needed to govern in a complex environment. And finally, the executives find it difficult to put forward sustainable concepts in a long-term perspective, facing citizens unwilling to give them decisional power and facing a parliament with changing majorities and a similar reluctance. Despite these shortcomings, there are no fundamental changes in local government in sight. Power sharing, direct democracy and laypeople politicians will continue to determine the functioning of most of the executives at the local level, and all the recent reforms in local government only aim at making them work better rather than differently.

Notes

1. Historically this dual form goes back to the French Revolution (see Wollmann, 2004).
2. In the German-speaking part of Switzerland, municipalities with 8000 to 10,000 inhabitants and more have a parliament, whereas in the French- and Italian-speaking municipalities this might be the case in much smaller municipalities. In the cantons of Geneva and Neuchâtel, all municipalities have a parliament, even those with fewer than 1000 inhabitants.
3. This is especially true for the canton of Zurich, where about half of the municipalities between 10,000 and 20,000 inhabitants have a municipal assembly.
4. The only exception is the French-speaking canton of Neuchâtel, where every municipality has a local parliament and where it is the parliament that elects the executive.
5. Many of the national MPs, however, nowadays make their living in jobs closely related to their political work (e.g. in unions, interest associations) and cannot be considered as laymen either.
6. Regardless of the voting system adopted, all important parties are usually represented in the executives due to the so-called 'freiwilliger Proporz' (voluntary proportionality). A shift from majority to PR voting cannot necessarily be considered a shift from a 'concentration of power' to 'power sharing' but rather a formalisation of an informal rule for power sharing.

9

The Swedish Model: Many Actors and Few Strong Leaders

Stig Montin

The organisation of the political executive in Swedish local government has its roots in the mid-nineteenth century. The view of local self-government held at that time was that lay representatives rather than civil servants should be responsible for all decision-making. However, during the 1960s there took place a cultural shift which has been described as a transformation from 'administration by laymen' to 'administration by professionals' (Strömberg and Westerståhl, 1984). The degree of professionalisation has increased ever since. Currently, more than one million people – some 21 per cent of the workforce – are employed at local government level, compared with 6 per cent in state employment. The municipality is often the largest employer in its local area.

Local governments in Sweden have a prominent position, as they are responsible for the major share of national welfare services. During the period of expansion, and particularly during the 1960s and the 1970s, the municipalities became strong institutions with substantial financial, legal, political and professional resources (Elander and Montin, 1990). Two amalgamation reforms were implemented in 1952 and 1974, reducing the number of municipalities from approximately 2500 in 1951, to 278 in 1974. During the last 20 years, a number of municipalities have been divided into two or more units, and now number 290, the largest being Stockholm (about 800,000 inhabitants) and the smallest Bjurholm (3000 inhabitants).

The Swedish local government system can be described as an integrative central–local government system (Montin, 2002). The Swedish constitution states that democracy 'shall be realised through a representative and parliamentary polity, and through local self-government'. Yet the concept of local self-government has never been clarified, and central–local government relations, at any given point, can best be understood as a negotiated order. About 80 per cent of the local government budget is related to national goals and policies regulated by law, such as the Social Security Act and the Education Act. So, although the main revenues come from local income taxes (about 65%), local self-government is actually restricted by national policies. On the other hand, the laws are framework laws; parliament (the *Riksdag*) defines what local government should do, but it is up to the local governments themselves to organise how they do it.

With the exception of 1960 and 1965, the post-war period was one of uninterrupted and substantial growth of municipal consumption. However, this period of expansion seems to be over. In the early 1990s, the Swedish economy underwent a severe crisis, with falling production and high unemployment. Faced with a reduced tax base, public finances showed heavy deficits, forcing both state and local governments to become more efficient. In the late 1990s, the economy once again became stabilised, and Sweden has now emerged from its acute economic crisis. However, many municipalities continue to face difficulties, including high unemployment rates, social problems, problems concerning the quality of services, decreasing turnout in local elections and mistrust among the citizens regarding the democratic institutions. These last few problems raise issues of political co-ordination and legitimacy (Montin, 1993).

Political organisation

The basic structure of municipal political organisation is regulated by the Local Government Act (LGA, which also regulates the county councils). The size of the municipal assembly (sometimes referred to as the municipal council) relates to the number of residents entitled to vote and consists of at least 31 members. The regular and deputy members of the assembly are directly elected (and nominated by political parties) at general elections every 4 years, on the same day as the county council and national elections. Normally, the assembly meets nine or ten times per year, but the number of meetings can be fewer, especially when there is a lack of policy matters to consider (Montin *et al.*, 1996). According to the LGA, the assembly decides on questions of major importance, such as goals and guidelines of activities; budget, taxation and other important financial questions; organisation and procedures of committees; election of committees and drafting committee members and alternates; election of auditors and their alternates and financial benefits for elected representatives and referendums.

The heart of the municipal government is the executive committee, which consists of at least 5, and normally 11 and 17 members. It is responsible for directing and co-ordinating the local government activities, and supervises the activities of other committees and municipal enterprises. It prepares or pronounces on business to be transacted by the assembly, takes charge of financial administration, puts assembly decisions into effect and generally performs the tasks entrusted to it by the assembly (LGA, 1991: ch. 6, section 4). The chairman of the executive committee, who is a full-time salaried politician (*kommunalråd*), has a position that can be described as that of an informal (modern) mayor (Bäck, 2004). The chairman, together with (at least) the first and second vice chairmen, constitutes the working committee. This committee is important for co-ordinating policy matters within the executive committee. The executive committee is elected proportionally in relation to the distribution of mandates in the assembly, but the chairman (and the vice chairman) of all committees, and full-time engaged politicians are appointed by the majority, which is often a coalition.

Standing (or specialised) committees to which members are also elected by the assembly are responsible for specific policy areas. They must ensure that activities in their field comply with the objectives and guidelines approved by the assembly and the applicable national legislation; and make decisions on matters delegated to them by the assembly. The standing committees have a degree of autonomy in relation to the assembly and to the executive committee. For example, the executive committee is not allowed to intervene in matters whereby the social service committee executes its authority according to the Social Service Act. Due to the growing financial stress, the financial co-ordinating role of the executive committee has become stronger in many municipalities during the last ten years. In some cases, where standing committees were considered to be too strong in their advocacy role for specific policy areas, the assembly has suspended them for a period of time in order to strengthen the central financial control (Granberg and Olsson, 1999).

The municipal assembly may also appoint ad hoc drafting committees, comprising one or more elected representatives. Drafting committees were introduced in approximately 30 assemblies during the early 1990s, and appear to have enhanced the role of the municipal assembly in local politics (Montin and Olsson, 1999). Since July 2002, it has been possible to co-opt outsiders with different background, experiences and competences to the drafting committees. However, this permissive power has not been used, and in 2004 there were no drafting committees with members from outside the assembly.

The Swedish local government system is complicated, and to many citizens it is unclear who really governs. A survey in Stockholm revealed that only 5 per cent of the electorate gave a correct answer to the question about the composition of the governing majority. Only 46 per cent had some idea about which parties are included in the governing coalition. Not even all of the assembly members in some municipalities know the correct composition of the governing majority in their own municipality (Bäck, 2003).

Administrative and professional organisation

Most local government staff work within schools, elderly care, childcare and other social services, all of which are politically supervised by standing committees. The service organisation is often organised into different 'result units', each responsible for its own budget. In some municipalities, these units provide service and social care on an internal contract basis, and are 'paid' for providing the service that the committee has 'purchased'. Within some policy fields, especially childcare, elderly care and compulsory education, it has also become quite common to form contracts with private providers. All of these alternatives are publicly financed, and the standing committees in the municipalities are equally responsible for private, as well as for municipal, provision of services.

Since the mid-1980s, when different kinds of organisational change started in several municipalities, administrative leadership became considered as increasingly important, with top managers expected to take more strategic responsibility. There are two types of top managers in the municipalities: the chief executive manager (*kommunchef* or *kommundirektör*) and chief administrative officers, including the chief accountant (*förvaltningschefer*). The chief administrative officers are responsible for staff and budget (the administrative organisation) with regard to their specific sector, and are accountable to the standing committees. The chief executive manager has an overall administrative co-ordinating role related to the executive committee and usually has no formal authority over the chief administrative officers. In several municipalities, they together constitute a formal management group (corporate management), while in others co-ordination is more ad hoc.

Delegation

Before 1992, the political and administrative structures of local governments were strongly influenced by legislation. In the so-called free-commune experiment of the second half of the 1980s, selected municipalities were allowed to design the structure of their committees as they desired. The 1991 Local Government Act gave the municipalities the right to organise themselves in different ways. Almost immediately, at least 70 per cent of the municipalities changed their political and administrative structure along these lines. Although there had been tremendous changes in the conditions for elected representatives due to the amalgamation reforms during the 1950s and 1960s, the rules concerning delegation were not reformulated in the 1976 LGA. The overall structure was transformed from 'administration by laymen to administration by professionals' (Strömberg and Westerståhl, 1984: 57), but the elected representatives were, according to the 1976 LGA, still supposed to handle day-to-day political matters (Björkman and Riberdahl, 1997).

One initiative of the 1991 LGA was to develop a new role for the elected representatives. By using new ways of steering, such as management by objectives (MbO), management by results (MbR) and purchaser–provider models, they should be able to focus on strategic issues, rather than on time-consuming day-to-day politics. In order to create this new political management, there had to be further delegation of decision-making to lower levels. According to the 1991 LGA, the inclusion of more recently made revisions means that decision-making can be further delegated to a select committee, an elected representative, or an employee of the municipality:

> A committee may authorise a select committee, a member or an alternate of the committee, or an employee of the municipality ... to decide a particular matter, or group of matters, on the committee's behalf ... (LGA, 1991: ch. 6, section 33).

However, there are restrictions. Decision-making power may not be delegated in respect of matters relating to the goal, focus, scope or quality of activities; proposals or statements to the assembly, and statements occasioned by an appeal having been lodged against a decision made by the committee as a whole, or by the assembly; matters relating to the exercise of authority in relation to individual persons, if these involve issues of principle, or are otherwise of signal importance or certain matters indicated in special provisions (LGA, 1991: ch. 6, section 34).

The main idea behind the change in legislation is that detailed political control is neither possible, nor suitable, in a complex municipal organisation, which should be characterised by strategic management, professionalism and flexibility. As a result of delegation and devolution, municipal organisation has become fragmented. A new, more professional, instrument of steering is required (Montin, 2000). However, the old idea of lay political responsibility is still strong, creating a tension between political and administrative professionalisation, on the one hand, and the part-time unpaid representatives on the other.

Salaried versus unsalaried politicians

In Sweden, there is a major difference between being an unsalaried lay politician and a part or full-time salaried politician. While, during the last 20 years, the number of representatives has fallen from around 70,000 to less than 45,000, the number of full-time engaged representatives has risen slightly and the number of part-time representatives has increased substantially (Gustafsson, 1999: 131; Hagevi, 1999). Between the years 1992 and 1999, the number of committees was reduced by 13 per cent (from 3940 to 3044). Each representative holds an average of 1.58 positions in 2003, compared to 1.4 in 1999 (Bäck and Öhrvall, 2003).

There is, then, a tendency towards an informal political professionalisation (Hagevi, 2000). A national survey found that more than half of all municipal representatives considered the leading councillors (kommunalråden) as having too much power (SOU, 2001: 48). The risk of power concentration and elite control is considered to be significant (Svenska Kommunförbundet, 2000; Hallström, 2001). The lay politicians have lost much of their day-to-day political control during the last 20 years. In the early 1980s, local government in Sweden is distinguished by the fact that the elected representatives participate directly in the handling of a matter at all levels, from drafting to decision-making and implementation, which means that their tasks include those which in the national administration are the sole concern of salaried officials (Gustafsson, 1983: 64). This description is now quite obsolete. While it is formally possible for the local political bodies (the assembly and the committees) to withdraw delegation from actors at lower levels, this does not occur. Strategic policy is now in the hands of full-time salaried politicians. Other matters have been delegated further down in the administrative and professional organisation. However, it is still quite common for administrators to accuse the politicians for intervening in their professional area. Among lower level administrators and middle managers, politicians are often referred to as an anonymous group of 'those up there', and sometimes there is a lack of trust among staff members (cf. Jönsson *et al.*, 1999: 116).

In April 2002, the Swedish Parliament passed a bill to revitalise democracy, including measures to increase the number of local representatives by 10,000 by 2010 (Government Bill 2001/02:80). It may be that in the longer run it will be necessary to make a choice between alternative models of local politics with

> A small number of full-time professional politicians, who interact with the public via mass media and occasional, brief encounters at public meeting, or the same small group of professionals surrounded by a broad group of unsalaried politicians who serve as a continuous, interactive link to the public at large (Jönsson *et al.*, 1999: 119).

The latter model is still the norm. The three largest municipalities (Stockholm, Göteborg and Malmö), for example, continue to form their political organisation along this line by having district councils (Bäck, 2002).

The role of parties

Generally speaking, the complexity of the local government political and administrative organisation has increased. The most important institution holding it all together is that of the political party. In accordance with the party-dominated representative system, every member of the assembly and the committees represent a political party. The party political control of the local government is illustrated in Figure 9.1.

The political parties nominate candidates for election. In the assembly and the standing committees, the members constitute party groups. The overall municipal organisation of the political party co-ordinates the policymaking, and controls the political positions among the members. In this process, the leading councillors (*kommunalråd*), such as the chair holder of the executive committee, have decisive power. But other full- or part-time enrolled politicians, such as the political secretaries, are important in the policy process. The role of the political parties at the local government level has increased during the last 20 years, particularly within the largest parties, whereby the local party organisation is important.

It is paradoxical that the co-ordinating role of the political parties has increased, while the trust in political parties among citizens has decreased. Since the mid-1970s, there have been several signs of crisis, such as declining membership (from about 1.5 million members in the mid-1960s to about 320,000 in 2003), and an increasing gap between the top and the bottom within the parties. In addition, the parties are

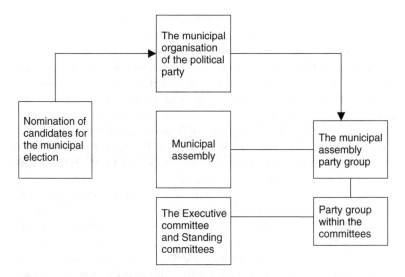

Figure 9.1 Party political control and co-ordination in municipalities (Gustafsson, 1999: 150).

not dependent on membership due to the party financing system, citizens are more often choosing other channels for political participation, and the trust in political parties as solvers of societal problems is considered to be low among citizens in general (Gidlund and Möller, 1999; Petersson *et al.*, 2000).

Because all local government representatives are nominated within the political parties, these strong tendencies of parties in crisis have negative effects on the recruitment of politicians. In 1979, 87 per cent of the local branches of the political parties had a sufficient number of available candidates for nomination to the local election. In 1998, this proportion had gone down to 72 per cent, which means that more than a quarter of the local branches had problems in recruiting new candidates in the late 1990s (Gidlund and Möller, 1999: 33). The strength of the local party system is an important factor in order to understand the local political structure of power in the Swedish municipalities, particularly in large ones (Bäck, 2002).

Leading councillors and chief executive managers

The chair holder of the executive committee has four important roles (Jonsson, 2003). First, he/she leads the decision-making process within the committee. This is a balancing act between representing his/her own political party, making sure that proposals are anchored among the leading politicians in the coalition, and making sure that proposals are feasible from an administrative point of view. Second, he/she leads the local government as a political organisation, which includes handling political and ideological tensions and conflicts. This mission is not politically party oriented. It is more about how to create trustworthy relations with the political opposition. It can be described as 'acting as a spider in the political web' (Jonsson, 2003: 116). Third, he/she leads the development of the local branch of the political party involving discussion of ideological issues concerning the future of the municipality. In leading the party organisation, the mission is to try to create common understandings and beliefs among fellow representatives. Sometimes this is carried out under a strong influence by national policies. Finally, he/she leads the local government as an actor in the wider environment to include co-ordinating activities together with other local governments in the regional area, representing the municipality in contacts with state authorities, national political organisations and international contacts.

The chief executive manager serves the executive committee. This includes activities like submitting reports and policy documents, making sure that different proposals are fully prepared and consider juridical, financial and democratic points of view, supplying information and knowledge concerning actual issues and receiving information for further distribution in the administrative organisation (Jonsson *et al.*, 2002). According to a national survey, the most important activities for the chief executive manager are to supervise, filter and distribute information in different directions (Värna and Örnfelt, 2003: 85).

Although the chief executive managers have close contact with leading politicians, they do not view these relations as an important part of the ideal work situation (Värna and Örnfelt, 2003: 86). Top managers want to keep a certain distance from the politicians, avoiding political processes that could threaten their autonomy and integrity. Mutual trust and close dialogue is of utmost importance in the relationship. It requires them to create and uphold a shared understanding of what are 'political', and what are 'administrative' or 'professional', matters. In some municipalities an issue may be political, but a similar issue may be considered as purely administrative in another. Furthermore, a policy issue may oscillate between being political and being administrative during the policy process. That is, if there turns out to be some sort of conflict among the politicians, then the matter is political, regardless of whether the issue, in reality, concerns deep ideological questions about authoritative distribution of values. Hence, both the top politician and the top manager have to act in the grey zone between politics and administration (Jonsson, 2003; Montin, 2002).

However, the relations between politicians and professionals differ, being closer in small municipalities and municipal organisations than in larger ones. Two different pictures of the relations between politicians and top managers can be drawn from the differing experiences of local governments. In the first, the role of top managers is highly political (Blom, 1994). They are expected to implement sometimes unclear and vague political decisions, leaving room for their different interpretations. They will often act as a guide or a coach for politicians, leading them down the road to the most appropriate decision. They often act as gatekeepers, having considerable influence on the political agenda-setting.

An example of this situation can be taken from a renewal process in Stockholm during the 1990s (Fridolf, 1996; Montin, 1998). In 1993, a competitive tendering programme for elderly care was introduced by the non-socialist majority. Several local representatives in the district committees (a district committee with responsibility for social policies) were ambivalent towards the programme, and so were some of the chief administrative officers (*socialcheferna*). Hence, the scope of the competitive tendering became varied between the 17 social districts. These variations could not be explained by exogenous factors, such as the proportion of old people, or the potential number of service producers. The explanation behind the variations was found in the actions among the politicians and the chief administrative officers. The latter had a strong influence on the process. In the districts where there was ambivalence among the local representatives, the influence of chief administrative officers could be decisive.

A somewhat different picture is presented by the evaluation of the district reform in Gothenburg, the executive structure of which is similar to Stockholm's. In 1990, the municipality of Gothenburg introduced district councils with responsibility for several policy areas. The 21 councils consist of appointed representatives and an administrative organisation led by a district manager. One of the objectives of the reform was to strengthen the position of political representatives. Questionnaire surveys and interviews with politicians and administrative personnel indicated that the politicians increased their insight into, and control of, municipal policies. They frequently requested reports and reviewed policies (Jönsson *et al.*, 1999: 116).

In the case of Stockholm, local representatives were ambivalent about an ideologically loaded reform. In the case of Gothenburg, district representatives handled day-to-day politics without any significant ideological conflicts. Thus, the relation between representatives and administrators/managers may differ in accordance to local circumstances and to the kind of political issues on the agenda. In some cases, the politicians may be in control of the policy process, but in other cases the managers are moving the politicians ahead. This relationship between politicians and chief managers has been described as an interaction between 'scrutinisers' and 'constructors'. If the politicians are defensive scrutinisers, the chief managers tend more to be active constructors. But if the politicians tend to be active, the managers tend more to be defensive constructors (Värna and Örnfelt, 2003).

Although the powers of the top managers derives from their expert knowledge and the amount of time they can spend on different subjects, they are always subordinate to the politicians and their position is an exposed one. If conflicts develop between a top manager and the politicians, the former may have to look for another job and, since the late 1990s, it has become more common for them to do so. Research on long-serving administrative officers shows that a relationship of trust with the politicians, and a diplomatic approach, with respect for the dynamics of political decision-making, is of great importance to their survival (Värna and Örnfelt, 2003).

Political accountability

The development of the executive structure in the Swedish local governments can be described as moving towards both fragmentation and hierarchisation (Montin, 2000). Since the 1980s, steps have been taking in order to strengthen the political leadership in several municipalities. However, the basic system of the executive still consists of many actors and leaders, which makes it difficult for ordinary citizens to gain insight into policy processes. Due to the increasing administrative professionalisation, delegation of decision-making and the NPM-influenced-ways of organising local government activities, the lack of transparency tends to increase. For example, according to several surveys during the 1990s, a majority of members of the Municipal Assembly considered that they ought to have more influence on local policymaking and implementation, and their role as political scrutinisers did not develop in the intended direction (cf. Montin, 1996; Montin, 2002). There are, however, some indicators showing that the system of drafting committees might improve the role of political scrutiny. In a comparative case study of four municipal assemblies, members in the one with drafting committees described the role of the assembly as more influential on local policymaking than did members in the other three cases (Montin and Olsson, 1999).

Although the instruments for political accountability, apart from the electoral arrangements, are institutionalised, it does not prevent different kinds of unethical behaviour among local politicians and administrators. Sweden is considered as one of the least corrupt countries in the world, but during the 1990s, several scandals were reported, especially at the local government level. According to empirical research, there are several 'danger zones' of corruption, or at least grey corruption. This is especially pertinent in relations with private business and public procurement where there is room for unethical behaviour. In comparing different cases, there are strong indications of variations concerning how delegation is structured, and the use of control mechanisms (Andersson, 2002). In general, economic and institutional changes (towards NPM-oriented solutions) during the 1990s have increased the number of danger zones of corruption, but in many local governments, the control system did not change to the same extent. It is interesting to note that the behaviour leading to the scandals were, in most cases, not discovered during the internal annual auditing, but by journalists in local and regional media.

From a perspective of political accountability, this leads to two observations. One is that the internal political auditing is somewhat inefficient, and the other is that local and regional media is an important actor in order to increase the awareness and knowledge of ordinary citizens. This not only relates to discovering scandals, but in a more general sense. Generally speaking, with reference to the knowledge ordinary citizens have about what is going on in local government politics and administration, the role of the local media has increased during the last decades, and is now, besides people's own experiences, the most important channel for information (Johansson *et al.*, 2001).

A second important development concerns citizen involvement. In 2002, a 'policy of democracy', entitled 'Democracy for the new century' (Government Bill, 2001: 02:80), was passed by the Swedish Parliament (*Riksdagen*), and has its main focus on the local government level. Its aim is to safeguard the traditional channels of representative democracy for exerting influence while enhancing citizen participation between the elections, especially for young people, the unemployed and those with a foreign background. Central government cannot force local governments to establish institutional arrangements for increasing citizen involvement, but the *Riksdag* can adjust the Local Government Act and encourage local leaders to introduce different arrangements. There are only a few municipalities that have adopted any overall strategy in order to increase citizen involvement, but different arrangements have been introduced, such as giving the right to all residents in the municipality to suggest items for the Municipal Assembly agenda, having different kinds of 'citizen panels' or other types of citizen advisory organisations, as well as youth advisory boards, and improving the use of ICT for administrative and democracy-oriented purposes. Many of these arrangements are not new and user boards in schools were, for example, introduced in many municipalities during the 1990s. However, the overall national strategy for improving citizen involvement is quite new. It is too soon to judge whether there have been any effects on political accountability.

Conclusion

Five themes may be drawn from this analysis of local government in Sweden. The first addresses the involvement of lay politicians. The representatives within the committees are engaged in the day-to-day execution of politics and they are interacting directly with the administrative staff, but to a much lesser extent than before. It is also worth noticing the difference between being a full-time salaried politician, interacting daily with chief administrators, and being an unsalaried representative, whose activities are conducted in leisure-time. In the discussion about modern local government structure, making a clear demarcation between politics and administration is high on the agenda. However, it is more accurate to conceive of a demarcation in which the top politicians and the top managers are on one side of the divide, and the unsalaried lay politicians and subordinate administrators/professionals are on the other.

This leads to the second theme – professionalism – which especially concerns the relation between political leadership and centralised administrative expertise. Due to the development of delegation, administrative leaders are handling matters which were previously considered to be political. How this works in practice depends on local institutionalised norms. Top administrators must be aware of these norms and follow them, if they want to remain in employment. Formally, all administrators are subordinate to the politicians (the committees), who can choose at any time to withdraw the delegation. However, this seldom happens, as mutual trust usually prevails between the top politicians of the majority party and the top chief officers.

When it comes to co-ordination, the most important actors are the political parties. All representatives in the municipal assembly and in the committees are nominated within the parties, and this makes it possible to co-ordinate the political executive decisions and actions. Besides this overall co-ordination, the chairman of the executive committee has an important role of political co-ordination. Furthermore, the chief executive managers have an important co-ordinating role vis-à-vis the administrative and professional organisation. Often, these two leaders – political and professional – work closely together. While the chairman of the executive committee has an important position, he/she is not directly elected. Nevertheless, the role of the chairman can, in many municipalities, be described as that of an informal executive mayor. However, the strength of a chairman's position depends on both personal qualities and historical factors.

Political accountability is brought into focus at election time, but throughout the period of the mandate, citizens are supposed to have continuous contact with 'their' representatives, getting involved in political parties or, as users, expressing their needs and demands to the service producers. It is in the latter sense that participation is growing among citizens as users and customers. In general, the local mass media are important for providing information about what is going on in local politics and administration. But policy processes are not transparent, and do not facilitate participation. They are largely dealt with by top politicians in co-operation with top administrative officers; sometimes, not even the representatives in the assembly know what is going on. Furthermore, Sweden's quasi-parliamentarism, with its combination of proportional and majority election of the executive, makes it difficult for citizens to keep themselves informed about the governing majority, and political accountability is weak (Bäck, 2003). In order to create more trustworthy relations between citizens and local representatives, some municipalities have introduced different kinds of participatory oriented activities.

At least a quarter of the local branches of the political parties have problems concerning recruitment of local representatives. There are different factors which can explain the recruiting problems. One factor is the perceived loss of power among lay politicians, but a more important explanatory factor is related to the political parties and citizens. People are at least as politically active nowadays as before, but they tend to turn to channels of influence other than the party channel, such as user organisations, new social movements and Village Action Movements (*lokala utvecklingsgrupper*). These tendencies towards non-party political involvement are, therefore, being taken seriously by the central government. Different types of citizen involvement in local matters are considered to be a basis for recruiting new members to the political parties (Government Bill, 2001: 02:80, p. 29).

In summing up the development of Swedish local government, we can find different tendencies and tensions. The complexity of the political and administrative organisation has increased during the last 20 years. Hence, there is a growing tension between different ideals of how to organise the political and administrative executive. The dominant ideal is the old idea of political control by many unsalaried representatives, close to the citizens. This system is challenged by a growing (informal) political professionalisation and the powerful position of chief administrators. Moreover, political participation among citizens has turned from the political parties towards other channels. User participation within specific policy areas is considered to be more efficient than more general political involvement, while the organisation of service production has turned into a more or less fragmented structure. The number of political influential actors has increased, while top politicians and administrative leaders have strengthened their positions. This leads to the conclusion that local government in Sweden can, to a large extent, at least in a comparative perspective, be described as a model with many actors, but few – if any – strong leaders.

10

Institutional Form and Political Leadership in American City Government

James H. Svara

The distinction between the mayor-council and council-manager forms of government for American cities is fundamental, yet until now not enough has been known about the impact of these two very different approaches to organising urban leadership. The alternative forms of local government used in the United States differ in structure and internal processes, and these differences provide the background to variations in political leadership. Both types of city government have an executive, either elected or appointed, and both have a mayor although they vary in the extent of their power. Finally, both types have a council but one is more like a European parliament in its scope of authority and the other more like an American legislature. This chapter examines the patterns of variation in political leadership with respect to their responsiveness to citizen preferences and their effectiveness in policy-making, as rated by council members and city managers themselves.

Aspects of political leadership in two forms of government

The council-manager form was devised in the early twentieth century and endorsed as part of the second edition of the Model City Charter in 1917.[1] It is now used in a majority of the cities between 10,000 and 250,000 in population, and in over 40 per cent of the cities outside that range.[2]

Under the council-manager form, the city manager is an executive with organisational and functional authority. This official also links the political sphere occupied by the mayor and council members and the administrative sphere. Long ago, it was recognised that the manager is a 'politician' (Bosworth, 1958), that is, one who forms policy and makes value choices, and the manager is expected to support the democratic process and encourage citizen participation.[3] Still, the city manager brings a professional perspective to policy leadership (Long, 1965; Stillman, 1977) and sees the world differently than elected officials based on his or her formal training and distinctive values (Nalbandian, 1994). Thus, the city manager contributes to policymaking and impacts the behaviour of politicians but operates as a professional rather than a politician.

The council-manager form is based on the unitary model of organising government. The council possesses all governmental authority, except as it delegates authority to the manager, and, thus, there is no separation of powers or checks and balances in the system. In this respect, it is similar to parliamentary government and the committee-leader and collective forms (Mouritzen and Svara, 2002), but unlike these, there is no formally or contextually strong political leader who serves as a key point of contact for the city manager with the political sphere. The manager is accountable directly to the entire city council with the mayor treated as the first among equals. The manager is appointed by the council with no voter involvement and serves at the pleasure of the council without term.[4] All other employees are hired under the authority of and report to the manager.

In the last forty years, many council-manager cities have altered the method of electing the council and/or the mayor to increase the linkages between elected officials and constituents.[5] There has been a shift from selecting the mayor within the council to direct election of the mayor in most cities. More council-manager cities now elect at least part of their council members from districts.[6] Instead of changing the form of government, a few large cities have considered altering the formal authority of the city manager vis-à-vis the mayor. Frederickson and co-workers (2003) argue that changes in the allocation of authority or changes in electoral institutions (along with the introduction of an appointed chief administrator in mayor-council cities) are creating a new melded type of city governments that are essentially alike regardless of form. The contrary view is that form continues to be a key variable (Svara, 2001).

The mayor-council form is based on separation of powers between the elected executive and council. As in strong mayor forms of government in other countries, the mayor is the political leader and has control over at least some staff appointments (although council approval is required in many cities) and directs the administrative organisation. In approximately two-fifths of mayor-council cities, there is a chief administrative officer (or city administrator) usually appointed by the mayor with the approval of the council who assists the mayor in handling administrative tasks and to some extent provides professional advice to the council.

There are institutional norms and practices that promote co-operation in council-manager cities and conflict in mayor-council cities (Svara, 1990: ch. 2). The characteristics of the council-manager form tend to not only promote co-operation but also to arrest and reverse conflict when it arises. The opportunity for the council to choose a person who matches their preferences promotes a positive working relationship. Managers come into office with broad expectations concerning their priorities and performance.[7] As new members come on the council, they in part adjust to the manager who is in office and the manager adjusts to the new members. Since the council can remove the city manager at any time, extended tests of will or stalemate between the council and manager are rare.

The interaction between officials is different in mayor-council systems. Strong mayor governments with separation between the executive and the council may experience sniping or warfare between the two seats of power depending on the nature of the relationship. Mayors and council members commonly have disputes about their respective powers and prerogatives. Both the election of the mayor and transition from one administration to another are likely to produce discontinuity and conflict. The mayor and political appointees may face resistance from career staff. As the end of the mayor's term approaches, opponents may choose to wait out the mayor and hope to have better luck with the successor. It is likely, therefore, that in the absence of special conditions that will overcome it, conflict will be commonplace in the mayor-council forms. Conversely, unless special circumstances are present, the council-manager form will not experience high-level, persistent conflict. Instead, co-operation, based on concentration of authority and shared goals, is likely to be found among officials. Surveys of council members and managers regularly find positive relationships (Svara, 1990).

All governmental structures provide for some combination of political and professional leadership. The council-manager form of government promotes a balancing of the two types of leadership. Although political supremacy of the council over the manager is formally assured, the dynamics of the form encourage respect of administrators by elected officials and deference by administrators to politicians. As we shall see, policy initiatives arise from both sets of officials. Department heads and other administrators also occupy an important place in the mayor-council form and professional perspectives are enhanced by the presence of a CAO. Still, the effort by the political executive in mayor-council cities to expand popular support, and the tensions between the mayor and council increase the likelihood that both sets of officials will adopt a transactional approach and attempt to exchange the positions they take for constituent support. As a consequence, professional perspectives are likely to be given less consideration in mayor-council cities.

Involvement of laymen in local government and characteristics of political recruitment

The laymen who sit on city councils may give emphasis to the governance role and/or the representational role, as described in Table 10.1

In council-manager cities, it is normally presumed that the governance role is emphasised at the expense of the representational role. The norms of council-manager government stress the involvement of elected officials in policymaking with minimal involvement in administration. Typically, the persons who filled elected office in these cities were civic leaders who held their office primarily as a service to the community (Prewitt, 1970). The trustee orientation, that is, acting in the best interests of the community, overrules the delegate orientation of speaking for constituents. Council members are less likely to assist constituents in dealings with government. They oversee the general performance of the manager and staff rather than getting involved in the details of constituent complaints. The conceptual design for the council-manager form assigns to the manager the responsibility of ensuring

Table 10.1   Council roles

	Governance role	Representational role
Policymaking	Shape goals	Express constituent demands and make individual policy proposals
	Review executive's policy proposals in terms of council goals	Review executive's proposals in terms of constituent and council interests
	Trustee orientation	Delegate orientation
Administration	Oversight of executive to determine whether performance matches intent	Investigate executive to determine whether council directions are being followed
	Refer complaints to manager	Act as ombudsman and intervene on behalf of constituent in administration

appropriate handling of citizen complaints, and council members do not take on the ombudsman function. Thus, in theory, council members would emphasise the governance role and give little attention to the representational role.

In mayor-council cities, a different set of norms prevail. According to the logic of the separation of powers between the mayor and the council, council members can be expected to stress the representational role, serving as delegates for constituents in assessing proposals from the mayor, investigating the mayor and departments and seeking to assist constituents in their dealings with city government. Following a delegate orientation, council members would be expected to propose initiatives that are demanded by constituents or are consistent with the interests of constituents. The mayor's veto can be used to restrain the policy preferences of the council if it indulges in excessive 'pork barrel' legislation – providing specific benefits to the districts of the council members backing the ordinance. Beyond this contribution, however, the council member in strong mayor cities is presumably not expected to make a major contribution to the policy process other than in reviewing the proposals from the mayor.

The hypothesised differences in council member behaviour regarding governance are supported by surveys of officials. When the self-assessment of elected officials from the two forms is compared, council members diverge in some areas (see Figure 10.1). For council functions

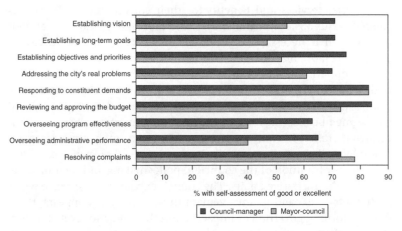

Figure 10.1 Effectiveness in handling major functions by form of government. (Self-Assessment by council members in cities over 25,000 population).

Source: Svara, 2003, fig. VII.1.

that involve goal setting and oversight, there are substantially higher ratings in council-manager than mayor-council cities.[8] Elected officials in the council-manager form devote more attention and achieve higher levels of effectiveness in establishing vision, setting long-term goals and annual priorities, overseeing programme effectiveness and overseeing staff performance than their counterparts in mayor-council cities. The differences in ratings are in the same direction but are more modest in addressing the city's real problems and budget review.

With regard to the representational role, however, the expected differences are not found. Officials in both types of cities give them-selves similar ratings of effectiveness in resolving citizen complaints and responding to constituent demands. The expectation of role specialisa-tion based on form of government must be revised. Rather than finding emphasis on either governance *or* representation depending on form of government, there is now emphasis on governance *and* representation in council-manager cities along with the stronger representational focus in mayor-council cities.

When examining other indicators, the normally expected differences are found, and council members in mayor-council cities demonstrate a somewhat stronger orientation related to the representational role. They are less likely to refer citizens with complaints to staff (43% mayor-council versus 52% council-manager), and more council members (48%) devote six or more hours per week to constituency services than do their counterparts in council-manager cities (38%). They are more likely to seek special services and benefits for their constituents (50% mayor-council versus 35% council-manager) and more likely to agree that their intervention is necessary to secure adequate staff response to citizen complaints (50% mayor-council versus 34% council-manager).[9]

To summarise, councils in council-manager cities continue their traditional function as a 'board of governors' for the city, whereas the council in mayor-council cities operates more as a 'board of delegates' whose members speak for constituents. An important change is that council members in council-manager cities increasingly stress represen-tation as well. In mayor-council cities, the executive mayor can limit both the contribution of the council to policymaking and their involve-ment in administrative affairs. The council encounters resistance when it attempts to expand its involvement in governance. It appears, then, that the form of government impacts upon the kind and level of leader-ship exercised by lay politicians. Council members help to set goals and oversee administrative performance particularly in council-manager cities. They interact intensively with individual citizens, and in cities with both forms of government they seek to help citizens in their dealings with government, although the representational role is more fully developed in mayor-council cities.

Professionalism in local government

The council-manager form is designed to provide for a high level of involvement by an appointed administrative professional. Executive powers are assigned to the city manager, and none are retained by elected officials other than appointment and removal of the city manager. In the mayor-council form, the professional attributes of staff in mayor-council cities steadily improved as the provisions for personnel and budgeting reform were adopted, and many cities have created a central administrative officer position (Frederickson *et al.*, 2003). Still, the executive is the elected mayor, and the political–professional balance is likely to be tilted somewhat more towards the political end.

City charters in council-manager cities commonly adopt language similar to the Model City Charter regarding the place of professionals in city government. First, the city manager is to be appointed based on professional qualifications. Second, the manager has full executive powers. Third, the administrative staff are insulated from interference by elected officials and the council members are to deal with staff only through the city manager.[10]

Structure, values and practice have led to substantial administrative autonomy in fact as well as in theory. This was not necessarily the case in early years of the form (Gilbert, 1978; Bridges, 1997: 118–24), but the use of professionally trained city managers has now become firmly established. City managers at the present time often argue that they must be vigilant to maintain administrative insulation to prevent political interference. Still, it does not appear that elected officials are subverting professional standards and the integrity of administrative procedures on a regular basis. City managers tend to call attention to the camel's nose as soon as it appears under the edge of the tent without waiting to see if the camel intends to move inside.

It is a major preoccupation of city managers to ensure policy stability and to establish priorities among conflicting demands. City managers view council members as overly responsive to specific current problems and constituent demands and see themselves as being focused on the 'real, ongoing work of the city'.[11] A top official in ICMA (Kellar, 2004) made a similar point about time perspective: 'Because we are appointed officials we often can take a longer view than politicians can, due to their frequent election cycles'. City managers find it is a recurring challenge to maintain support for the long-term policies adopted by previous councils. Councils are constantly under pressure to find resources to deal with specific, current problems and may abandon prior long-term commitments.[12]

The adoption of management innovations occurs more rapidly in council-manager cities. For example, in the early 1990s, citywide use of strategic planning was more common in council-manager (30%) than mayor-council cities (17%) (Poister and Streib, 1989; Streib and Poister, 1990). In present times, incorporation of e-government provisions is more likely to occur in council-manager cities (Pavlichev, 2004). Substantial attention is given in the professional development activities of the International City/County Management Association to educating local government administrators about 'best practices' and sharing information about implementing them.

The orientation of city managers is more to the profession and their own career rather than to a particular local community. The persons who serve in larger cities typically worked in other cities before their current position. To illustrate, the characteristics of the city managers in 33 cities with population over 200,000 can be examined.[13] The average age of these managers is 55, and 9 in 10 have a master's degree. They have spent an average of six years in their current position. Three in 5 had previously held the position of city manager in another city, and had served over 12 years on average as a city manager in all positions. Nine in 10 had experience as either a city manager or assistant city manager, and the total years in local government service was over 28 years. The managers who occupy these prized positions in the largest cities are mature, well educated and experienced municipal administrators. Most have worked in more than one city rather than rising through the ranks in the city where they are currently the manager.[14]

A final indicator of the professional orientation of city managers is a comparison with strong mayors as organisational leaders. City council members in cities with population over 25,000 rated the executive in their cities in three areas of performance. Table 10.2 indicates the proportion of city managers and mayors, respectively, who received very good or good ratings. A majority of the executive mayors perform well with respect to these measures, whereas most of the city managers do so. City managers not only support excellence in the organisational process but also openness in the democratic political process.

Table 10.2 Performance of the executive as organizational head, by form of government

Per cent of council members (mayors excluded) who agree with the following statement: The executive [manager or mayor] –	Council-manager form	Mayor-council form
Maintains high standards of personal conduct for self and staff	90	61
Seeks to improve efficiency of city government	86	61
Insures that city government is open to participation of all groups in the community	76	64

Source: Svara, 2003, table IX.4

Co-ordination and relations between politicians and bureaucrats

There is great emphasis currently on improving the co-ordination of the component parts of government. Vertically, this involved 'rationalising' the relationship between politicians and administrators. For example, the reinventing of government movement and NPM reforms stress the importance of elected officials focusing on 'steering,' that is, setting the direction and course, rather than 'rowing', or doing the work of moving vessel along. This approach may be described as establishing objectives to set the terms for management, or management by objectives as an approach to governance in contrast to the internal managerial focus of MBO in the United States 20 years ago. Horizontally, co-ordination involves linking the performance of departments to better deal with cross-cutting policies and programs. The overall goal is 'joined-up government' (Pollitt, 2003).

There have been two long-standing approaches to increasing co-ordination in American cities. The political approach to overcoming the 'ungovernable' city with poor vertical and horizontal co-ordination was to increase the leadership and power of the mayor (Yates, 1977). The reform approach is to adopt the council-manager form of government. As discussed in the previous sections, the prescribed roles in the council-manager form are close to the steering concept: the council stresses the governance role by setting broad goals and overseeing performance in meeting them; the city manager offers professional advice to the council in its legislative function and ensures the co-ordinated response of an integrated administrative organisation.

Implicit in the latter approach is the maintenance of distinct though overlapping functions. In council-manager cities, there is a moderately high degree of distinctness between elected officials and administrators when it comes to the administrative sphere. Still, the interest in constituent services is increasing, and council members are increasingly likely to intervene to help constituents with complaints and to seek special services for them even if they do not feel that their intervention is needed to insure adequate response from staff.[15] Co-ordination may be negatively impacted if council members either push for specific remedies that undercut general policy responses or if attention to constituent matters distracts council members from their governance role.

The city manager contributes to co-ordination by encouraging the council to adopt broad, proactive policies. A survey of council members and administrators in cities over 200,000 in population indicates general agreement, from both sets of officials, that the city manager is extensively involved in all dimensions of the governmental process, including establishing the mission and goals of the city. Furthermore, there is acceptance by both elected officials and administrators that the actual level of involvement is appropriate, that is, it matches the respondents' preferred level of involvement for the manager and staff.

City managers recognise the distinctness of elected and administrative office. Nalbandian (1994) argues that the two sets of officials differ substantially in values and orientation. A key responsibility of city managers is to bridge this gap and help council members understand the perspective and recommendations of administrative specialists, on the one hand, and help administrators understand the policy intentions of elected officials, on the other. The manager is not part of the political sphere, but he or she has insights about it. City managers encourage the adoption of cohesive approaches presumably based on sound analysis and at the same time attempt to support individual members in pursuit of their separate goals. A county manager described his advice to commissioners this way at a recent conference:

> I recommend what I consider to be a sound budget. If one commissioner wants to cut the budget, I tell him why I think he should support my recommended budget and then help him identify ways to make cuts. If another commissioner wants to increase the budget, I tell him why I think he should support my recommended budget and then help him identify ways to make additions.[16]

City managers are nostalgic about the past when elected officials focused more exclusively on the governance role. They are frustrated when council members focus too much (in their view) on immediate problems, short-term solutions or constituent concerns. They would prefer that council members identify problems and then let the manager and staff propose solutions, although they report that council members increasingly advocate their own preferred approaches.

There is sufficient difference in perspectives between council members and city managers to produce a modest degree of tension that underlies the overall positive working relationship. Nine out of ten council members agree that they have a good working relationship with the city manager (Svara, 2003).[17] Still, council members in conversations express concern that managers are sometimes aloof and committed to their own 'professional' view of what the city should do and how it is done. They complain that managers shield them from more direct interaction with and supervision of department heads. About one council member in five (22%) would favour having the power to approve the appointment of department heads.

The wariness conveyed by the sentiments of council members and administrators probably helps to preserve a constructive rather than complacent working relationship. The council-manager form promotes co-ordination but at the margins the council pushes for more short-term political responsiveness and more administrative flexibility than managers are comfortable with, and the city manager pushes for more coherence in policy and consistency between policy and practice than council members would wish to see.

Political control of the administration

City managers are not just active in generating policy proposals, as we have seen; they also view themselves as having substantial influence. In fact, when compared to other actors, the city managers rated their own influence as higher than the mayor or the council in both the budgetary process and economic development. On a scale where 100 indicates very high influence and zero indicates no influence, city managers rate their influence in budgeting as 92 (Svara, 1999a). It is higher than the rating they assign to either the mayor (63) or the city council (74) in budgetary decisions. City managers also rate their influence (78) higher than the mayor in economic development (68). These patterns are consistent with those of cities in all countries that use the council-manager of government (Mouritzen and Svara, 2002: 206–8). The city manager is a key official in shaping decisions in both the internally oriented function of budgeting and the externally oriented function of economic development.

In view of the extensive involvement of city managers in policymaking, the issue of political control in council-manager government is a critical one. From the beginning, the unique character of the city manager's office as a 'controlled executive' has been stressed (Childs, 1913). Given the great scope of the manager's influence and authority, some feel that the form weakens public control (see, for example, Jones, 1983: 368). Others contend that democratic government is not jeopardised. Although an influential member of the community elite, Loveridge (1971: 163) observes, 'the close and jealous supervision of the city council requires that the city manager be highly responsive to their preferences and interests'. High acceptance of the manager's recommendations may reflect managers' responsiveness to council members as well as the manager's influence.

The council has the power to remove the city manager at any time. Newland (1985: 8) has contended that 'executive authority can safely be great, because limits on the executive are even larger, and they may be exercised swiftly and decisively'. When the reason for the current incumbent manager's immediate predecessor leaving the office was examined in a 1997 survey, almost half of the city managers in the United States reported that their predecessor had problems in their relationship with elected officials – higher than in any of the other thirteen countries studied (Svara, 1999a).[18] City managers in the United States are subject to pressure and risk of removal from office by the city council.

The relationship of elected officials and administrators is not simply superior and subordinate in council-managers cities. There is reciprocal influence and interdependence between the two sets of officials. The absence of *complete* control of administrators by elected officials does not mean the absence of *any* control. In city government across countries, most city government CEOs are neither dominated by elected officials nor autonomous from them (Mouritzen and Svara, 2002: ch. 9).

Political accountability

The norms of the council-manager form and the council's ability to select and remove the city manager imply a high level of accountability by the manager to the council. City managers, however, also demonstrate professional independence in their views and are attentive to citizens, bringing a professional perspective to their work rather than being politically responsive to the council majority. In the United States, only 27 per cent of the city managers agree that it is advantageous for the manager to have the same political opinion as the majority of the council. This attitude reflects the prevailing opinion of CEOs in 13 other countries (Mouritzen and Svara, 2002: 86–7). Furthermore, only 31 per cent in the United States agree that the manager should be primarily responsible to the political leadership compared to 54 per cent of managers in the other countries. Thus, more city managers see themselves as servants of the public as well as, or rather than, servants of the council than in other countries. These views may serve to promote openness and transparency in the governmental process since managers must be guided by their responsibilities to the council and to the public.

For CAOs in mayor-council cities, the method of appointment has a bearing on attitudes about political accountability. When the council makes or approves the appointment, over seven in ten of the CAOs agree that they should be equally accountable to the mayor and the city council. When appointed by the mayor alone, only 28 per cent share this view (Svara, 2001).

Political leadership by the mayor

Mayors provide types of political leadership that are not provided by other officials. These include advocating goals and setting priorities for city government, developing innovative solutions to problems, mobilising public support and building coalitions. An important question regarding the council-manager form is what impact it has on political leadership by the mayor. Weakness in focused political leadership has been viewed as a shortcoming of the form and a feature that makes it poorly suited for large and diverse cities. Even with increasing use of direct election, the mayor has been characterised as a figurehead because of the lack of formal powers and the absence of informal resources that can be used to acquire leverage over other actors (Pressman, 1972). Still, mayors may provide a different kind of leadership than the power-based entrepreneurial leadership that is the ideal in mayor-council cities. The facilitative leader is well suited to co-operative conditions of council-manager government and exercises leadership by enhancing communication among officials and promoting the accomplishment of shared goals (Svara and Associates, 1994).

Council members in a 2001 survey identified the important initiators of policy in their cities. When mayors are compared, 37 per cent of the mayors in council-manager cities are cited as very important sources of policy compared with 57 per cent of the mayor-council mayors. When the *most* important policy initiator is identified, however, the differences in the mayor's office are dramatic. In almost half of the mayor-council cities, the mayor is the most important policy actor compared to only one in ten council-manager mayors. Thus, mayors in mayor-council cities are stronger leaders in the visible political tasks of initiating policy proposals and presumably in the related tasks of mobilising public backing and building coalition support for mayoral priorities. Another measure in this survey reveals a similar pattern. In council-manager cities, 42 per cent of the council members (excluding respondents who were mayors) agreed that the mayor is a visionary leader compared to 57 per cent in mayor-council cities.[19] The potential for mayoral leadership is not being realised in a majority of council-manager cities, whereas visionary leadership is present in a majority of mayor-council cities.

Although it is common to associate political leadership with the behaviour of a single elected official, the collective leadership of the council can contribute to the overall leadership from politicians. As indicated earlier in Figure 10.1, councils in council-manager cities rate their performance in establishing vision, setting goals and setting priorities higher than do their counterparts in mayor-council cities. The enhanced council performance may be attributed to the council's unified authority in policymaking, the co-operative interactions among officials and to the mayor's leadership within the council. In addition, most council members view the city manager as effective at accomplishing goals set by the council and at providing sufficient information (see Table 10.3). The city manager as a professional leader enhances the performance and increases the involvement of political leaders.

Table 10.3 Performance of the executive in tasks related to the functions of the council, by form of government

Per cent of council members (mayors excluded) who agree with the following statement: The executive [manager or mayor] –	Council-manager form	Mayor-Council form
Accomplishes the goals established by the council	80	42
Provides the council with sufficient alternatives for making policy decisions	75	41
Provides the council with sufficient information to assess the effectiveness of programs and services	74	41

Source: Svara, 2003, table IX.4

The executive mayor who is a political leader may diminish or, least, not enhance the contribution of legislative body. The logic of the mayor-council form assumes that the mayor and council have divergent official interests and an adversarial relationship. Only two-fifths of the council members in mayor-council cities view the mayor as effective at supporting the council. Mayors commonly expect the council to support the goals established by the mayor and come to the council seeking their approval for the mayor's policy proposal rather than providing options. Most mayors do less than a good job at giving the council information needed to support oversight. The mayor has significant formal and informal resources although the council may seek to hold the mayor in check using their own more limited resources.

Thus, in council-manager cities, the mayor may be perceived by the public as the focal point of political leadership, but the entire council exercises leadership, with substantial contributions to policy decisions and council performance coming from the city manager. For the council as a whole to provide this leadership, the members must be able to work together effectively. Using facilitative techniques rather than positional power, the mayor is capable of contributing to goal formation and promoting positive working relationships, but the number of mayors who do *not* make this contribution is greater than the number who do offer effective facilitative leadership.

There is no source of power within the governmental structure that can compel cohesion when council members each pursue separate agendas and have difficulty reaching agreement. A major issue in local government at the present time is whether the mayor's position should be 'empowered'.[20] The empowering provisions may enhance leadership by giving the mayor additional tools to use in assembling a coalition of supporters where it does not naturally emerge and, perhaps more important, by attracting more assertive leaders who are put off by the perceived limitations of the mayor's office. The question that cannot be answered without further research is whether these provisions will make mayors better leaders, attract better leaders to be candidates for mayor or have no positive effect on leadership at all.

The alternative considered recently in a number of large cities including Kansas City, Missouri; Cincinnati, Ohio and Dallas, Texas – and approved in Richmond, Virginia – is change of the structure to the mayor-council form. The primary goal of this change is to enhance political leadership, but the overall impact may be mixed. Having an elected executive mayor and council in a separation-of-powers structure increases the likelihood for political leadership from the mayor, but tends to reduce the contribution from the council and can de-emphasise professional leadership from the top administrator. The supposedly strong mayor can also be constrained by conflict with the council and the 'checks and balances' in the form.

Conclusion: contrasting, not converging, patterns of political leadership

City governments in the United States offer two contrasting patterns of political leadership. In mayor-council cities, more or less strong mayors have the responsibility to develop a policy agenda and direct the work of city staff with the council acting as delegates for constituents, endorsers of the mayor's policy proposals and checkers of the mayor's performance. In approximately half of the mayor-council cities, mayors provide visionary leadership and work well with the council. In the other half, one or both of the conditions is absent. Given the centrality of the mayor's office in the mayor-council form, there can be negative consequences for overall leadership and the contribution of the city council if mayors are either not strong at goal setting or have their own agenda that they pursue independently of the council. A majority of the council members surveyed feel that the mayor does not do a good job in supporting their policymaking or oversight activities. When a chief administrative officer is present, this official heightens the level of professionalism and may serve as an agent of the mayor or as a bridge between mayor and council depending on how the CAO is appointed.

The council-manager form combines a council acting as a board of governors with extensive policy and professional leadership from the city manager. The mayor can enhance policy focus and co-ordination among the actors in city government, although in over half of the cities the mayor does not do this very well. Unlike the mayor-council city, however, other members of the council can fill a leadership vacuum on the council and the city manager – if well chosen and well supervised – should offer a consistent quality of policy advice that combines responsiveness and professional considerations even if the mayor is weak as a facilitator. Members of these councils are also extensively involved in the representational function – more so than in the past –, and they and the city manager must develop ways to channel citizen concerns into the governmental process without fundermining sound administrative practice.

Beyond expanded attention to constituent concerns in council-manager cities, there are other changes that affect political leadership. There is increased activism by elected officials in initiating policy proposals and more hesitancy about accepting substantial leadership from the city manager. Council members are becoming more actively involved as advocates for specific policies, proponents of solutions to current problems and ombudsmen for their constituents. At the same time, they are less engaged in long-range goal-setting and systematic oversight. To adjust to the change in the behaviour of elected officials, city managers are extensively involved in developing broad-range, long-term and citywide proposals as well as continuing to be very active in proposing middle-range policies. In many cities, elected officials promote change in management methods, for example, more privatisation, and want a hand in – or to be informed in advance about – key decisions. Beyond appraising the city manager, they would like to know more and have more impact on management below the level of the manager.

These trends do not amount to a reversal of roles between elected officials and administrators since managers have long been active in policy development. But there is a greater need for city managers to promote shared goals and coherence in the policy process. Rather than operating under the general direction of a homogeneous group of council members drawn from business circles whose world view is similar to the manager's, city managers now relate to diverse councils with activist members and must devote more attention to blending specific initiatives and filling gaps in the city's agenda. Furthermore, they must raise long-term policy issues and prevent new projects from diverting too much time and resources from established policy commitments.[21] Mayors are emerging as more important leaders, but it appears that some focus on advancing a political agenda of their own rather than enhancing the council's cohesion and sense of common purpose.

Nor do these trends amount to a convergence of the mayor-council and council-manager leadership patterns. There is similarity in the sense that the governmental process is becoming more 'politicised,' council members have similar level of emphasis on the representational role, and mayors are more uniformly assertive in the policy arena. Still, the dynamics of political leadership continue to be differentiated by form of government. Having an elected executive mayor in a separation of powers structure affects the role of the council and the contributions of professional administrators in mayor-council cities. Having a council with unified authority affects the council's role, the nature of the mayor's leadership and the status and contributions of the city manager and staff. Citizens and scholars continue to need two roadmaps to explore political leadership in American cities.

Notes

1. The Model Charter has been published by the National Civic (originally Municipal) League since 1897 as a body of recommendations about how city governments should be organised to promote and balance effectiveness, efficiency and democracy. It is periodically updated, and the eighth edition was published in 2003.
2. A small proportion of cities use a town meeting form of government – especially in smaller cities in the New England region – or the commission form in which the members of the city council also direct departments of city government.
3. ICMA Practices for Effective Local Government Management. See Newell (2004: appendix B).
4. It is becoming increasingly common for managers to have a contract that sets forth their rights and benefits in office and compensation if removed from office, but the contract usually does not specify a term nor restrict the council from removing the city manager.
5. The second Model Charter also supported either a small number of districts in large cities – in contrast to councils with 30–50 members elected from small districts that were common at the time – or the use of proportional representation. Hardly any of the council-manager cities, however, adopted these electoral mechanisms that would have increased the representativeness of the city council and opted for at-large elections.
6. Still, differences persist. Two-thirds of the council members from council-manager cities who responded to the 2001 survey in cities over 25,000 people were elected at-large. In contrast, 60 per cent of the council members from mayor-council cities were elected *from districts*.
7. Flentje and Counihan (1984) find that in Wichita, the desire for change and reorientation was reflected in the selection of an outsider who meets the qualities desired by the council, whereas periods of consolidation are overseen by managers selected from inside.
8. Despite these favourable self-assessments, there is evidence that elected officials in council-manager, cities devote less attention to governance activities than in the past (Svara, 1999b), and these council members' actual attention to goal setting and establishing policy principles is not as high as city managers would prefer it to be (Mouritzen and Svara, 2002: 192–3).
9. Council members in large cities are more likely to feel that staff members are less responsive to citizens and that their intervention is necessary although the difference between forms persist (66% mayor-council feel that their intervention is necessary versus 42% council-manager in large cities).
10. *The Model City Charter*, eighth edition. Denver: National Civic League, 2003.
11. A city manager expressed this view in private conversation. Perhaps it is not coincidental that this manager was fired by the city council within a year of making this statement.
12. One manager reported this method of maintaining discipline and defending established goals. He 'hid' money from the council by not emphasising reserves held in a number of special funds but rather focusing on the balance or deficit in the current operating budget.
13. Data from 'Who's Who' biographical files available to ICMA members.

14. Nelson (2002) reports that CAOs in the largest mayor-council cities are also likely to have professional degrees although not as commonly as in public administration. They are less likely to have had previous experience in other cities than city managers, although more likely to have worked in state or federal government or in business.
15. Some council members appear to recognise that constituent service is a useful means to secure electoral support, and they seek out opportunities to provide it. Three in ten council members in the 2001 survey do *not* feel that their intervention is necessary to secure adequate response from staff but still encourage citizens to go through a council member in lodging a complaint.
16. Graham Pervier, County Manager, Forsyth County, North Carolina, at a meeting of the North Carolina Association of County Commissioners, Greensboro, NC, 16 August 2003.
17. In fact, the percentage agreeing that the relationship is positive has gone up slightly in cities of all sizes since 1989.
18. In comparison, in other countries in the UDiTE study, the average was 37 per cent leaving due to retirement whereas only 8 per cent of the US city managers retired. This suggests that the local CEO's position is the culmination of a stable career to a greater extent in other counties than in the United States.
19. The self-assessment of the mayor was much more positive. In council-manager cities, 84 per cent agreed and, in mayor-council cities, 96 per cent agreed that they were visionary leaders.
20. The methods proposed are giving the mayor powers to appoint citizens to serve on boards and commissions without council concurrence, exercise the veto, receive the annual budget prepared by the city manager and present it with comments and suggestions to the council (or preparing a mayoral budget in addition to the manager's), nominate the city manager to the council for approval and initiate the dismissal of the manager.
21. City managers in the large and small cities alike also report that it now takes more effort to persuade council members to follow their own or their predecessors' policy until they explicitly choose to change the policy.

11

The Powerful French Mayor: Myth and Reality

Eric Kerrouche

For many observers, the legal status and powers of the French mayor remain exceptional among the Western democracies. It is true that, seen from without, the mayor's authority, and the way in which the French municipal council is organised, may come as a surprise: everything seems to have been designed to ensure the continuity of the mayor's power. Over and beyond the mayor's extensive prerogatives, however, there is another observation to be made. While voter turnout in France has generally undergone significant erosion since the 1980s, it has remained relatively firm in local elections. Moreover, the French mayor, elected by more of his fellow citizens than is the case for any other political representative, remains extremely popular.

We cannot speak, however, of the office of mayor without bearing in mind the prevailing institutional context, that of a fragmentation of *communes* which is unique in Europe. A few figures shed light on French territorial reality. Today, with its 36,565 metropolitan *communes*, France alone has 42 per cent of the total number of *communes* of all the 25 EU member states combined. Only 1739 *communes* have more than 5000 inhabitants, and a mere 841 (3%) have more than 10,000. France has an average of 1548 inhabitants per *commune*, although more than 60 per cent of the French population live in *communes* exceeding 5000 inhabitants. It is against such a background that the functions of local councillors are to be understood. The territorial reality of France also shows us that, for a population of some 60,000,000, there are currently 497,208 elected *commune* representatives including mayors and local councillors. In 2001, when the last local elections were held, more than 1,100,000 candidates stood for election. This 'atomisation' of *communes* is accompanied by another characteristic: its permanence. This phenomenon is all the more puzzling as most of France's European neighbours had themselves managed to reduce the number of their own local entities.

Despite the problem of *commune* fragmentation in France, the competences accorded to all *communes* are considerable. The principal statutes dealing with French *decentralisation* have not radically changed this general state of affairs.[1] The *commune*, the basic local territorial unit, besides serving as an administrative constituency for the State, also possesses a wide range of powers that stem from the notion of local public interest. As for other aspects, the provisions of the Acts of January and July 1983, dealing with the allocation of jurisdiction between the different authorities, conferred, for each of the major areas of activity, a specific jurisdictional domain for each administrative level, be it *commune*, department or region. In practice, however, these two Acts did not do away with earlier laws organising *commune* intervention in more traditional matters. Equally, other more recent laws have been introduced to detail or extend *commune* jurisdiction. Moreover, and notwithstanding the statutory definition of *commune* jurisdiction, a *commune* can still act to complement the action of another administrative authority, such as a county council. This is an implicit example of what is known in France as 'municipal socialism'[2]: the aptitude of a *commune* to deal with an activity simply because doing so corresponds to the interests of its inhabitants.

The French *commune* remains, more than ever, at the heart of the French local administrative system, both as regards its *commune* aspect, and the attachment of citizens to their municipality and, often, to their mayor. Within the specific terms of this territorial equation, the mayor remains the benchmark for elected representatives, a local figure who must always be taken into account. As regards the relationship between council and mayor in France, several empirical findings confirm that the importance of the mayor as *representative of the citizenry* is increasingly shifting towards what has been termed 'urban presidentialism' (Kuhlmann, 2004). In many respects, the mayor constitutes the cornerstone of French territorial organisation. Due to his central position within French local government, the mayor is also a powerful manager and a community leader.

The mayor as cornerstone of French territorial administrative organisation

The pre-eminent stature of the French mayor is based on two, mutually reinforcing characteristics. The first stems from the legal basis of the role.

The second characteristic underpinning the status of the mayor arises from the ways in which French territorial administrative system has evolved.

The mayor and the progressive institutionalisation of power

The French *commune* possesses a very definite mark of originality: the State, in its efforts to establish a perfectly interlocking network for the whole of its national territory, has made of the *commune* an administrative constituency. The State, however, does not delegate to any representative, since it makes use of the mayor, who thus wears two hats: that of a local agent and that of an agent for the State. As State agent, he serves as the lowest-level representative of deconcentrated government and is, as such, subject to the hierarchical power of the Attorney General or to that of the prefect. This explains certain of the mayor's administrative responsibilities, such as officially publishing and applying laws and by-laws in the *commune*, organising elections, issuing certificates and applying measures of public safety. It also underpins his judicial duties, with the mayor as a registrar, celebrating civil marriages, keeping various registers concerning the population and also exercising a certain number of police powers.

Nonetheless, all these functions are somewhat minor, when compared with his other responsibilities. Not only does the mayor serve as an agent of the State, but he also has a number of other important administrative obligations of local origin. In particular, he is charged with carrying out the decisions of the municipal council. His responsibilities include representing the *commune*, negotiating and signing contracts and preparing the budget, as well as managing *commune* assets. The mayor also exercises other functions delegated to him by the municipal council and, at least in theory, is answerable to it for his actions. The delegated functions embrace a wide range of domains, including, for example, the allocation of *commune* property, taking out loans, creating classes in schools and handling lawsuits, and these can all be revoked at any time. The mayor is likewise invested with his own specific authority regarding the assignments and management of *commune* staff. He also has authority over the local police force, and must ensure public law and order, as well as public safety, security and health.

Over and above such competences, the importance of the mayor stems from a long historical and institutional evolution. Initially and, indeed, for quite a long period, the mayor was appointed to his post, which led to his being considered essentially as a local agent of the State's authority. The law of 5 April 1884, however, which introduced his direct election by the local council, has gradually allowed a new type of political practice to be established. Universal suffrage has put the finishing touches to the mayor's previously acquired historical legitimacy (Le Bart, 2003). It should be borne in mind, however, that even if the relevant laws indicate that it is for the local council to elect its mayor, it is the mayor who co-opts the council. When the mayor draws up his electoral list he establishes his authority over the municipal council, rather than having to depend on the council to designate him. The fact that he is not elected by universal suffrage in no way prevents him from taking the lead role on the local political stage, thereby easily keeping control, as party or majority coalition leader, over the local assembly. The mixed electoral system introduced in 1983 for *communes* with more than 3500 inhabitants certainly helps in this respect. In essence, the system favours the majority, due to the rule of the greatest average, and to the eliminatory barrier of a 10 per cent minimum requirement. The list of those in the lead benefits from a guaranteed majority: more than three-quarters of the seats, if the list is first-past-the-post after the first round; or more than two-thirds, if the list is elected after the second round, even should only one-third of the votes be cast. We must remember, too, that the period of 6 years, for which the mayor and his list are elected, is an unusually long term.

Thoenig (1996) has clearly demonstrated the atypical place occupied by the mayor, by contrasting his situation with that of the President of the Republic. The mayor is chosen by the local council from among its members, whilst the President of the Republic is elected directly by universal suffrage. The mayor simultaneously heads the local council and ensures the execution of the decisions legitimised by the council, whereas the President of the Republic, who appoints the Government, does not have a seat in Parliament. The separation of powers, in particular, between the legislative and executive branches, is far more marked nationally than it is locally. Parliament is made up of two houses; the municipality has only one council. Although one and the same parliamentary party may, at times, hold the majority in both houses, and have the President of the Republic coming from its ranks, the mayor's majority governs the council for 6 consecutive years.

Such a comparison offers an interesting point of view as to the place of the French mayor within the local system. This state of affairs was initially made possible by the privileged bonds maintained by mayor and representatives of the State (Worms, 1966), as well as by the natural tendency of local worthies to make their weight felt. In this sense, the local worthy is a product of the integrative and representative mechanisms characterising French peripheral power (Duran and Thoenig, 1996). Decentralisation and territorial transformations have developed this phenomenon even further, both by increasing the capacities for mayors to intervene and by putting the necessary means at their disposition.

The mayor at the heart of territorial organisation

The decentralisation of 1982, with the various attributions and responsibilities that it conferred, gave a boost to the powers of elected representatives of territorial authorities, including those of mayors (Rondin, 1985). It would be a mistake, however, to think that the increased activity of mayors dates from that time. As early as the Third Republic, French local government was based on the resolution of urban problems in the largest sense. Many of these are at the very heart of welfare institutions: problems of poverty and social aid, as well as those concerning hygiene, health or housing (Gaudin, 1985). Dominique Lorrain (1991) has shown how very responsive municipal institutions are on a daily basis. There are, too, other indications of municipalities' capacities to innovate. The innovations of the 1950s and 1960s, in particular, qualify the commonly accepted idea of an all-powerful State prevailing during this period (Borraz, 1998). That tendency only started to change after 1977, with local society insisting on being taken into account, and with the mayor-as-worthy being superseded by the mayor-as-militant. This shift marks the passage from a legitimacy due to the provision of access to the services of the State, to one founded on the theme of local democracy and the accessibility of the town hall's services.

The system arising from the decentralisation laws gave birth to a new type of mayor. Since the end of the 1980s, the general situation has been considerably modified, and the mayors have become much freer as regards taking initiatives. The logic and rhetoric of local development – that is, their capacity to transform local society (Marie, 1989) – has become essential, both in shaping mayors' discourse and the way in which they act (Darviche, 2000). The model of the entrepreneurial elected representative has now become the dominant one, to the extent that local economy and developmental capacity are now seen as one (Lorrain, 1993; Thoenig, 1999). Equally, the letter of the law has been disregarded in the allocation of competences between local authorities; at every level, especially at *commune* level, there is the temptation to intervene in as many domains as possible.

The most significant change, however, concerns the way of thinking of mayors: they no longer see themselves as the irrational agents of social needs but, increasingly, as accountable managers. We are witnessing,

Table 11.1 Perceived importance of the mayoral tasks

Mayoral tasks	Of utmost importance (%)	Of great importance (%)	Of moderate importance (%)	Of little importance (%)	Not a task of the mayor (%)
To implement the programme of his/her political party/movement	2	13	30	22	29
To manage the implementation of his/her personal policy choices	5	18	38	23	14
To contribute through local experience to the general consolidation of his/her party action	1	11	31	26	29
To ensure good quality of local services	49	49	1	0	1
To encourage new projects in the community	38	56	4	0	0
To create a vision for his/her city	65	32	2	—	0

Note: N = 588

then, a growing focus on the accountability of elected representatives. It is in this light that we must interpret the way in which different styles of managing local public services have been chosen, with the traditional ideological reflexes fast disappearing. The priorities of mayors show this new situation rather clearly. A survey in 2003 of French mayors in *communes* with more than 3500 inhabitants shows how political concerns clearly give way to the needs of service and management, as confirmed in Table 11.1 which shows responses to a question about the importance of the Mayor's several tasks.[3]

Local political action, in comparison with the past, seems to have been considerably toned down, whether in respect of the implementation of personal political preferences or party considerations. This sidelining of party politics as being outside the mayor's domain is particularly revealing. Two types of explanation need invoking here, one of which is sociological. Although the survey only deals with *communes* of more than 3500 inhabitants, this same tendency to banish politics can be found, to an even more extreme extent, in the smallest *communes*. The root *commune* is to be found in the word *communauté*, a shared feature which is far from being neutral: at a local level, *commune* and *communauté* merge, so that any political divisions within its *communauté*, which might well harm its very existence, are spurned. This way of seeing things has been the case in the smallest *communes* and has even been 'imported' by certain urban centres. There is, however, an additional explanation: the image of the mayor-as-manager has come to be held in increasingly greater esteem. It seems quite understandable, then, that the very nature of local projects, and the absolute need to ensure that services are of good quality, mean that these two points are brought to the fore by the mayor. In such cases, the assertion of political stands and points of view gives way to the need for effective management.

It certainly seems as though the mayor-as-manager tries to find optimal solutions to offer the best service for the lowest cost, thus putting economic considerations above all others. Despite an increase in local expenditure, due essentially to the number of very costly transfers of jurisdiction, most observers agree that there has been an improvement in the financial management of all French local authorities. This general evolution has also been sustained by other factors. The *commune* accounting reform (*nomenclature M14*), however conventional it may be, has proved very helpful. It allows a far better appreciation of a local authority's situation and reinforces senior territorial executives in their aim of developing a management-minded culture.

The mayor as manager and community leader

It is true that the status of mayor is ensured by certain specific legal dispositions; but the mayor also benefits from the fact that additional institutional and organisational resources for elected representatives and mayoral services are put at his disposition.

From the outset it should be noted that the distinction between a deliberative assembly and an organ which merely executes has practically fallen into disuse, since it is the executive which now wields all the powers. It is in this sense that the council itself can be said to be an organisational resource at the mayor's disposition (Le Bart, 1992). Furthermore, the institution of a collegial organ, applying a distribution of tasks, is something which seldom prevails since the mayor keeps those elected on a very tight rein indeed (Mény, 1992). As Hoffman-Martinot (1999) observed, if local councillors are at liberty to air their grievances and to promote various requests and projects, it is for the mayor to choose whether he will govern alone or by delegation, helped by his collaborators, including, in the biggest communes, deputy mayors. After all, there is no question of deposing the mayor by a vote of no confidence. On the contrary, it is the mayor who holds the dissuasive power of being able to deprive his council deputies of their delegated authority. 'Municipal presidentialism' can be seen at work here in all its glory (Mabileau, 1995). The mayor, who is more freely accessible, benefits from better advice, and is kept better informed than his councillors on all issues, essentially monopolises decision-making. What is more, the mayor controls the executive board, in addition to the various municipal commissions of which he is *ex officio* president, even if, at his request, one of his deputies may stand in for him.

The only real modification to such a picture is to be found in the increasing role that mayoral deputies are coming to assume. Certain of these deputies may, within the scope of their own particular sector of community life (sports, economy, culture, etc.), effectively exercise full responsibility, inasmuch as they work in very close collaboration with the principal actors involved in their domain (Borraz, 1998). In such cases, in which deputies possess far greater expertise than their mayor, they sometimes behave like specialised local administration departmental heads (Hoffman-Martinot, 1988; Lorrain, 1991), making them less dependent on their mayor. Nevertheless, it is the mayor who remains the ultimate orchestrator, not only because he is completely free to arbitrate, amongst his different deputies, especially as regards the budget, but also because it is he who represents municipal business for his fellow citizens. Moreover, with the number of functionally specialised deputies growing apace, the mayor remains the only factor of integration in a system that bears the imprint of growing complexity. So, we can conclude that a distributed pattern of municipal work is not incompatible with municipal presidentialism.

As for the mayor, he can equally ensure his leadership by counting on the services of the municipal staff, for his executive staff can be said to be just as dependent on him as his elected representatives are. It is clear that the personalisation of the French municipal system implies that municipal executives agree with the mayor's political orientations. This means that CEOs realise that they are at the mercy of a political changeover. The only constraint is to be found in the Territorial Civil Service Statute, which limits the mayor's room for manoeuvre by obliging him to make his choice from within a population that respects certain criteria. Yet, detailed analysis by Roubieu (1999) concludes that elected representatives apparently enjoy complete freedom in choosing their closest collaborators, which allows us to better understand the spoils system applied in the wake of an election. In 1995, for example, out of 40 towns of over 30,000 inhabitants in which the mayor changed, only one CEO was kept on, and more than 4000 executives (General and Deputy-General Managers) were obliged to move out.

Collaboration between mayors and CEOs is made easier by the fact that they increasingly share the same conception of commune management, one impregnated by managerial culture, and disseminated notably by professional periodicals. Under the influence of inter-municipal structures, this model has spread to communes with fewer than 5000 inhabitants, in which case the term 'CEO' is replaced by that of 'Municipal Secretary'. Mayors nowadays realise that they are judged on their aptitude to assume and master the development of their local authorities. Globally, the senior executives of the territorial civil service share this dynamic vision of management, which corresponds very well to the training they have had. The French part of the UDITE survey showed that the CEOs, whose general training level has risen, prize their image of professional executives, akin to that of the mayor-as-manager.[4] The CEO–mayor partnership seems, moreover, to be considered a mutual privilege. Partnership with the mayor, based as it is on mutual trust, is essential for a CEO, far more than is his relationship with the municipal services, the other local political actors, the general public and the local population. It is equally true to say that the same type of partnership is very much appreciated by the mayor. The mayor's necessarily close professional partnership with his CEO, together with the importance that he accords to the smooth running of the *commune* in general, can be seen clearly in the replies given by mayors to the question: *Many different tasks are associated with the mayor's position. How important do you think the following tasks are?* (Table 11.2).

There is additional confirmation of this tendency to be found in the average time set aside by the mayor for his weekly meetings with his

Table 11.2 Mayors' views about the importance of administrative tasks

Administrative tasks	Of utmost importance (%)	Of great importance (%)	Of moderate importance (%)	Of little importance (%)	Not a task of the mayor (%)
To ensure the correctness of the political-administrative process	6	42	37	10	2
To set goals for transforming the administrative structure	4	47	38	6	3
To guide the staff in their day-to-day activity	5	36	33	7	17

administrative staff, which, at 5.55 hours, is almost as much as that set aside for meetings with the local council (5.84 hours), and is close from that reserved for citizens and societies (6.62 hours).

All this description would be incomplete if it were to neglect the particular role played, in sufficiently significant communes, by the mayor's own cabinet.[5] Cabinet collaborators can be freely recruited for their abilities, for political reasons or in both. They are recruited from outside the councillors and their career depends solely on the mayor; as a consequence, these collaborators often make up the mayor's close political guard. They depend entirely on the mayor who has hired them, and their duties duly come to an end when the mandate of the territorial authority who recruited them is over. Their personal relationship with the mayor is of primary importance. If the CEO's role is to control the budget and the other departments, it is nonetheless, the principal private secretary who is politically closer to the mayor, although this is disputed by the appointed members of the mayor's cabinet.

Neither the occurrence of conflicts nor the ascendancy of one entity over another can be entirely excluded, however. An example would be when the cabinet, which cuts across departmental divisions, short-circuits established administrative procedure. All these considerations are borne out by a certain number of answers by French mayors to the Survey on European Mayors. A question such as: *On the basis of your experience as a mayor in this city, and independently of formal procedures, please indicate how influential each of the following actors are in your local authority's activities?* elicited the replies shown in Table 11.3.

Table 11.3 Mayors' assessment of the influence of other local actors

Local actors	No/weak influence (%)	Medium (%)	Moderate/ high influence (%)	No answers (%)
Other leaders in the council	27	40	29	5
Single influential councillors	10	40	48	2
The presidents of council committees[6]	13	34	50	3
The heads of department in the municipality	4	28	66	2
The executive board	4	9	86	2
The municipal chief executive officer	2	10	86	2
The mayor	—	0	99	1

The table clearly highlights the structure of relationships within the municipal council, whose equilibrium revolves around the mayor. His influence, in turn, may be affected by two different channels. The first of these is administrative, largely dominated by the CEO and, to a lesser extent, by the departmental heads. The place of the member(s) of the cabinet – not mentioned in the table – varies neatly from one commune to another and in some, the cabinet can literally replace the CEO. The second channel is an elected one, dominated by the mayor's deputies and their assembly (the executive board) and, in part, by the presidents of commissions (even if, in practice, the two functions very often tend to coincide). As for the other actors (other council leaders, and influential municipal councillors), they are somewhat pushed into the background. The figures given in the table allow us to understand, even more clearly, both the role of spectators assigned to the other municipal councillors, and the quasi-exclusion of opposition members. The relationships evoked can best be schematised as shown in Figure 11.1.

The type of organisation presented by Figure 11.1, essentially centred around the mayor, means the *de facto* marginalisation of municipal councillors. However, whereas municipal councillors of the majority may ultimately be able to express their grievances and have some moderating influence on projects set in motion by the mayor, this is not at all the case for councillors of the opposition. What we are witnessing, in fact, is a very real marginalisation of political opposition within the municipal council. The representatives of the opposition are, in the first place, the victims of the particular form of voting scheme applied in communes of more than 3500 inhabitants. The comfortable majority awarded to the victor leads, in turn, to adversaries being underrepresented, bearing in mind that the leader of the opposition is, above all, the one who has lost the municipal elections. Defeat, moreover, confines adversaries to the *de facto* role of spectators, inasmuch as they cannot really sanction the mayor himself during his mandate. In this respect, votes cast against the council majority's decisions are purely demonstrative and symbolic, which means that issues must be debated outside the institutional sphere and aired, for example, through the local media. Moreover, even those measures which have been taken to guarantee a certain capacity for the minority in the municipal council to intervene fall short of investing the opposition with a real status; for example, the *démocratie de proximité* (proximity democracy) bill 2002 gave oppositions in municipal council some new rights, especially in the field of information.

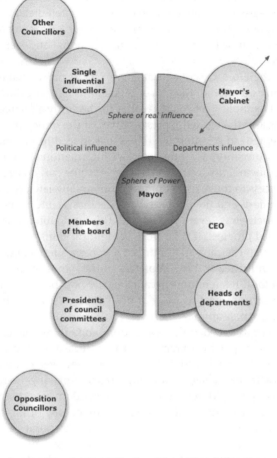

Figure 11.1 A power based on a particular vision of local democracy.

Yet, such omnipresence poses a real democratic problem. The powers at French mayors' disposition allow privileges to the detriment of transparency towards citizens. Democracy is, in essence, representative: this is equally true at a local level of government (Aubelle, 1999). Indeed, in the *commune*, perhaps even more so than in the case of other ballots, everything happens as though the elections ought to embrace and exhaust all the democratic virtues, as if the public domain could not construct and renew itself legitimately other than through the elective process (Caillosse, 1999). The corollary of this logic is that it allows elected representatives to systematically disqualify other modalities of democracy – including referendums – as being prejudicial to the representative model. French mayors are in favour of a *government-based* policymaking based on majoritarian decisions and representative democracy.

We can, therefore, describe local democracy as procedural democracy, in which the situation of the mayor is guaranteed for the duration of his mandate. To simplify, we could say that the law only envisages the right for citizens and the elected representatives of the minority (where they are represented) to be informed. There has indeed been some progress in public information. Citizens can have information about the budget, access to documents concerning the running of delegated public services, access to the register of resolutions and by-laws, the announcement of sessions and the publication of decisions concerning economic affairs. Nonetheless, even though all this undoubtedly amounts to much-needed progress, it is far from being sufficient.

Equally, even the capacity for direct action via a referendum is tightly controlled in France and is completely in the hands of the mayor. The date when local referendums became legally possible in France is quite revealing in this respect. It was not until 1992 – 10 years after the first laws on decentralisation – that the Territorial Administration of the Republic Act was to codify the referendum, something that certain mayors had already put into practice before a legal framework had been determined. This newly codified referendum, however, came with many restrictions. In particular, it was not decision-making in nature, but purely consultative. Moreover, all such referendums are stamped with a markedly representative (and not participative) type of logic since it is the elected representatives who interpret and respond to the results (Blatrix, 1997). It was not until 2003 that the revised article, N°72–1, of the constitution authorised the implementation of a decision-making local referendum within the province of *commune* jurisdictional competencies, and made it possible for citizens to ask for an issue to be debated within the municipal council.

New challenges to be met

Notwithstanding the personal and institutional resources available to French mayors, their situation can be challenged by two concomitant types of evolution. The first is the assertive rise of inter-municipality, and the second is the transformation at work in the sphere of local governance.

Commune transformations and inter-municipal hierarchies: A threat to mayors' powers?

The rise of the phenomenon of inter-municipality in France is quite recent, but its development seems unstoppable. Admittedly, co-operation between *communes* has always existed but, since the beginning of the twentieth century, legislation has introduced a number of different mechanisms. These mechanisms have imposed themselves as a quasi-obligatory functional necessity for *communes* which are too weak, and often completely unable either to deal with local requirements, or to cope with the demands of modernisation.

All this makes it easier to understand the success of inter-municipal co-operation as reformulated by the legislature. The Act of 1999, a simplification and systematisation of the framework sketched out in 1992, has revolutionised the landscape of French *communes*. The law has foreseen three types of community based on demographic criteria. The greater urban community is for areas with more than 500,000 inhabitants, the urban agglomeration community for those with between 50,000 and 500,000 inhabitants, the *commune* community for areas with fewer then 50,000 inhabitants. In 2004, 83.3 per cent of the French population was included in the perimeter of an inter-municipality. It must be noted that the law foresees that the *communes*, when they create a joint community, must necessarily abandon certain attributions which are, thenceforth, jointly employed by the newly formed group. This allows us to infer two essential consequences arising from the development of inter-municipality. The first consequence is that the *commune* relinquishes a certain number of its prerogatives: the inter-municipal structures are accorded a number of key strategic attributions. The *commune* and its mayor are not completely called into question as regards their daily operations, but only as regards their medium- and long-term orientations.

The second consequence concerns the hierarchisation of mayors between themselves. It must be noted that the community council, the legislative organ of the community, is made up of municipal councillors from each of the *communes* making up the community. The representation of *communes* in this community council varies in terms of their demographic size, thereby giving an advantage to the biggest town, an advantage limited, nonetheless, whatever the circumstances, to a maximum of half the number of seats. The president of the community is elected from among the community councillors and, not surprisingly, it is often the mayor of the biggest town who is elected to this post. The mayor of the main town thus becomes the spokesman for an extended area, which leads to the mayors of the *communes* in the community being sidelined. This system, which is still relatively recent, could well produce, in the long run, a hierarchisation of mayors by creating a category of 'super' agglomeration mayors. This development would represent a real challenge for most of the other mayors that may lose a noticeable part of their real prerogatives.

New limits on mayors' local supremacy

The multiplication of the number of actors acting locally, together with the disengagement of the State, has transformed the mayors' capacities for action. The mayor's legitimacy no longer depends on the possibilities of his access to the State, but on his ability to develop a capacity for action in a particular territory in terms of some local interest. But the recomposition of this model has led to the municipal authority's capacity for integration being weakened, including a real limitation as to the way mayors can exert their authority.

Equally, French urban mayors have to deal with the challenge of France's metropolitan growth (Hoffmann-Martinot, 1999). A comparison between France and other Western democracies shows quite clearly that the growth of French towns, other than that of Paris, is fairly recent. On the other hand, the big French centres have undergone a series of radical transformations since the 1980 s to form vast urban groupings that are highly differentiated as regards the ways they are populated and their space occupied and used. The 'agglomerated' and radio-centric model which once characterised France and other parts of Europe seems now to have had its day, giving way to a general, widespread urban sprawl. It is increasingly difficult to give a pertinent definition of vast urban areas.

At the same time it has become clear that the official municipal boundaries are completely out-of-date, first because of the centrifugal distribution of dwelling places and activities, and second, because the average citizen is no longer even aware of *commune* boundaries. Suburbanisation, the constitution of suburban zones, has superimposed itself on a movement in which the peri-urbanisation of rural areas has been accentuated. Thus, between 1975 and 1990, demographic growth was essentially located in the suburbs and neighbouring rural *communes*. Nonetheless, it is obvious that these inhabitants of the outskirts are largely dependent on their main town, both as regards activities and collective services. These evolutions represent a real challenge for French mayors (Heinelt *et al.*, 2005).

The situation of rural mayors has, equally, been transformed. Even if the percentage of farmer-mayors remains relatively high, it has nonetheless been decreasing. Indeed, the rural areas are also undergoing their own mutation, but this is taking place somewhat unequally. Certain rural areas are still in a state of decline, whilst others are particularly dynamic because they are at the intersection of the outskirts of the biggest urban areas. More generally rural society has for several years now been fast emancipating itself from the agricultural reference marks which used to make up the basis of its political life. This is not without consequence for the different forms of local management. The concept of 'rural urbanisation', a term coined fairly recently in France, merely retranscribes this modification of the way in which rural territories are apprehended, leading to greater co-operation between *communes* in order to gain access to new services and implement specifically rural territorial projects. In such a context it comes as no surprise to find that the election of new mayors is no longer based on the traditional factors of eligibility (dominant families, and professions intimately bound up with the agricultural history of the village), and these factors are now on the way out.

The implementation of functional and managerial approaches within *communes* gives rise to an ever-stronger opposition between political issues and those involving public opinion: territorial management apprehended in a rational mode and recognition of the citizen's place within that territory are not automatically complementary. This could be a major problem for French mayors due to their need for democratic legitimacy.

Conclusion

Despite the challenges with which he is confronted, the French mayor can still be considered as belonging to the category of 'strong mayors'. There is, nevertheless, a major difficulty, one that cannot be gainsaid in what concerns French mayors: it is not possible to speak of them all in the same vein. There is a real variation of power amongst them resulting from the heterogeneity of French communes.

The fact that there is a myriad of tiny communes contrasting with a rather limited number of big municipalities means that different mayors find themselves confronted with a host of very different situations to which they have an unequal ability to respond. The disparity of potential fiscal income *per capita* varies so significantly with the size of the *commune* that, as Perrin (1996) pointed out, a local grocery is only to be found in *communes* exceeding 1250 inhabitants, and a full range of equipment, facilities and services requires more than 30,000 inhabitants.

Below a certain threshold, the *commune* has only a purely legal existence. It is quite obvious, then, that any comparison of French mayors' real power must take into account such very unequal situations. How could we possibly compare the administrative services offered by a town with more than 10,000 inhabitants with those provided by a part-time secretary and a local village jack-of-all-trades in a village of fewer than 500 inhabitants? In this context, it is easy to understand that the generalisation of inter-municipality will accelerate the hierarchisation of mayor and leave the weakest of them with very few prerogatives.

Another difficulty would be connected with the lack of a real professional status in touch with the prerogatives and responsibilities of mayors. Monetary compensation alone, however, could not be the only response to this increase in mayors' work and the ever-growing specialisation of their duties. For a mayor to carry out his duties in the best conditions possible also implies that work flexibility must be taken into account. Acknowledging the difficulties faced by someone trying to reconcile his elective duties with his other professional activities, the French legislature introduced a law in 1992 allowing mayors and their deputies in all *communes* and local councillors in *communes* exceeding 100,000 inhabitants to benefit from a set number of hours to administer their local authority (a number which has been progressively increased).[7] It remains true, however, that a perfect representation of all those who make up a particular population is but a pipe dream (Rosanvallon, 1998).

Both the present situation and the laws currently in force still favour certain professions and age groups and, more generally, favour men, notwithstanding the law of 3 May 2000, to promote the equal access of men and women to electoral mandates and elective offices. Despite a drop in average age in 2001, mayors are still to be found in the higher age-brackets: only 5 per cent of French mayors are under 40 (2% in 1995); 66 per cent are between 40 and 59 (51% in 1995). Almost one-third of them (29%) are retired people reflecting both the ageing of the population in rural areas and the need for a mayor to have sufficient free time to carry out his duties. As for the participation of women, their rate is particularly revealing: the application of rules concerning an equal number of men and women has, it is true, enabled the proportion of women councillors to rise to 48 per cent. This has led, however, to only a very slight increase in the number of women mayors (from 8% in 1995 to 11% in 2001). Evolution of the composition of the body of mayors presents a key challenge for French local government in the coming years.

Notes

1. The three major cities do have their own special status with the two Acts of 31 December 1980, known as the PLM Acts for Paris, Lyon and Marseille, establishing a special system of internal deconcentration at the level of the *arrondissement*, an administrative subdivision of the *commune*.
2. This expression has been widely used at the beginning of the twentieth century.
3. This questionnaire had a response rate of 21 per cent, which is relatively high for a survey addressed to French elected representatives.
4. The survey on CEOs was conducted from 1995 to 1997. This survey (the so-called U.Di.T.E. Leadership Study) covered Belgium, Denmark, England, Finland, France, Ireland, Italy, the Netherlands, Norway, Portugal, Spain, Sweden as well as Australia and the United States. In France the U.Di.T.E. study has been carried out by Katherine Burlen and Jean-Claude Thoenig. It was based on a sampling drawn from among municipalities with more than 5000 inhabitants and reached a response rate of 35 per cent.
5. The Law of 16 December 1987 stipulates the maximum number of mayoral cabinet collaborators: one person, when the *commune* has fewer than 20,000 inhabitants; two, when the population is between 20,000 and 40,000 inhabitants; one person for each additional bracket of between 1 and 45,000 inhabitants (when the *commune* has between 40,000 and 400,000 inhabitants); and one person for each additional bracket of between 1 and 80,000 inhabitants (when the *commune* has more than 400,000 inhabitants).
6. In theory, the mayor chairs all municipal committees. In fact, the presidency of each committee is given to an *adjoint* (deputy). The executive board gathers all the deputies.
7. The number of usable hours allotted is established on a quarterly basis, and depends on the particular elected representative's office, the size of his *commune*, as well as other characteristics, such as district administrative centre or tourist centre, etc.

12
Transformation of the Political Executive in Belgian Local Government

Johan Ackaert

In 2001, the responsibility for municipality legislation was transferred from the Belgian federal state to the regions. The Flemish, Walloon and Brussels regions are granted the power to settle the structure of local government and organise their municipalities, including the form of their local political structures, bureaucracies and relations with citizens. Today, the Flemish region is the most advanced in developing new arrangements for local governance. This chapter reviews the traditional system of local government before examining the main features of the proposed transformation and its consequences for the roles of lay politicians.

The traditional system: councils, boards and bureaucrats

The autonomy of Belgian municipalities is guaranteed by the Constitution. Their organisation and competencies was laid down in the municipality law of 1836, later rewritten in 1989. Belgium has 589 municipalities: 308 in the Flemish region, 262 in the Walloon region and 19 in the Brussels capital region. Each municipality has a council, whose members (7–55 in number) are directly elected for a six-year term. Among its members, the council elects between two and ten aldermen.[1] They usually belong to the political (single-party or coalition) majority in the council. Finally, the mayor, as chief executive of the municipality, is appointed by the King for a six-year term. Such an appointment is rooted in a nineteenth-century tradition since when the influence of the King in politics decreased considerably with, in practice, nominations being made by the Home Department minister (Stengers, 1992: 279). Since the transfer of the municipality competences to the regions, nominations to mayor are to be made by the regional minister of interior affairs.

The council has competence to decide on all matters of local interest. It is also an organ of the central authorities for the purpose of administering matters of general interest. The mayor and aldermen together constitute the executive board of the municipality.[2] The board is the executive organ of the council, but is also responsible for certain duties delegated by higher government. Municipalities are responsible for all the issues that are not formally allocated to higher administrative levels. In practice, autonomy is limited by the requirement for municipalities to comply with higher rules and norms. In reality, the debate about the nature of 'local autonomy' is eclipsed by the recognition of the growing complexity of public administration.

The law allows councils to install standing committees in order to prepare council decision-making. These committees comprise members of the different parties represented in council in proportion to their strength. Such committees exist in nearly half of the Belgian municipalities. The councils can also be assisted by advisory bodies on which council members are outnumbered by outsiders. Some of these bodies are statutorily required, as in the case of environmental planning or the administration of public libraries. Others are established by the council itself, to cover such areas as road safety or international co-operation. Although the council is in principle considered to be the 'heart' of the local political institutions, in practice the executive board is pre-eminent. The board is not only responsible for the execution of decisions taken by the council, but also prepares the council diary and formulates the decisions presented to the council. Only in exceptional cases are board proposals rejected by the council. Party loyalty and discipline, the growing complexity of local administration and policy, combined with the lack of organisational and financial support needed for policymaking – resources that are controlled by the Board – put the council in a weak position relative to the board. In 1998, municipalities were given the option to empower council members by improving their access to the local administrative staff and information. They were also permitted to grant financial resources to the political fractions and support training programs.

The municipality secretary is the highest functionary within the local bureaucracy. In recent decades, his function shifted from a traditional notary role towards a CEO role. He is no longer simply responsible for editing decisions taken by council, board or mayor, but also for the preparation of policy presented in the different political arenas within the municipality. Under a law of 1990, he is recognised as the leader of the administrative component of local government but can only exercise his power 'under the authority of the board', a vague term which resulted from a compromise between the Flemish and Walloon politicians. The Flemish were in favour of a stronger role for the CEO within the administration, while the Walloons latter feared the impact of the CEO as a potential danger for their political control of the administration. The position of the CEO as link between board, council and mayor on the one hand and bureaucracy on the other hand is undermined by the tendency of board members to assume 'cabinet' positions giving direction to the various service heads (Plees and De Leemans, 1997: 7). In law, board members do not possess individual executive competences; decisions are taken by the board as a college.

The mayor has two main functions. First, as administrative chief of the police, he is responsible for maintaining law and order in the municipality. Second, he is the first magistrate of the municipality. He presides at meetings of the council and the board. In practice, the mayor is also the political leader of the majority, and thus chief policymaker. In order to summarise the roles mayors ascribe to themselves, we constructed role-categories based on Faber (1967, 1974) and Derksen (1980) and asked the mayors to rank them.[3] Table 12.1 presents the results.

The importance attributed to the 'head of the police' role in administrative handbooks is not reflected in the role-ranking as perceived by the mayors. Instead, the role of leader of the political institutions in the municipality prevails. Then comes the role of confidante. The role of lobbyist also obtains a high score in the ranking. This role is followed by

Table 12.1   Role-ranking

	Mayors		
Roles	Flemish	French-speaking	Belgian
Leader of council and board	2.91	2.54	2.76 *n.s*
Confidante	2.60	4.56	3.37
Lobbyist	5.00	3.18	4.23
Leader administration	4.92	3.58	4.35
Policymaker	3.88	5.90	4.73
Head of the police	5.07	5.21	5.12 *n.s*
Promoter of direct participation	5.62	5.66	5.64 *n.s*
Reconciliator of population	6.34	6.26	6.31 *n.s*
Promoter of party	8.10	8.08	8.09 *n.s*
(Base)	138	96	234

the leader of the administration. The last three roles deal with patronage in politics. The first concerns the relations between the politician and citizens, the second, the relations between the politician and other administrative levels and the third, the control of administration by politicians. In the context of party rule and patronage, a more important place for the role of party-promoter might be expected. The data show the opposite, and this role obtains the lowest score of all.

Since a mayor plays multiple roles, it was necessary to investigate possible combinations. We accordingly ran a cluster-analysis on the data collected in the survey among Belgian mayors and found a satisfying solution with four clusters. The largest proportion of the respondents can be labelled as the traditional mayor (42.4% of the mayors). The traditional mayor is in the first place the confidante of his citizens, considers himself as the leader of council/board and bureaucracy but pays less attention to policy-development. The promoter mayor (23.1%) is quite the opposite. He does not recognise himself in the role of confidante but is overall the leader of council and board, taking a close interest in policymaking. The lobbyist mayor (9.5%) is neither confidante nor policymaker but emphasises his role in having contacts with other administrative levels and private groups in order to collect benefits for his municipality. Finally, the co-ordinator mayor (25.1%) is, like the traditional mayor, the confidante of the citizens, but combines this role with promoting direct participation and concern for policymaking. It is remarkable that the role of reconciliator does not feature in any of the four types, nor does the role of party-promoter, whose weak scores were noted earlier.

Main features of the proposed transformation

The competence for municipality legislation was transferred in 2001 to the Belgium regions. The remainder of this discussion focuses on the Flemish region which is far ahead on the adoption of change and has already presented a comprehensive proposal to the Flemish Parliament. To prepare the new Flemish local government act, a group of academics was invited to write a 'proof of the local government act'. Their report called for the election of the mayor from within the council, while giving the Flemish Government the option to oppose the council's choice in the event that the elected mayor was judged not to meet the necessary moral conditions. In such a case the local council would be required to elect a new mayor from within its members (Maes and Boes, 2001: 137–8).

On 17 July 2002, the Flemish Government presented their proposal for a Local Government Act. It had hoped to pass its proposal in Flemish

Parliament before the 2004 regional elections (which coincided with the European Parliament elections) but failed. New proposals were brought forward including provision for the direct election of the mayor. In spring 2005, the Flemish Parliament will debate two proposals. The first is a government proposal for the global transformation of local government. The second embodies the introduction of the directly elected mayor introduced by the liberal party VLD, part of the Flemish Government majority. This is the result of an ambiguous compromise between the different parties supporting the current Flemish Government, whereby the liberals are the strongest defenders of that idea and the Christian-democrats the strongest opponents, with the socialist party holding a centre position.[4]

The main aims of the reform proposals are to strengthen democratic administration and improve the functioning of the political bodies that determine policy for the municipality. They seek also to improve management, provide the administrative component of local government with increased responsibility and introduce strategic planning, human resources management and introduce modern financial management, strengthen the internal auditing and reduce the external control. Reform is also intended to allow municipalities sufficient discretion for organising their internal and external autonomous administrative structures and provide for self-regulation, as well as offer them a new framework for private–public collaboration and enlarge the involvement of the citizen with provision for citizens consultation on given issues and the introduction of complaints management.

The proposal puts political responsibility for policy preparation and implementation into the hands of the board of alderman and the mayor. The board is also responsible for the matters delegated by the council to the board and for the administration and management of the municipality organisation. In order to allow the council to act in an independent way, the election of a council president is proposed, together with options for delegating some competences to the board of alderman and the self-regulation within the council of advisory committees. Final decisions belong to the council which decides on proposals elaborated by the board of alderman which in turn is accountable to the council for the functioning of the administration. The proposals also provide for council members, president and political parties to be compensated for financial loss.

There are no reforms envisaged concerning the selection of the alderman. They will – as in the current system – be elected within and by the council. Nor do the current proposals make fundamental changes in the duties, competences and role of the mayor, with the exception of his position vis-à-vis the council and the administrative staff. A council-elected member will replace the mayor as president. The mayor will act as an independent partner, and no longer as member of the board, in the production of the note of agreement between the administrative staff, board and the mayor.

The current legislative proposal also includes some innovations in the task distribution and the collaboration between the political and administrative components of the municipality. Policy preparation and execution of strategy, together with citizen-oriented service presuppose an organisation with sufficient administrative autonomy in order to realise programmes and acts. Individual politicians like mayor, alderman or council members are not allowed to operate as administrative chiefs. The administration is to be headed by the municipality director, who will replace the present municipality secretary, will head the personnel function and lead the different services, reporting to the board. He will advise the various bodies on policy, administrative and juridical matters. As spokesman of the management team, he agrees with the board and mayor on matters relating to the functioning of the administration. His position, compared with the present secretary, is to be strengthened as he will act as a budget-holder and decide on appointments of personnel. The proposal foresees a central role for a financial manager and local auditor who will replace the municipal-receiver.

Anticipated consequences of the reforms

In order to evaluate the intended and unintended potential consequences of the proposals, we first present information on the current transformation in the role behaviour of Flemish mayors. Table 12.2 links the typology based on the cluster analysis described earlier with age and level of education. In order to do this, we constructed two dummy variables. Age was recoded (based on the marginal distribution) in the group of mayors younger than 57, and equal to or older than that age, while we coded education according to whether or not mayors had a university or equivalent degree

It is clear from Table 12.2 that mayors of traditional orientation tend to be in the older age group and lacking university education. There is also quite a strong tendency for the promoters and co-ordinators to be younger and, in the case of promoters, to be university educated.

There is a strong interaction between age and education, making it difficult to identify their independent effects on mayoral orientations.

Table 12.2   Flemish mayors: determinants of typology

Typology	Age			Education		
	Young	Old (%)	Total	Non-university	University (%)	Total
Traditional	31.7	55.0	41.5	57.8	28.4	42.0
Promoter	28.0	21.7	25.4	12.5	36.5	25.4
Lobbyist	1.2	1.7	1.4	1.6	1.4	1.4
Co-ordinator	39.0	21.7	31.7	28.1	33.8	31.2
(Base)	82	60	142	64	74	138

$Chi^2 = 8.424$, D.F. = 3, p = .038 $Chi^2 = 15.223$, D.F. = 3, p = 002

To address this problem, we examined the relationship between the mayor's orientation and education, controlling for the age category (table not included) and found only a significant relation between education and orientation for the younger mayors. Younger mayors with a lower educational level seem to identify themselves with the traditional roles and less with the role of promoter.

The changing role of the mayor

In the summer of 2002, 42 mayors in the Limburg province were sent a questionnaire which repeated some questions of the previous survey. This made it possible to assess the extent to which the mayoral role was undergoing change. In this survey, 38 mayors (or 86.5%) responded. Table 12.3 presents the role-ranking of the Limburg mayors and compares it with the Limburg sample of the 1993–4 survey.

Compared with the 1993–4 survey, mayors profile themselves much more as policymakers than as people's confidante. In their relations with citizens, mayors are replacing the traditional parochial clientelistic style by an approach based on participation and co-ordination. This finding is not unique. Clark and others described the worldwide emergence of a new political culture, characterised by a decline of clientelist patronage-based relationships between politicians and voters, a change more pervasive among younger and more educated local politicians (Nichols-Clark and Hoffman, 1998: 12–13).

This transformation of Flemish mayors can, then, be partly linked to the changes in their social-demographic background. We have already noted that the more educated a mayor is, the more strongly he is oriented towards general policy problems. Today, 58 per cent of the

Table 12.3   Transformation in the role-ranking of mayors

Roles	2002–3	1993–4
Policymaker	2.62	3.67
Confidant	3.29	2.40
Leader administration	4.47	5.15
Lobbyist	4.50	5.19
Leader of council and board	5.06	3.05
Head of the police	5.24	5.53
Promoter of direct participation	5.56	5.68
Reconciliator of population	5.85	6.26
Promoter of party	7.71	7.74
(Base)	34	22

Limburg mayors have a university degree compared with 47 per cent in 1993–4. Moreover, there are indications that a move away from the traditional role occurs within the career of a local political leader. Newton showed, for example, that seniority leads to concentrating on general policy issues and less on dealing with individual service rendering. The longer a local politician keeps his seat, the more his role behaviour is affected by fellow councilmen and less by citizens and voters (Newton, 1974: 631–6). Our survey contained a question about the socialisation agents training the mayor in filling their role. Nearly 70 per cent of the respondents indicated the CEO (the municipality secretary) as the main socialisation source. This proportion varies significantly with the seniority of the mayors; the respondents leading the municipality for a first term mentioned the CEO in 63.7 per cent of the cases. This share increases to 71 per cent for the mayors in the second term and ends at 79.5 per cent for the mayors in a third or following term. The mayors were also asked to identify the sources of resistance. A little more than 80 per cent referred to the opposition members of the local council, as might be expected (the duty of the opposition is to oppose). In second place come individual citizens (38% of the cases). They are more important than local press, action groups, local committees, etc. This proportion does not vary with the seniority of the mayors, but we found a significant relation between quoting individual citizens as the main source of resistance and the role of the CEO as socialisation agent. Nearly 80 per cent of the mayors mentioning individual citizens as source of resistance described the CEO as the main socialisation agent while this was only the case for 64.3 per cent of the mayors not suffering that kind of obstruction.

Both surveys indicate a transformation in mayors' role behaviour. Slowly, the traditional parochial style (whereby the mayor is the boss of the political organs and treats the citizens as individual clientele) is being replaced by a new type of leadership that emphasises policy-making, linking the citizens as group to local government and running as go-between between several authorities, groups, policy-networks, etc. We explained this shift mainly by transformations in the social-demographic background of mayors. Not only is the individual background of mayors changing, but also the administrative framework and political context differ from the past. Although administrative law handbooks still portray the municipality as led by the council and board, the reality is much more complex. The shape of a local society is no longer formed by council and board decisions, but by multiple inter-actions in a multipolar network consisting of several local public and private actors (Bouckaert, 1997: 118).

The profile of mayors is changing. The younger and the higher edu-cated a mayor is, the more the chance he has to identify himself with the role of promoter and co-ordinator and less with the traditional role. Comparative research concluded earlier that political attitudes and skill of MPs derives from the individual educational and professional back-ground (Blondel, 1973: 132). De Winter arrived at the same conclusion for Belgian MPs (De Winter, 1992: 296, 365). Education develops those skills that are necessary for a successful career pattern. Furthermore, the orientation towards general policy issues increases (and the orientation towards individual problem solving decreases) with educational level. The difficulties that lesser-educated MPs encounter when they cope with complex and abstract political issues drive them to emphasise the 'easier' errand boy role (De Buyst, 1967: 398–9). The kind of activities associated with this role requires less intellectual skills and leads faster to visible success and personal satisfaction. It seems that these findings apply equally to the mayoral cadre. Although the proposed new local government act gives the future 'municipality director' (the local CEO) greater autonomy in leading services and recruiting personnel, it seems possible that this aim will again be traversed by the influence and power of a directly elected mayor.

Political accountability and leadership

A major reason for introducing the directly elected mayor was to bring a greater transparency in the selection of board members and mayor and to strengthen the impact of the voter in this process. This would, in the eyes of the defenders, increase the participation of the citizen in local politics. It is not clear that this reasoning fits with reality. First, the electoral system is characterised by compulsory voting. At the 2000 local elections in Flanders, the turnout was 93.1 per cent. Taking the turnout in other countries into account, and knowing that the turnout at Belgian local elections is already higher than at the general elections (Ackaert *et al.*, 1992: 216), it seems difficult to increase that figure. Second, in nearly half of the municipalities, the voter determines directly the party composition of the board. Third, voters also have a large impact on the individual selection of council members. Fourth, although parties play an important role in coalition formation in the other half of the municipalities and the selection of board members and mayor, they cannot neglect the number of preference votes cast on individual candidates. So, it is by no means evident that the lack of transparency in the selection of board members and mayors is as great as the promoters of the proposal suggest. Finally, the expected transparency might be reduced by the existence of the running mate. The proposed local government act foresees the replacement of a sitting mayor in the case of his or her election for parliament by the running mate. About 15 per cent of mayors today are member of one of the Belgian Parliaments (Ackaert, 1994b: 596; Fiers, 2001: 185). This means that in these municipalities, voters will have no certainty that their preferred candidate will in fact become the mayor.

If the parliament accepts the liberal proposal concerning the direct election of the mayor, this might be one of the most spectacular changes in the local electoral system since the adoption of the first municipality law in 1836. However, the proposal combines elements of representative and majority political systems. This exercise of political engineering would even be impeded since the government stated that the council elections will in the future be organised on a more representative system (by replacing the Imperiali seat distribution method by the D'Hondt system). Moreover, local politics in the recent decades has been characterised by a trend towards fragmentation. After the 1976 local elections, Flemish municipalities contained four political groups, a number that increased to five after the 2000 local elections. It is not clear how the introduction of elements of a majority system could be combined with the growing political pluralism among the voters.

The consequences of the proposed reforms for the political-institutional framework are considerable, and will transfer the balance between council, board and mayor. This is not immediately obvious. At first sight, the shifts in checks and balances between council, board and mayor are limited, for the current proposals do not allocate important competences to the mayor; on the contrary, the government wishes to maintain the collegial model of a board. Further, the proposal aspires to reinforce the role of the democratically elected council in strategic decision-making. Yet, this aspiration is likely to be negated by the political weight of a directly elected mayor, who will be able to cite his electoral base when the opinions of council and board members diverge from his own. Second, although the proposal assigns the elected mayor a significant role in the majority formation, it does not prevent the possibility of 'cohabitation' which would increase the risk of a political stalemate in the administration of the municipality.

Final remarks

At the time of writing, the new Flemish Parliament is to discuss the new shape of local government. The debate concerning the direct election of the mayor overshadows the advantages in the government proposal. The larger part of the government proposal seems to be attractive for different players in the local area, but this is not the case for the issue of the direct election of the mayor. That idea is supported by the liberal members of the Flemish Government. But it receives support neither from the High Council of Interior Administration, nor from the Flemish Union of Municipalities, the present council and board members in Flemish municipalities, the present mayors and local bureaucrats (Meire *et al.*, 2002: 40; VVSG, 2003: 5). The acceptance of this proposal among the present municipality leaders is by consequence very low.

The democratic benefits of the introduction of the directly elected mayor remain uncertain. Moreover, the cost of this innovation is likely to harm the intended improvement of local government performance. Earlier, we noticed among the mayors an evolution from a traditional leadership style towards a more modern style that emphasises co-ordination roles and policymaking. Knowing that a direct election will *de facto* produce a more powerful mayor towards board, council and local bureaucracy and a more dependant mayor towards individual citizens requests, it is likely that we are facing the renaissance of the traditional mayor.

Notes

1. In eight (linguistic sensitive) municipalities, the aldermen are distributed on a representative way between the parties according to the number of party votes.

2. Although the revenue system for local politicians has been improved in 2000, aldermen as well as mayors are part-time politicians, with the exception of the largest cities of the country.
3. The empirical evidence in this contribution is drawn from two surveys, undertaken between September 1993 and September 1994. In a random sample of 340 mayors of which 172 were Flemish and 168 French-speaking mayors, a response rate of 80 per cent was achieved. The second survey was based on a questionnaire sent to all mayors in the Flemish province of Limburg. Conducted in 2002, this survey focused on the effects of the police reform and the role behaviour of mayors (Ackaert, 2003).
4. During the previous legislature, the Christian-Democrats belonged to the opposition and were then already opposed to the idea of the directly-elected mayor. The socialists belonged to the government and they accepted within a global framework of compromises this proposal, yet without much enthusiasm.

13
Institutions Count but Resources Decide
American Mayors and the Limits of Formal Structure

Clarence Stone

American mayors are often cited as examples of policy leadership and problem-solving energy,[1] and some European scholars have looked at the American mayor as a model of how to revitalise local politics. It is a highly visible office and one that is often associated with innovation. Yet caution should surround any effort to transplant a practice from one place to another. Reforms often fail to yield intended results. It is well to remember that leadership is rarely a matter of relying on the formal features of the office. The experience of mayors in the United States shows that leadership rests on informal arrangements, not simply on the formal powers of those who hold local executive offices.

No American mayor has a ready-made mechanism available for executive control. Any apparatus of policy leadership has to be knit together with the mayor as only one actor. As Robert Dahl noted in his famous study of New Haven's Richard Lee, the 'centrifugal forces in the system' are 'persistent and powerful'. Dahl observed of Lee: 'The mayor was not at the peak of a pyramid but rather at the centre of intersecting circles. He rarely commanded. He negotiated, cajoled, exhorted, beguiled, charmed, pressed, appealed, reasoned, promised, insisted, demanded, even threatened, but he most needed support and acquiescence from other leaders who simply could not be commanded' (1961: 204).

The wherewithal to govern is not in place for use by the institution of the mayoralty. Instead, the office of mayor is one of the leverage points from which a governing coalition can be raised. Consider experiences from four cities.

Business and civic co-operation: the Atlanta Case

Sociologist Robert Crain concluded a multicity study by observing that 'one of the most complex issues in the study of American local government [is] the phenomenon of the businessmen and others who, without holding formal office, make up a civic elite that influences the government's actions' (1968: 356). A compelling example of Crain's insight occurred with the election of Andrew Young as mayor of Atlanta in 1981. Before becoming Atlanta's second black mayor, Andrew Young had long service in the civil rights movement as one of Martin Luther King's lieutenants. He had also been a member of the US Congress, and he was US Ambassador to the United Nations during the presidency of Jimmy Carter. Young therefore brought strong credentials to the position of Mayor of Atlanta, and he was elected to that position by a solid majority. Yet, before he took office, he felt that it was necessary to meet with representatives of the city's business sector, most of who had supported his opponent. At an informal luncheon with city business leaders, Young opened up with the comment, 'I didn't get elected with your help,' but he repeated a statement made during his campaign: 'I can't govern without you' (Stone, 1989: 110).

Atlanta is by no means a typical American city, but business involvement in governing coalitions is not a rarity. Atlanta, however, has an exceptionally unified and engaged business sector. Organisationally business operates through the Chamber of Commerce (which has no official link to the governmental sector) and Central Atlanta Progress, a downtown business association. Labour unions are weak, and the city has no history of philanthropic foundations playing a large, independent role in the city's civic life. Locally, the Metropolitan Community Foundation is a significant player, but it is an arm of the business sector. So also is Research Atlanta, a non-profit organisation that conducts studies of local issues. Business executives also lead such activities as the United Way (the major local charity drive) and the Arts Alliance. The daily newspaper has also functioned as an integral part of the Atlanta business community. There are a variety of service organisations, but Atlanta has no powerful advocacy organisations that speak for the city's social needs. In Atlanta, most civic pathways lead to and from the city's business leadership. All things considered, 'if one is seeking credit, donations, technical expertise, prestigious endorsements, organizational support, business contacts, media backing, or in-depth analyses of problems, then very likely one is thrown into contact with the civic network that emanates from the activities of the downtown business elite'

(Stone, 1989: 192). This is the civic context in which Mayor Andrew Young acknowledged that he could not govern the city without the co-operation of Atlanta's business leadership.

In 1973, a new city charter gave Atlanta the strong-mayor form of government, a form in which executive authority over such matters as budgeting and administrative reorganisation rests in the hands of the city's elected executive. That is not a trivial fact, recognised in an accompanying limit of two consecutive terms for the mayor as a check against concentrated executive power. Yet the form of government is less important than informal arrangements that make Atlanta's biracial coalition the city's governing force. From 1946, when a black voter mobilisation paved the way for an alliance with white business executives, to the present, governance has had a biracial foundation. In 'the city too busy to hate' black electoral clout has served the policy needs of the white business elite, and white business leaders have used their influence in state government first to move Georgia away from the position of diehard segregationists and second into partnership in such undertakings as the hosting of the 1996 Summer Olympics. The biracial coalition enabled Atlanta to transform its rail-centred downtown of the industrial age into an auto-centred/airline-served downtown of the post-industrial age. In the process, it also became a Mecca for the black middle class. This transformation turned very little on the formal structure of government, but greatly on the city's biracial coalition and its ability to secure support from the state government.

Governmental authority and resources are part of what made the biracial coalition possible, and black electoral power was crucial in providing the coalition control of local government. Atlanta's black community itself has an extensive civic structure, including the colleges that make up the Atlanta University system, black churches, substantial black businesses and a network of non-profit and voluntary organisations. Yet, by itself, this African American civic structure would be a weak foundation for governing. It is the complementary resources of the white business elite, the civic structure it heads and its access to state officials that give the coalition a formidable capacity to govern. Could business on its own have provided the resources for an effective arrangement for governing the city and transforming its economic base? Not likely. Urban redevelopment on the scale executed in Atlanta is costly, controversial and laden with conflict. Support from elected officials provided an essential element, and large expenditures of public funds were a necessary part of the process.

The remarkable feature of Atlanta's experience is how a stable governing coalition was created around two highly contentious issues, those of racial change and urban redevelopment. Yet, captured in the slogan 'the city too busy to hate', these two issues provided an agenda on which the biracial coalition could be built and which the complementary resources of the coalition partners could sustain. The coalition has had its tensions and its moments of crisis, but it has also made use of informal means to restabilise from time-to-time and maintain the level of co-operation needed to sustain the coalition as a governing force. For the past few decades, a key means of pursuing co-operation has been Action Forum, a non-governmental organisation that links the white business elite with top-level black leaders. Its deliberations are closed to the public, and it keeps no written records. Action Forum perpetuates a tradition of behind-the-scenes negotiation outside the formal channels of government.

Governance in Atlanta occurs through a coalition that includes, but extends far beyond, local government officials. The coalition brings together partners with complementary resources that in combination are sufficient for tackling large and controversial issues. The coalition works as a governing arrangement because a largely informal network of interpersonal and inter-organisational ties facilitates the level of civic co-operation needed to deal with contentious issues. Complementary resources, a congruent agenda around which coalition is built and an effective scheme of co-operation are the key elements. The office of mayor is an important part of the picture but only one part in a very complicated whole.

Atlanta's business sector has a long history of engagement in community affairs. New Haven, Connecticut, represents a different pattern (Dahl, 1961; Rae, 2003). The city's politics was long dominated by ward-based politics oriented primarily to patronage and personal favours. Business had a presence through the Chamber of Commerce, but most business leaders resided in the suburbs and viewed city government warily. The Chamber of Commerce backed the idea of downtown redevelopment, but nothing much happened until Richard Lee was elected mayor in 1953. Lee seized on downtown renewal as the centrepiece for his administration, created a special redevelopment agency directly under his wing and recruited a team of bright and capable planners, policy technicians and professional administrators to pursue federal grants and put together an ambitious program me.

To protect redevelopment from the politics of patronage and to engage business leaders and investors in the programme, Lee created a

Citizens' Action Commission (CAC). Eleven of the 24 members lived in the suburbs, and more than half were what Dahl termed 'Economic Notables' (1961: 71). Yale University and organised labour were also represented. The body consisted of what Mayor Lee called 'the biggest set of muscles in New Haven' (1961: 130). Though a formally constituted body, the CAC operated outside the normal channel of city government. Lee's effort to strengthen the administrative power of the mayor's office under a new city charter failed in a 1958 referendum. Despite the failure of efforts to give the mayors executive authority a stronger foundation, the city's redevelopment effort continued apace. The coalition embodied in the CAC, the talented staff, the availability of substantial federal and state money and the mayor's leadership skill in holding the arrangement together provided the mix of purpose and resources able to move ahead. The special redevelopment agency and CAC, drawing mainly on external funds, enabled the mayor to bypass the Board of Aldermen and its penchant for patronage politics. That ability to bypass the usual political channel kept business engaged and facilitated private investment in the redevelopment process. The mayor was a central player and an essential sparkplug for redevelopment, but, without the co-operation of business and the investment of private funds, redevelopment would not get off the ground. To assure that business and Yale University were fully integrated into the redevelopment process, Mayor Lee constructed ad hoc arrangements for that purpose.

Both Atlanta and New Haven have pursued redevelopment vigorously, with New Haven having more difficulty sustaining its effort. In a nation with little translocal regulation of land use, private investment decisions are not easily channelled into the central city (Sellers, 2002).

The two cities have had little success in pursuing social regeneration. New Haven made an early effort, relying largely on external funding. Following the same model as in redevelopment, the mayor created Community Progress Incorporated (CPI), an independent agency closely tied to the mayor's office (Murphy, 1971; Rae, 2003). With a tilt towards social agencies, CPIs board brought together much of the city's organised 'muscle'. It, however, had no effective representation of the grass roots, and in an era of 'maximum feasible participation' found itself caught in a series of debilitating controversies. Despite recruiting a talented staff, similar in many ways to the one at the redevelopment agency, CPI could not overcome the alienation and distrust of the city's poor and minority population. Creative programme ideas had only limited impact; their target constituency saw these programmes as imposed from outside.

Atlanta did extraordinarily well in integrating the black middle class into the city's civic and business life. However, Atlanta as 'Black Mecca' is strictly a middle class phenomenon. Unrepresented through such channels as Action Forum, the city's poverty population has been left on the sidelines. Several recent initiatives have proved disappointing.

During the planning for the Summer Olympics, an explicit anti-poverty initiative known as the Atlanta Project got underway. Sparked by former president and Georgia governor Jimmy Carter's social conscience, and bolstered by corporate concern about Atlanta's image, the initiative attracted wide business sponsorship, and gave rise to a temporary surge in volunteerism. With an aim of 'community empowerment', the architects of the project chose to bypass local government agencies, but failed to develop an integrated plan of action. The result was a host of specific but not well-connected projects, ranging from child immunisation to housing improvements. Lacking a firm direction, the overall project was spread thin. The Atlanta Project never connected fully with the non-profit sector, and such important actors as the city's black clergy were never integrally involved. Without the inclusion of government agencies, resources were inadequate, and the volunteer base proved to be short term. After a five-year run, the project faded into a small, university-based activity.

Where the Atlanta Project bypassed the governmental sector, Atlanta's federally funded Empowerment Zone failed to engage the city's major businesses (Rich, 2003). From the planning stage onwards they kept a distance. The programme itself underwent a succession of management failures, and the city saw its effort falter from early on. Another ill-fated initiative, the Renaissance Program, was launched by then mayor Bill Campbell (mayor from 1994 to 2002). This initiative sought to build on the Olympic Games and promote both economic development and neighbourhood renewal. Although Campbell appointed a 'blue ribbon' commission, including Coca Cola's CEO, the mayor gave the commission only sporadic attention, and the commission itself developed no coherent plan on its own. After two years of meetings and hearings, the Renaissance Commission ended with a report acknowledging 'a lack of consensus among the city's political and business leaders regarding Atlanta's future direction'. The final report highlighted 'an environment of cynicism and distrust among each of the city's major constituencies' (Saporta, 1998).

Bringing political and economic elites together is no sure-fire path to success, as both Atlanta and New Haven illustrate with their social regeneration initiatives. Elites may not develop a shared mission, and, even if they do, they may be unable to elicit the kind of grass roots co-operation needed. Governing 'muscle' effective in tackling some problems may turn out to be ineffective in tackling others. The nature of the problem is a key consideration, and for some issues the crucial factor is one of how to overcome citizen alienation and distrust. This is a challenge to which a small number of American cities have responded.

Hampton's dynamic duo

For a period of a decade and a half, Hampton, Virginia, was led by a mayor and city manager open to innovation and receptive to ideas about reinventing government.[2] The mayor, James Eason, was first elected in 1982 and served for 15 years. An accounting executive by occupation and a civic activist by inclination, Eason saw city government as an important channel for problem-solving. Shortly after taking office, Eason recruited as city manager Robert O' Neill, someone known for creative thinking about administrative issues. In search of administrative flexibility, O'Neill replaced the rigidity of functional specialisation with a new administrative structure built around task forces to take on complex issues that cut across traditional lines of administration. Part of Eason's and O'Neill's strategy for governing was to recruit, develop and retain able professionals by giving them latitude in which they could take on challenging projects. Hampton's police chief, for example, was a pioneer in community policing. The head of the Planning Department was strongly sympathetic to ideas about community and citizen engagement. Another significant player on the scene was a nonprofit, Alternatives Inc.

Two convergent experiences led the city to redefine its relationship to the citizenry. One involved the planning process. Faced with vociferous opposition to a proposed highway, the city turned to a conflict-resolution group and the use of a consensus process in which the city government was a participant but bound by the need to arrive at a consensus among all parties. This put citizen knowledge and concerns on the same plane as the city's planning expertise. Both had to be satisfied.

The second experience grew out of a response to a teenage drug problem, particularly at the high school level. School officials acknowledge that they were at a loss about how to deal with the issue. The police chief, school superintendent and Alternatives Inc., put in place a plan that started with police surveillance, but involved engaging youth, working with PTA and neighbourhood volunteers in a programme based on a youth-development approach. The initiative provided a major instance of community-based collaboration of the kind O'Neill sought through his evolving management strategy. Combined with the consensus process and planning, this youth initiative laid a foundation for new directions in city policy.

As the 1980s gave way to the 1990s, several forces converged on a human-capital agenda for the city. The mayor and city manager focused on the link between a changing economy and the city's social problems. In December of 1989, city manager O'Neill formed a working group, ranging from city and school officials to executives from NASA, the military and a nearby shipbuilding company to brainstorm for ways to curb dropout rates, drug use and other problems for at-risk children (Lerman, 1990). In his 1990 State of the City message, the mayor put forward workforce development as a top priority. He cited a 'serious mismatch' between jobs and available workers, and called for renewed attention to education, including early childhood programmes.

Concurrent with these developments, Hampton created the Coalition for Youth as a means by which the city could pursue a collaborative approach in giving more attention to its young children and teenagers. Cindy Carlson moved from the position of director of school and community programmes for Alternatives, Inc., to become director of the city's Coalition for Youth. In 1990, Hampton obtained a grant from the federal government's Center for Substance Abuse Prevention, which was used to launch a community-wide planning and consultation process under Carlson's direction.

The Coalition developed a plan of action based on an 'extensive research, dialogue, and community outreach process involving over 5,000 Hampton youth and adult citizens'. The proposal called for four initiatives: a focus on youth; considering youth as resources, by creating opportunities for them to be involved in community decisions and engaged in community service; partnership with neighbourhoods and expanding the system of support for families.

The first initiative evolved into a focus on asset building, and eventually an 'asset inventory' conducted in the Hampton City schools. The second initiative gained institutional focus as a Youth Commission, composed entirely of youth, to provide advice to the city council and various agencies, on a range of matters from pending legislation to the location and design of community facilities. The Planning Department employs two youth planners, recruited through the Youth Commission. The Commission also receives an appropriation from the city council to make grants for youth-serving activities to various community groups. In a parallel development, Alternatives, Inc., shifted from an NGO concerned with treating drug problems, to one concerned with youth development.

The third initiative, known as the Healthy Neighborhood Initiative, involved creation of a Neighborhood Office as a department of city government. Charged with leading the effort to improve neighbourhoods, it approached the task by increasing city responsiveness to neighbourhood needs. The chief of planning moved to become the head of the Neighborhood Office. In this new role, she was also put in charge of a Neighborhood Task Force as a means of focusing city departments on neighbourhood concerns. However, given limited city resources, the Neighborhood Office also seeks to build capacity for neighbourhoods to meet their own needs, following a four-fold approach of outreach, organising, planning and developing projects generated by groups based in the neighbourhoods. The Neighborhood Commission provides grants, but the city promotes a process through which the community shares in building assets for problem-solving.

The Neighborhood Office provides a major line of connection between the city and its citizens. Its grants and programmes are guided by a Neighborhood Commission, composed of commissioners from each of the ten districts into which the city is divided, plus additional members to represent business, the faith communities, the school system and other city agencies, together with two youth members from the Youth Commission. The city council appoints the Neighborhood Commission, but ten district nominees are selected in meetings held in the respective districts.

The fourth proposal resulted in a new entity called the Healthy Families Partnership or HFP. It represents a complex of programmes, with parenting classes, information on parenting and a newsletter on child development available to all parents in the community. With a special appropriation from the city and a strong record of grant-seeking, HFP also runs a programme of support for families deemed to be at risk for child abuse. HFP is led by a steering committee composed of several city departments along with private partners, particularly hospitals. HFP operates on an 'investor' principal – members of the steering committee represent institutions that can contribute resources to 'invest in' the programme. When these initiatives took shape, Hampton possessed a new agenda concerned with children and youth.

City Manager O'Neill and Mayor Eason played central parts in establishing a partnership approach in which the city and the community both contributed to problem-solving. Citizens, including youth, served as sources of information and understanding. They also contributed resources. Instead of seeing an active citizenry as a troublesome body to be neutralised and be held at bay, city officials treated citizens as contributors to the well-being of Hampton. Efforts to align city government and the community also gave citizens opportunities to appreciate better the role that city staff play. As one of the participants in the planning process commented, 'the biggest thing I got out of the consensus group was that the city government and the staff were not the enemy' (Plotz, 1992: 37).

Hampton, it should be noted, is not a city with a huge poverty population. It is more or less evenly balanced racially between blacks and whites with a significant black middle class. Moreover, its programmes are designed to work mainly with citizens of modest means and counter any drift towards poverty and neighbourhood deterioration. What is significant about Hampton is the extent to which the city has embraced an approach that treats citizens, including young people, as a source of energy and resources in governing. Because Mayor Eason was elected when the city was in a financial squeeze, his administration has been guided by a desire to enable citizens to be more than service recipients and become contributors to the governance of the city. Hampton's approach also involves searching for ways in which citizens provide resources; whether in the form of time volunteered or matching contributions from grant-seeking or by self-help. None of this happens without tensions, but Hampton has a coherent approach for merging city efforts with those of citizens and nonprofits.

Boston: aligning the planets of school reform

Boston provides a telling contrast with Atlanta. At a time when Atlanta was hailed as 'the city too busy to hate', Boston went through an ugly conflict over school desegregation.[3] City schools performed badly, and acquired the reputation of being a fiefdom of jobs and connections for Boston's Irish population. Neighbourhoods were portrayed as having 'fortress schools', more oriented towards keeping the community at a distance than providing educational opportunities, particularly to its black students (Kozol, 1967; Schrag, 1967). In this period, Boston had an elected school board called the School Committee. It was a source of resistance to desegregation, and some of its members stirred up fear and anger among segments of the population, leading eventually to a period of violence equal to that experienced in such places as Little Rock and New Orleans.

Later (1993), Boston abandoned its elected School Committee for one appointed by the mayor. At that stage, a period of high turnover in the office of school superintendent gave way to stability. Subsequently,

Boston was cited as an example of effective school reform (Cuban and Usdan, 2003). Looking back on the shift to a favourable climate for school reform, one observer said: 'All of the planets have to be lined up' (Portz *et al.*, 1999: 98). Clearly institutional arrangements matter, and the mayor of Boston brought stability to the city's school politics and provided political protection for the superintendent to pursue a far-reaching reform agenda. Boston, however, is also an example of how an effective institutional design is constructed as part of a succession of steps and altered relationships extending over several years. At the time when a federal judge took over the school system to see that racial segregation was ended, Boston's civic elites were thoroughly disengaged from the schools. Many lived in the suburbs or sent their children to private schools. Public education in Boston did not touch them personally.

What changed? First of all, when the federal judge took charge in the desegregation crisis, he set about changing the city's civic relations. He created a Citywide Coordinating Committee to monitor compliance with the courts desegregation order, put in place district advisory counsels and racial-ethnic parent counsels for each school and sought to build a structure of community support for the schools. The judge also initiated several school–college and school–business partnerships. In short, he pressured 'business, higher education institutions, community organizations, and parents to become more involved' (Portz *et al.*, 1999: 89).

For its part, business proved to be a willing participant, reversing its earlier pattern of disengagement and recognising its growing need to have a literate and reliable workforce in an emerging high-tech economy (Cuban and Usdan, 2003: 39). Business wanted a comfortable platform for involvement, and that came through its participation in job training. The business group, known as 'the Vault', had no infrastructure of staff and programmes. But its involvement in the Private Industry Council (PIC) created under the federal Job Training Partnership Act 'provided an independent umbrella for the development of business-school programs' (Portz *et al.*, 1999: 88). It became the entity for creating and housing the Boston Compact, initially an agreement between the school system and the business sector involving a pledge by business to provide summer jobs and hire graduates in exchange for a promise by the school district to pursue improvement. Although the Compact had an uneven history, it focused attention on academic achievement and enlisted a growing number of partners – higher education, labour organisations, the Boston Human Services Coalition and the Boston Cultural

Partnerships. From early on, the goals of the Compact included that of increasing college enrolment among public school students. Business funding helped create a nonprofit, the Boston Plan, as a spin-off of the Compact. Among other activities, it became home to a scholarship and mentor programme to boost college attendance among high school students.

Even with an expansive business role, the enlistment of other partners, and the emergence of the local education fund as a significant player, Boston's education politics still had to overcome a difficult history. Conflict centred in the elected school committee and frequent turnover in the office of superintendent perpetuated a pattern of 'incessant political controversies' (Cuban and Usdan, 2003: 40). In reaction, business played a major role in replacing the elected body with one appointed by the mayor. Institutional realignment, that is, the move to an appointed school committee thus proved to be important, mayoral leadership was a keystone in sustaining and enlarging the move to reform public education in Boston. Still, as one author points out, the change in governance structure to one centred on the mayor's office was not the product of a single choice made at one point in time: 'Far from being a quick process, the change that occurred in Boston was the result of a series of demands, responses, and changes that occurred over a 25-year period' (Yee, 2003: 101).

Overall, Boston's experience shows us that a change in institutional structure can play an important part in how a community is governed. At the same time, the change in formal structure was only part of a more far-reaching effort to realign Boston's civic relations, involving business more directly in education and also enlisting labour unions, institutions of higher education and others. Engaging parents and community-based organisations was also a significant part of the shift that occurred. Boston's era of fortress schools ended not merely because of the mayor's role in school governance, but because a range of community elements was enlisted to become active participants.

Discussion

In a classic treatment of corporatism, Stein Rokkan offered the aphorism 'votes count but resources decide' (1966: 105). In Rokkan's assessment, elections are not the fulcrum around which politics revolve. Strategic resources are fundamental, and in the Norwegian corporatism of Rokkan's era, governance involved a central policy role for society's major economic sectors. Politics in America has conventionally been characterised as pluralist, with fluid alignments. Whether the term pluralism is apt can be debated, but governing arrangements in American local politics are highly informal.

Across the four cities examined here, a variety of non-governmental entities entered the picture in important ways. Business played a prominent part, but as the physical reshaping of the city gave way to increasing concern for social reconstruction and the development of human capital, policy innovation involved a substantial role for grass roots groups and processes.

Changes in the executive structure of local government appear at various points in the four cities considered here, but those changes were often overshadowed by tectonical shifts in civic relations. Atlanta adopted a new city charter in 1973, remaking the mayor's office into a strong-mayor form with a full panoply of executive powers. Yet, that change amounted to much less than the continuation of the city's biracial coalition and its reliance on such extra-governmental means as Action Forum.

Mayor Richard Lee's effort to change New Havens executive structure to the strong-mayor form was rejected in a city referendum, but that decision did not sidetrack the city's huge redevelopment effort in and around the central business district. Nor did it figure into the ineffectiveness of the city's attempt to bring about social regeneration in its lower-income neighbourhoods.

Allocating executive control over the school system to the mayor of Boston proved to be a vital step in reducing conflict and turbulence in the city's education politics. But that was a step that came late in a long series of moves, many of which involved efforts to reduce the isolation of the schools and engage various elements of the community more heavily in education.

Hampton is the only council-manager city among the four, but the mayor proved to be an important political leader despite his lack of administrative authority. The development of the city's human capital agenda involved a prominent role for the city manager and other professionals in local government, but it also took shape through a process of community consultation and planning. Moreover, an important actor in the process was Alternatives Inc., a nonprofit working with youth, initially on drug treatment and later on youth development more generally. Non-profit organisation and public–private partnerships also figure prominently in the picture in Boston.

Hampton underscores a vital point that runs through the experience of all four cities. Resources come in many forms and derive from multiple sources. The expertise of policy and administrative professionals is one source, and a key to effective governments is to create conditions in which they are motivated to be innovative and to make special efforts to see that new initiatives are put in place and work. Civic elites are important, of course, but note that in Hampton business played little role in shaping that city's human-capital agenda. Hampton shows that the co-operation of ordinary citizens can occupy important ground. They have local knowledge particular to the situation that the training and experience of professionals do not provide. Citizen time and energy as well can contribute to governance. It is therefore important that citizen distrust not impair the relationship between officials and the people.

In the United States, local political leadership and local political mobilisation are often organised around a problem-solving agenda. Who is engaged depends on the issue and the channels for engagement. The mayor's office is an important institution in governance. More often than not, the school district is an independent taxing authority and in many instances a separate power base. Other independent authorities are sometimes significant players as well. The Atlanta Housing Authority, for example, is an independent agency. Although its members are named by the mayor, they are appointed for long, staggered terms of office. Perhaps equally significant are the many nonprofit organisations that play a variety of roles. Sometimes they are designed to foster a particular problem-solving effort, such as school reform. Whether in the form of expertise, skill in such matters as staff development or monetary grants, resources may come through various channels, and their convergence may stem from civic co-operation rather than executive authority. Because municipal government is never more than a partial source of the capacity to address local problems, effectiveness may rest on informal proclivities to co-operate more than on formal authority to issue mandates and send executive orders.

There is much we do not know about informal schemes of co-operation, but they are important because they expand the base of resources that can be brought to bear on the complex problems faced by many of today's local governments. Experiences in Atlanta and New Haven remind us, however, that schemes of co-operation and resource bases adequate for some agendas are inadequate for others. As civic relationships are brought to bear, it is important that the scope of resources mobilised be commensurate with the problem to be addressed. That is why institutions are important, but ultimately resources decide and efforts to mobilise them can lead to a variety of relationships, both formal and informal.

Notes

1. Useful sources on the American mayoralty include: Greer, 1974; Kotter and Lawrence, 1974; Ferman, 1985; Svara, 1994; Holli, 1999; and Henig and Rich, 2004.
2. Parts of this section are drawn from Stone and Worgs, 2004.
3. Parts of this section are drawn from Stone, 2005; it also benefited particularly from Portz, 2004. On Boston's Mayor Thomas Menino, see Keller, 2001.

14
Transforming Political Leadership: Models, Trends and Reforms

Helge O. Larsen

This chapter revisits some of the key themes in local government modernisation and reform. Drawing upon experiences of the several countries presented in this collection of essays, it examines some of the reasons for the shift from the classic model of local government – the council-committee model – to more executive-oriented models, like the parliamentary and the presidential models as well as hybrid forms. Special attention is given to the direct election of mayors, adopted in several countries as a way of strengthening the political executive. Central to this shift is the attention given to aspects of laymen rule, collegiate organisation and collective decision-making. These processes have developed over some time, resulting in a professionalisation of political leadership roles, and of the role of mayor in particular (Larsen, 1996, 2003) and the de-collectivisation of political decision-making in local government (Larsen, 2002).

Comparing reforms: problems and pitfalls

An explicit aim for several of the reforms has been to strengthen the political executive in local government, and to increase the formal authority of the mayor. Svara's contribution to this volume shows just how such shifts from council-manager models to mayor-council models came about in the United States in order to enhance mayoral leadership. Elsewhere, the introduction of direct election of the mayor has been seen as only one among several means to strengthen political leadership.

In Norway, for example, local authorities were allowed to experiment with direct election of their mayor in the local elections of 1999, and the number was increased to 38 in the 2003 elections. In the 1999 elections, no change was made in the powers associated with the position. In 2003, a small number of authorities were also allowed to experiment by introducing some changes in the formal authority of the mayor. Letting the voters decide who should be the mayor of a local authority instead of having the councillors do it means that both the council *and* the mayor have a direct mandate, and may claim the legitimacy of such, but does not necessarily imply a change in the formal authority of the mayor. Direct elections provide the mayor with a separate mandate from the council, even if it may not be a clear one. In relation to the citizens, it is reasonable to assume that such a mayor will have at least some additional legitimacy compared to one elected by his or her fellow councillors. In relation to the council, however, the situation may be different. Again, institutional rules may differ, and be of importance. Access to top political positions may be more or less strongly coupled to access to council positions. Commonly, a candidate would have to serve a period as councillor before moving on to the executive body or to be mayor or vice mayor. In some reforms aiming to strengthen the local political executive, there has been a de-coupling of councillor seats and positions in the executive, and the latter are sometimes equipped with separate portfolios and administrative responsibility. Such de-coupling was introduced in the Netherlands with the new Act of 2002 as Denters's contribution to this volume shows.

Laymen rule and collective decision-making under pressure

The democratic principles that justify local government are no different from those pertaining to the national level (Mill, 1861: ch. xv), even if local government possesses a greater capacity for educating people about representative government. But since local authorities are numerous, and in many respects closer to the citizens, they are well placed to make the point that political activity at the outset is essentially a layman activity. The essence of democratic rule is that authority emanates from the people: from the citizens of a polity. Each of them should have an equal say and an equal right to participate. A further implication is that everyone by definition is *competent*; no particular skill, expertise or education is required in order to participate (Offerdal, 1989).

For most of us, participation in national politics is limited to casting a vote on polling day. At the local level, the situation has traditionally been quite different. The most extreme form of participation is the *town meeting*, still upheld as the highest authority in a number of New

England local authorities and reflected in some Swiss local authorities, as shown by Ladner in this volume. But even in representative systems, decision-making involves a large number of people. For one thing, the ratio of council members to voters has been high in quite a number of national systems. Taking the Nordic countries in the mid-1980s as examples, councillors in Norway made up 0.45 per cent of the voters, in Finland 0.36, in Sweden 0.21 and in Denmark 0.12 per cent (Larsen and Offerdal, 1994). In Norway, candidates for local elections made up more than 3 per cent of the electorate, and on average, only slightly more than 200 voters were represented by each councillor. In addition came the extensive use of committees in local authorities, a practice which often brought other citizens into local governance.

Recent years have witnessed a more dramatic reduction in the number of elected posts in local government, generally paralleled by an increase in the number of salaried professional administrators. In Sweden in 1963, there were about 186,000 council and committee posts to be filled, while by 1980 the number had been reduced to 83,000 (Gidlund, 1983). Local government reform in several Australian states in the 1990s meant a considerable reduction in the number of councils as well as the number of councillors, in South Australia by 31 per cent and by a massive 73 per cent in Victoria (Kiss, 2002: 141).

The ideal of (local) politics as a laymen activity, or laymen rule, has come under strong pressure (Mauritzen and Svara, 2002). Partly, this is due to what the editors of this volume term 'professionalisation of politics', in which officials are increasingly likely to be compensated full or part-time for their political participation. For these, politics has become less of a vocation, and more of an occupation.[1] Partly, the handling of local matters has been transferred from fellow citizens in committees to administrators with their professional expertise. These processes may to some extent be mutually re-enforcing, since a dominant motive behind proposals to have more full-time politicians often is the need to match the capacity and the professional expertise of the bureaucrats.

The organisational form most commonly associated with local government has been that of collegial organisation. Councils and committees usually function by according members the same rights and obligations, their votes and views are – at least formally – accorded the same weight. The leader of such collegiate bodies primarily functioned as speaker and chairperson, sometimes with the right to cast the decisive vote in the case of a tie.

The emergence of a more hierarchical political structure is a major theme running through this volume. As some of the contributors show, the political executive has been strengthened in local authorities, in some cases by the re-organisation of committee structures, empowerment of the leading political positions, the introduction of cabinet-like structures and an even more marginalised political role for backbenchers. The growth of a municipal bureaucracy and the rise of the new managerialism have also brought more hierarchic structures and processes in their wake.

The collegial organisational form is closely associated with collective decision-making. Representatives of the people are expected to reach decisions that are recognised as legitimate, and hence binding. Such decisions are supposed to be made on the basis of a free and open debate among the representatives. Stoker draws attention to 'the distinctiveness of the political realm as a focus for collective decision-making' (Stoker, 1996: 21). Arguments have to be advanced and defended, for 'democracy belongs to the sphere of the *political*, which is the sphere of collectively binding rules and policies, and of the resolution of disagreement about what these policies should be' (Beetham, 1996: 29). It is defined as the activity by which different interests within a given territory are conciliated (Crick, 1964: 167).

Political solutions cannot be calculated on technical grounds, and nor will conflicts of interest simply disappear through political discourse. A commonly found argument is that collective decision-making in collegiate bodies composed on a proportional basis is conducive of a certain policymaking style: that of consociational politics. It would be misleading to make this contention either an inherent normative ideal or an actual description of collective decision-making in collegiate bodies. These are essentially arenas for finding legitimate answers to political problems, which may or may not arise from conflicts of interests. 'There is simply one type of governmental system which is inherently concerned with conciliation based upon a recognition (both sociological and ethical) that civilized communities are internally diverse' (Crick, 1964: 167).

The council-committee model under attack

There hardly exists one classic model of local government organisation. Even if some classification is possible, no two national systems are identical (Goldsmith, 1995). In general, though, the highest authority lies with a directly elected representative council. Apart from that, the allocation of functions, responsibilities and powers vary considerably. Indeed, some systems might be characterised exactly by a weakly developed or specified executive function. It is in this sense that Wollman calls the British system as 'monistic', where political power centres on the council, which together with the committees is also responsible for executive decisions. As Rao observes, 'the British system of local government, rooted in its nineteenth-century tradition, was essentially "government by committee" '. Decisions were made through council committees, and all councillors, including those from the minority parties, were able to participate in decision-making. Rao concludes that the working of the committee system itself was the basic reason for the discontent with the local government system in Britain.

The Nordic countries share many features in their local government structure. As for the way the executive function is organised, there are interesting differences, however, as Montin in Sweden, shows, the council appoints a strong executive committee, with considerable separation from the council. Members of the board may come from outside the council. The leader of the council is not the chairman of the board; in Finland, the chief executive officer may even be appointed as chairman. In Denmark, as Berg shows, the committee model reigns, and there is no proper executive body, even if the finance committee is regarded to be the most important and influential. In contrast to the other Nordic countries, however, the Danish mayor (who is a member of, and elected by, the council) has a dual function as leader of the political as well as the administrative part of a local authority. The traditional Norwegian system is based on a model where the executive body is elected by and from amongst the council on a proportional basis. The mayor is the leader of both; also elected by and from amongst the council members. Apart from the mayor, the Norwegian model resembles the Dutch system before the reforms of 2002, with council and a board of aldermen. These aldermen did not have any separate portfolios, however, and the Norwegian mayor was never a powerful executive figure.

There have been at least three major criticisms levelled against the 'classic' committee model in local government. Lack of accountability and transparency is the most frequently raised criticism against the committee model, it being argued that voters should be able to hold someone accountable for political decisions. Collective decision-making blurs the political differences between the various parties, groups and representatives. Those supporting such a style would argue that even if compromises and conciliated decisions sometimes may dilute pure political stances, they may produce solutions with a high degree of legitimacy and, as such, have a greater likelihood of being implemented. Others have blamed just such features for producing political apathy among citizens, and a declining turnout in local elections. The second objection relates to the 'slow and cumbersome nature' of the committee system. Rao's chapter rehearses the shortcomings of the committee system in terms of its inability to produce clear policies, speedily and effectively. It is not uncommon to find local bureaucrats being frustrated by their politicians, whom they see as unable, and perhaps even unwilling, to produce rational and consistent political decisions. The decision-making process itself may take time since matters are to be dealt with at several levels and a good deal of duplication may be involved if an issue first is to be decided on by a (policy sector) committee, and later by the full council. The communication process in local authorities is such that politicians and administrators interact at several stages in the process, and may even form alliances within specific policy areas. Administrators may be confused as to chains of command, since they may relate to the political leadership of a committee, to their administrative superiors in the central administration, as well as to other political leaders. Because of the long and often cumbersome process, the latter may experience a lack of control because they enter the process at the later stages only. Mayors have often expressed frustration because matters are discussed and frontlines formed in committees, in the media and elsewhere long before they have had any chance to deal with the issue in the executive committee or in the full council.

Third, it has been argued that the committee system fails to produce a clear and meaningful role for councillors. Council meetings are designed to legitimise issues by being open to the public, and through debate, deliberation and decision. They provide an arena for parties, groups and single representatives to justify and defend the positions they have taken, and to identify flaws in those who hold other opinions. As such, they are symbolically important. Such heroic visions of councillor life have come under increasing scrutiny. Studies have shown that most councils are segmented, in the sense that political power and influence is unevenly distributed. Sometimes, only a handful of politicians have enough information and oversight to be able to exert real influence, particularly over budgets and other complicated matters. In reality, matters are often settled before an issue reaches the council, and the debates often have no consequence for the final outcome. As a result, councils may have become less attractive. Parties find it more difficult to recruit people to stand as candidates, as there is little prestige in being a councillor. Turnover between elections is high in some countries, and service as councillor has become less of a stepping-stone for obtaining political positions at regional or national level.

The changing political organisation of local government

Reforming local government in general, and the political executive in particular, is on the agenda in a number of countries these days (Caulfield and Larsen, 2003). It is noteworthy that several organisational forms may be found within one and the same country; partly because organised experiments are being carried out, and partly because local authorities have been granted more freedom as to what kind of forms they want to adopt. Typical in this respect are the Nordic countries. During the 1980s, the so-called 'Nordic free commune experiments' were carried out (Baldersheim and Ståhlberg, 1994). Lessons from these were later used when countries, such as Norway and Sweden, passed new local government acts during the early 1990s (Amnå and Montin, 2000). A common feature of this new legislation was that the local authorities were given increased freedom as to how they could organise their structure and activity.

Despite these variations, the reform of local government has taken three basic forms. The first contains more incremental types of reform, in which the traditional committee model is retained, but given new content and characteristics. The second option implies a move in the direction of introducing a parliamentary type of model, strengthening the executive powers of the political leadership of an authority. The third is to move in the direction of a local presidential system of which introducing direct, popular election of the mayor is one example.

The council-committee model retained

In a classic paper, Luther Gulick (1937) described four basic principles for organisation, based on territory, function, clientele or process, and versions of all these four can be found in local authorities. Balancing the need to organise for specific policy areas with the co-ordination of the overall activity of an authority can be problematic. To a large extent, reforms have focused on streamlining the decision-making structure. One remedy for the fragmentation of the decision-making process has been to rationalise the committee structure, bringing the number of committees down radically. Another measure has been a consolidation of positions. Ideas about participation, laymen rule and the desire to spread power often led authorities to involve large numbers of people. In general, the practice has changed towards more concentration. In a similar vein, many countries and authorities have sought to reduce the size of the council by bringing the number of councillors down.

This move often goes hand in hand with an increasing professionalisation of politics, in the sense that in order to increase political steering capacity, central politicians are compensated on full or on considerable part-time basis. As observed by Denters in this volume, 'nowadays, councillors are semi-professionals rather than amateurs'.

While a major goal in many local government systems has been to strengthen the political executive, there has also been a concern about the declining role of the council itself, and ways have been sought to restore its position, including a strengthening of the position of councillors (Stewart, 1995: 79). Remedies have varied, and efforts to re-invigorate the council as a forum for real debate and deliberation have been undertaken. Efforts have concentrated on turning the council into a more strategic body, with a responsibility for goals, priorities and to some extent scrutiny and oversight. In such a perspective, it makes good sense to reduce the element of political amateurism in local authorities, to have fewer councillors and to strengthen the managerial and executive functions.

Despite these developments, the conception of councillor roles as primarily having to do with policy- and decision-making has been questioned. Some would claim that the role of politicians as agenda setters with the power to take initiatives always has been exaggerated, and that such functions in reality belonged more to the realm of administrators. In this case, it is more a question of adjusting expectations to practice. Others hold that it is no longer possible nor desirable that ordinary council members should aim for a role as agenda setters and policymakers. Instead, they should in a sense see themselves as auditors, whose job it is to secure legitimacy in decisions, and to help constituents get what they want. Not least in the British debate, the role as *scrutiniser* has been offered as the new road to be taken by councillors in general, and backbenchers in particular.

Majoritarian models

Majoritarian or ministerial models represent a break with the traditional way of composing the political executive in local government. Here, the city council elects an executive body or board, which forms a sort of city cabinet. In order to enhance their governing capacity, only the council majority is represented. The executive functions are left with this body, and parliamentary mechanisms are introduced. If a vote of no confidence is passed in the council, the executive will have to resign. Another feature is that the position of mayor is retained, but the influence of the post is severely reduced. He or she is left with chairing the council (as speaker), and representing the local authority at various occasions.

A new position as leader of the executive is created, as an equivalent to the position of prime minister at the local level.

Members of the executive may be drawn from the council, or they may be picked from outside. Likewise, they may or may not be equipped with separate, administrative portfolios. A major motivation behind the introduction of such models generally has been to increase accountability and also governability. Partly in response to fiscal stress, the model was introduced in Oslo, the capital of Norway, in 1986. It has been modified in the early nineties, but is still retained, and an account of this model is given by Baldersheim in this book.

Presidential models

In national political systems, the relationship between the legislative and the executive branch of government is generally organised either along parliamentary lines, or as a presidential system. Building on classical ideas from Montesquieu, the latter involves a more strict separation of powers, and the mandate of the president usually stems from a direct, popular vote. This is not to say that all presidents are equally powerful, since in some systems, this position is mostly of a symbolic nature. But in contrast to the parliamentary model, the executive branch does not depend on the confidence of the legislative body in order to stay in office. An essential element, however, is a system of checks and balances, meaning that in order to get something done and to realise political goals, the executive depends on support from the legislature.

By and large, such models for the political organisation of local government has been of rather limited interest. Recent developments have changed this, however. In principle, the introduction of directly elected mayors, and mayors with – sometimes strong – executive powers clearly increases their relevance also for local government. Current reforms of the system of political governance in local authorities not only involve the way the executive is elected or selected, but also the way power relations between executive and the council are structured. It is within this domain we find the most vigorous and also most numerous reform efforts in Europe today, and the rest of the chapter is devoted to a discussion of these.

Directly elected and executive mayors – two fashionable ideas

Direct election of mayors is gaining ground in Europe, even in the northern parts, where such an arrangement has not been an element of the traditional structure of local government. Germany illustrates this development, where the model has been spreading from the southern Länder (where it has been practised for a considerable amount of time) to the north and east. In the spring of 2000, Londoners went to the polls to elect the new mayor of London.

While some form of local government is found in more or less every nation-state in the modern world, this is not the case for the position of a mayor as the political leader of an authority, and particularly not if this position is associated with executive responsibilities. In many European countries, executive responsibilities lie with a collective political body, or, alternatively, with an appointed administrative executive. The issue is not only about functions and responsibilities, but of language and terminology as well. The point is also observed by Clarke and colleagues:

> there is confusion arising from the language itself. This is a particular problem for British audiences; in England and Wales the title of mayor suggests a ceremonial and social role but not one which involves exercising political authority. In many systems, ... the title 'mayor' is used to describe what is in effect the political leader of the authority. (Clarke *et al.*, 1998: 8–9).

To the extent there is another internationally used term, it is probably the German term *Bürgermeister*, which literally means 'the master of citizens', and refers to a position equipped with both ceremonial and executive functions. Mayoral position, then, represents the highest political position, which involves chairing the supreme political body (the council), and representing the municipality both legally and ceremonially. In most council-committee systems, the mayor is also the chair of the executive board. Sweden and Finland provide exceptions, and the positions are also split in municipal parliamentary systems.

In local government, the relationship between the council and the executive body is not necessarily based on a majoritarian principle, but more often on proportional representation. Directly elected mayors, particularly when coupled with executive functions, pull the system in a presidential direction.

Clearly, we need to distinguish between a more executive political position in local government – an executive mayor – and the electoral arrangements for selecting a person for a mayoral position, be it executive or not. These two concerns have most often been coupled, and in England as well as in Germany, the emphasis has been on the executive dimension. This is in contrast to Norway, where the current experiment was undertaken virtually without change in the formal authority of the position. New Zealand represents a case where the stress is on electoral reform, and with a deliberate desire *not* to equip the popularly elected mayors with real political powers, but instead to underline the symbolic, representative and possibly integrative aspects of the role as mayor. This may seem a little odd, at least at first glance. It would be reasonable to assume that a mayor elected directly by the citizens would enjoy and make claims to a different and stronger legitimacy than one chosen by the councillors.

Reforming the executive and the office of mayor

Political authority is a product of both structure and action. In most places, attempts to make mayors more visible and influential have been pursued by means of various structural or institutional reforms. Some of these emphasise administrative or managerial aspects of local government leadership, while others are more directed towards the purely political. Executive mayors are akin to the first, where they are given a more clearly defined function in carrying out the policies and decisions of a local authority, often leading to a de-collectivisation of local decision-making. The Italian reform is an example of this, as is also the case with some of the German Länder.

In the Netherlands, as Denters' contribution to this volume shows, the most recent reform changes the relationship between the council and the executive, in the sense that aldermen no longer can be council members, and do not have to be recruited from among the elected councillors. A clearer division of tasks is also sought, in the sense that the council is to concentrate on legislative matters and general principles, while the board of mayor and aldermen is allowed to decide on all administrative matters. A proposal by the Royal Commission on local government to introduce directly elected mayors has not been adopted, however.

Although given the opportunity to introduce directly elected mayors by the Local Government Act of 2000, English local authorities were given three options to choose from including mayor-cabinet, mayor-city manager and leader and cabinet model. In this last, a small executive body of councillors will provide for community leadership, while the majority will play only a representative role. The vast majority opted for the leader-cabinet model, with around 12 authorities adopting mayor-cabinet councils and one with a mayor-council manager model.

Among the Nordic countries, it is only the Danish mayor who is the formal head of not only the political side of local government, but also the administration. In Norway, as in Finland and Sweden, the authority to instruct the administration still lies with the executive committee. In all these countries, it is noticeable that an increase in professionalisation among the politicians has been accompanied by a concomitant rise in officer influence. By far the strongest chief administrative officer is found in Finland, and the weakest, perhaps, in Sweden, as Montin demonstrates. Here, the position is not identified in the Municipal Act as it is in Norway, and the CAO does not usually have formal authority over the other sectoral leading administrative officials.

Electing mayors by direct popular vote aims to strengthen their position in municipal decision-making processes. The Norwegian experiment, aimed primarily at increasing voter turnout, was also designed to enhance the political authority of the mayor. However, most reforms combine elements from both the political and the administrative spheres, as is the case, for example, in England.

Differing motivations

Even if the idea of having a directly elected and/or executive mayor is being realised in several countries, the motivations for such a reform varies considerably. Five principal arguments for change have been identified, including the importance of giving national prominence to local government and to strengthening its place, its influence and its side of the partnership between central and local government; strengthening local democracy and encouraging greater involvement, particularly in elections; providing a focus for community leadership; strengthening internal leadership in local government and providing for more effective direction and cohesion; and transforming the impact of party politics (Clarke *et al.*, 1996: 13–14).

One of the principal objectives of providing for a visible and effective political leadership at the local level is most clearly expressed in the British government's White Paper on the governance of London. This argued that strong executive mayors elsewhere in the world have made a positive difference to the lives of their citizens and the communities they serve. London needs leadership, and Mayor was given sweeping new powers, duties and responsibilities designed to ensure that the programme on which he or she was elected could be delivered (DETR, 1998: 8–9). It may be that England looked across the Channel with some envy in these matters. Not only is local and regional government more important in France, with the French mayors seeming omnipotent in comparison with an English mayor, but being *Maire de Paris* has often proved to be a stepping stone to the highest political offices in the land. French mayors are powerful on the local political scene, but many of them also enjoy a high visibility in national politics, not least due to the institution of *cumul des mandats*.[2]

In one sense, the reform experiments in Norway lie at the other end of the scale. Here, the dominant goal has been to promote participation in local elections. Having enjoyed a traditionally very high turnout in local elections, the steady drop in turnout throughout the 1990s caused a lot of concern among national and local politicians alike, and became a prime reason for embarking on the experiment of having 20 municipalities (out of 435) elect their mayor by popular vote in 1999.[3] The motivation – and expectation – of an increased local turnout in these municipalities was clearly voiced by the political leadership of the responsible ministry, but also strongly expressed by candidates standing in the mayoral elections.[4] Both the 1999 and the 2003 elections, however, failed to fulfil these expectations.

Another motivation, not explicitly acknowledged by reformers at the national level, pertains to the coalition-formation processes in the council after a local election has been held. When seats in the council are distributed among the parties or groups in proportion to their election result, it is nowadays rare for one party to command an overall majority. Consequently, the parties and their candidates for the top positions start to negotiate. Since the various parties do not necessarily make it clear to the voters before the election who they will co-operate with, or enter into alliance with, voters remain uncertain as to who their next mayor will be until long after the election. The coalition talks are seen by many as an unwelcome part of the political process (Pederson, 1997) and this is particularly so when bargaining results in a candidate with the least number of votes becoming or retaining mayor.[5]

Making mayors strong(er) – reorganising structure or reinventing roles?

Electing mayors by direct popular vote and creating mayoral positions with an executive function are both measures to make the position of mayor a more influential and powerful one. At a somewhat less general level, we have seen that there may be varying intentions both nationally and locally for strengthening the position of the mayor in local government. Many factors contribute to the strengthening of the Mayor. It is also a question of 'strong' in what sense, and in relation to what and whom. At a systemic level, it is linked to the question of the relative strength of local government itself. This is an aspect of what Dahl and Tufte in their discussion of size and democracy have called 'system capacity' (Dahl and Tufte, 1973). A French mayor may enjoy a very strong position in his or her commune. But it is important to bear in mind that French communes on average are among the smallest in Europe, and play a less central role in the implementation of national welfare state policies than do, for example, their Nordic counterparts.[6] The same point is observed in the American context by Stone who argues in this volume that, in order to appreciate the strengths and weaknesses of the office, one needs to see it in context. The United States has a weak-state tradition in which public authority is viewed sceptically and the word 'politics' carries negative connotations.

The desire to strengthen the political governance capacity of local activities has been seen in many countries, prompted by the fiscal stress experienced in the 1980s and early 1990s (Clarke, 1989). In the face of fiscal austerity and increasing demands from citizens as well as national authorities, local politicians have been called upon to provide political leadership and settle clear priorities. This coincides too with the emergence of new public management (NPM) doctrines that set out how public sector organisations should be led, and called for the need to distinguish more sharply between what are considered political matters on the one hand, and administrative ones on the other (Marshall *et al.*, 1999: 34–57).

In this managerially inspired way of thinking about good government, one slogan has been to 'let managers manage', implying that politicians should restrict themselves to setting some general (policy) goals, giving the administration considerable freedom in selecting means, interpreting rules and deciding on single cases. Such management by objectives is often associated with, for example, the Thatcher years of public sector reforms, but dates, of course, even further back to ideas about good management in private sector enterprises.

Such NPM-inspired ideas about governance bring strong institutional pressures on the role of politicians, including that of the mayor. The normative idea in these doctrines is of an elected representative who sets (broad) goals, decides on master plans and budgets, but very much leaves the day-to-day business of public administration to the professional administrators of a local authority. In most European settings, such a conception of the role of local councillors is quite at odds with the traditional way of filling that role, and there is a lot of evidence emerging of the way councillors of today struggle to redefine their political work, or at least to come to terms with the new conceptions of how they should act in their role. In Denmark, for example, Berg identifies a very strong norm as to what a good local politician is (Berg, 2000). The core of this idea, or 'institutionalised standard' as it has been called, contains elements from values like rationality and efficiency, and a leadership focus which gives priority to tasks of a general nature, at the expense of particular issues and matters. Management by objectives is seen as the quintessential tool for good governance, and politicians who concern themselves with 'small' and particular matters are given little credit. Among other things, Berg shows that the Danish Association of Local Government Authorities currently acts as a very strong proponent of such a conception.

It is not difficult to see why such managerialist conceptions of how politicians should act, in many ways is at odds with the very logic of politics itself. As Harold Wilson said 'in politics, a week is a long time'. To administrators, there are virtues in goals that are clear, stable and easy to operationalise. For politicians to act accordingly would severely restrict their room to manoeuvre, and few would tie themselves to the mast in such a way as to make managers happy. This is particularly pertinent in a local setting. One could argue that a local government system in which local politicians are not allowed to concern themselves with particular or even individual concerns makes councillors, as we have known them, more or less redundant, and in the long run undermines the legitimacy of local government.

It is perhaps too early to judge whether or not the actual behaviour of local politicians and of mayors have changed markedly in the direction that NPM prescribes. It is not unlikely that there may be more talk than action in this field so far. There can be little doubt, however, that the representational role of local councillors is under pressure, at least in their capacity as decision-makers. We observe tendencies towards an increased differentiation between roles, in that the position of mayor is increasingly professionalised, and given a more executive orientation, while that of councillor is pushed in the direction of policy review and scrutiny. This seems to be an emerging picture in the case of Britain and Netherlands as contributors to this volume have shown.

Electing mayors directly may represent a move in the direction of giving more weight to responsiveness than to representation in local government. It is argued that electors today are not much concerned with greater representativeness, at least not in the social sense of the term: 'popular expectations of the representative process have abandoned representativeness in favour of responsiveness' (Rao, 1998). In a survey following the mayoral elections in the 20 Norwegian municipalities, one of the clearest findings was that the citizens had strong expectations that the new arrangement would make mayoral candidates more responsive to the voters. As many as 68 per cent of the voters subscribed to such a view, while only 13 per cent held the opposite expectation.

But this was obviously not enough to make people rush to the polling stations. The Norwegian experiment was very much motivated by a desire to try out institutional changes that would presumably turn the trend of a steady decline in voter turnout in local government elections. If not an outright failure, it was definitely not a structural change, which produced the desired outcome in turnout. In this way, it adds to the conclusion drawn by Michael Clarke and colleagues in their review of international experiences in relation to the introduction of executive mayors in Britain:

> Although there are powerful arguments about using the introduction of executive mayors to re-invigorate local democracy, the effect of mayoral systems on local democracy is not clear either. Certainly there is a lack of evidence to suggest that even the directly elected executive mayor leads to a markedly higher electoral turnout. (Clarke *et al.*, 1996)

Thus, the relationship between institutional reform and the intended consequences is not a straightforward one.

Notes

1. In his book *The Amateur Democrat* (1962), James Q. Wilson offered the definition 'An amateur is one who finds politics *intrinsically* interesting because it expresses a conception of the public interest. The amateur politician sees the political world more in terms of ideas and principles than in terms of persons. ... The main reward of politics to the amateur is the sense of having satisfied a felt obligation to 'participate' (pp. 4–5).
2. An arrangement which makes it possible to accumulate mandates. A mayor of a big city may thus be a member of a regional assembly or parliament at the same time.
3. The turnout in local elections in Norway rose from 71.5 per cent in 1947 to a high of 81 per cent in 1963, and remained above or around 70 per cent until the election in 1987. In the 1990s, the turnout rate has dropped to 60 per cent in the municipal elections in autumn 1999, and 56 per cent in the regional (county) elections.
4. I wish to thank my research assistants Helen Sagerup and Tord Willumsen for carrying out these interviews.

5. Since the Norwegian system allows for an element of preferential voting, it may even be that a candidate having received a severe beating in the polls still emerges as the final victor.
6. In 1988, local government expenditure made up 19 per cent of all public expenditures in France, while the same share amounted to 47 per cent in Denmark in 1986; cf. Anders Lidström (1996): *Kommunsystem i Europa*. (Local Government Systems in Europe) Stockholm: Publica.

Bibliography

Ackaert, J. (1994a), 'Het gebruik van de voorkeurstem bij de gemeenter-aadsverkiezingen. Een terreinverkenning in de provincie Limburg', *Res Publica*, 36(2), pp. 107–18.

—— (1994b), 'De nationalisatie van de gemeentepolitiek. Een onderzoek naar de verwevenheid tussen nationale politiek en gemeentepolitiek op het niveau van de politieke mandatarissen', in *De gemeenteraadsverkiezingen en hun impact op de Belgische politiek. Handelingen van het 16de Internationaal Colloquium van het Gemeentekrediet*, Brussels: Gemeentekrediet van België, pp. 587–604.

—— (2003), 'Verteren burgemeesters de politiehervorming?' *Politiejournaal and politieofficier*, 3, pp. 7–12.

Ackaert, J., L. De Winter, A. Aish and A. Frognier (1992), 'L' abstentionnisme élec-toral et vote blanc et nul en Belgique', *Res Publica*, 34(2), pp. 209–26.

Amnå, E. and S. Montin (eds) (2000), *Towards a New Concept of Local Self-Government*, Bergen: Fagbokforlaget.

Andersson, S. (2002), *Corruption in Sweden: Exploring Danger Zones and Change*, Umeå: Umeå University, Department of Political Science, Research Report 2002: 1.

Armstrong, H. (1999), 'The key themes of democratic renewal', *Local Government Studies*, 25(4), pp. 19–25.

Ashworth, R. and S. Snape (2004), 'An overview of scrutiny: a triumph of context over structure', *Local Government Studies*, 30(4), pp. 538–56.

Ashworth, R., C. Copus and A. Coulson (2004), 'Local democratic renewal: an introduction', *Local Government Studies*, 30(4), pp. 459–66.

Aubelle V. (1999), 'Le sens de la démocratie locale' , in CURAPP, *La démocratie locale, représentation, participation et espace public*, Paris: PUF.

Bäck, H. (2000), *Kommunpolitiker i den stora nyordningens tid*, Malmö: Liber.

—— (2002), *Fragmentation and Consolidation in the Big City: Neighbourhood Decentralisation in Six Scandinavian Cities*, Paper presented at the XIII Nordiske Statskundskabskongres 15–17 August 2002, Aalborg universitet.

—— (2003), 'Vad krävs för en fungerande valdemokrati?' in M. Gilljam and J. Hermansson (eds), *Demokratins mekanismer*, Malmö: Liber.

—— (2004), 'The institutional setting of local political leadership and community involvement', in M. Haus, H. Heinelt and M. Stewart (eds), *Urban Governance and Democracy: Leadership and Community Involvement*, London: Routledge.

Bäck, H. and R. Öhrvall (2003), *Det nya seklets förtroendevalda. Om politikerantal och representativitet i kommuner och landsting 2003*, Stockholm: Svenska Kommunförbundet, Landstingsförbundet och Justitiedepartementet.

Bains, M. (1972), *The New Local Authorities: Management and Structure*, London, HMSO.

Bakker, J. M., P. Castenmiller and A. J. H. Smallenbroek (eds) (2000), 'De alledaagse praktijk van het decentraal bestuur', in *Staatscommissie Dualisme en lokale democratie: Rapport van de Staatscommissie Dualisme en lokale democratie (onderzoeksbijlage)*, Samsom, Alphen aan den Rijn, pp. 5–141.

Baldersheim, H. and K. Ståhlberg (eds) (1994), *Towards the Self-Regulating Municipality: Free Communes and Administrative Modernisation in Scandinavia*, Aldershot: Dartmouth.

Baldersheim, Harald and Torodd Strand (1988), *Byregjering i Oslo kommune, Hovedrapport fra et evalueringsprosjekt*, Bergen: Norwegian Research Centre, in Organization and Management. Report No. 7.

Beetham, D. (1996), 'Theorising democracy and local government', in D. King and G. Stoker (eds) *Rethinking Local Democracy*, Basingstoke: Macmillan.

Begeleidingscommissie Vernieuwingsimpuls (ed.) (2003), *Dualisering in de steigers: Eerste Jaarbericht van de Begeleidingscommissie Vernieuwingsimpuls*, VNG Uitgeverij: Den Haag.

Begeleidingscommissie Vernieuwingsimpuls (ed.) (2004), *De positie van de wethouder, De toekomst van het verleden. Tweede Jaarbericht van de Begeleidingscommissie Vernieuwingsimpuls*, VNG Uitgeverij: Den Haag.

Berg, R. (2000), *Den 'gode' politiker'. Et studie af politiske ledelsesværdier i kommunerne*, Odense: Odense Universitetsforlag.

Berg, R. and S. Pedersen (2001), *Fra små kongedømmer til moderne republik?* Odense: Syddansk Universitet, Samfundsvidenskab.

Berveling, J. (1994), *Het stempel op de besluitvorming: macht, invloed en besluitvorming op twee Amsterdamse beleidsterreinen*, Thesis, Amsterdam.

Björkman, U. and C. Riberdahl (1997), *Det kommunala förtroendeuppdraget: rättsliga villkor och förutsättningar*, Stockholm: Publica.

Blatrix, C. (1997), 'Le référendum local, une procédure de démocratie participative? Bilan et perspectives' , in D. Gaxie (ed.), *Luttes d' institutions*, Paris: L' Harmattan.

Blom, A. P. (1994), *Kommunalt chefskap. En studie om ansvar, ledarskap och demokrati*, Lund: Dialogos.

Blondel, J. (1973), *Comparative Legislatures*, Englewood Cliffs, NJ: Prentice-Hall.

Bogumil, J. (2001), *Modernisierung lokaler Politik*, Baden-Baden: Nomos.

Bogumil, J., D. H. Gehne and L. Holtkamp (2003), 'Bürgermeister und Gemeindeordnungenim Leistungsvergleich' , in *Eildienst, Informationen für Rat und Verwaltung*, Heft 10/ 2003, pp. 337–9.

Borraz, O. (1998), *Gouverner une ville: Besançon 1959–1989*, Rennes: Presses Universitaires de Rennes.

Bosworth, K. (1958), 'The Manager is a Politician' , *Public Administration Review* 18 (Summer), pp. 216–22.

Bouckaert, G. (1997), 'Proliferatie van locale besturen: Beleids- en beheersinplicaties' , *Res Publica*, 39(1), pp. 109–23.

Bridges, A. (1997), *Morning Glories: Municipal Reform in the Southwest*, Princeton, NJ: Princeton University Press.

Brugué, Q. (2002), 'Nuevos Ayuntamientos, concejales diferentes: del gobierno de las instituciones al gobierno de las redes', *Revista Española de Ciencia Política*, 7.

Brugué, Q. and J. M. Vallés (1997), 'Los sistemas de representación y gobierno', in F. Longo (ed.), *Informe Pi i Sunyer sobre Gobierno Local en España*, Barcelona: Fundació Carles Pi i Sunyer d' Estudis Autonòmics i Locals.

Brugué, Q., R. Gomá and J. Subirats (2001), 'Les polítiques municipals a Catalunya: Cap a una governance de proximitat, estratègica i relacional', in R. Gomá and J. Subirats (eds), *Govern i polítiques públiques a Catalunya (1980–2000), Coneixement, sostenibilitat i territori*, Barcelona: Edicions Universitat de

Barcelona i Universitat Autònoma de Barcelona-Servei de Publicacions (Manuals de la Universitat Autònoma de Barcelona, 27).

Brunsson, N. and S. Jönsson (1979), *Beslut och handling* (Decisions and Action). Stockholm: Liber.

BZK (Ministerie van Binnenlandse Zaken en Koninkrijksrelaties) (2000), *Kerngegevens Overheidspersoneel, Stand ultimo 1997, 1998 en 1999, Den Haag:* Ministerie van Binnenlandse Zaken en Koninkrijksrelaties.

—— (Ministerie van Binnenlandse Zaken en Koninkrijksrelaties) (2002), *De eerste klap is een daalder waar: Evaluatie eerste fase Wet dualisering gemeentebestuur,* Den Haag: Ministerie van Binnenlandse Zaken en Koninkrijksrelaties.

Caillosse, J. (1999), 'Eléments pour un bilan juridique de la démocratie locale en France', in CURAPP, *La démocratie locale, représentation, participation et espace public,* Paris: PUF.

Caulfield, J. and H. O. Larsen (eds) (2003), *Local Government at the Millennium,* Opladen, Germany: Leske and Budrich.

Chester, D. N. (1968), 'Local democracy and the internal organization of local authorities', *Public Administration,* 46(2), pp. 287–98.

Childs, R. S. (1913), 'The Theory of the New Controlled–Executive Plan', *National Municipal Review,* 2, January, pp. 76–81.

Clarke, M., H. Davis, D. Hall and J. D. Stewart (1996), *Executive Mayors for Britain? New Forms of Political Leadership Reviewed,* Birmingham: Capita.

Clarke, S. E. (ed.) (1989), *Urban Innovation and Autonomy: The Political Implications of Policy Change,* Newbury Park, CA: Sage.

Copus, C. (1999), 'The Local Councillor and Party Group Loyalty', *Policy and Politics,* 27(3), pp. 309–24.

Council of Europe (1998), *Structure and Operation of Local and Regional Democracy,* Switzerland, Strasbourg.

Crain, R. L. (1968), *The Politics of School Desegregation,* Chicago, IL: Aldine.

Crick, B. (1964), *In Defence of Politics,* Harmondsworth: Penguin Books.

Cuban, L. and M. Usdan (eds) (2003), *Powerful Reforms with Shallow Roots,* New York: Teachers College Press.

Daalder, H. (1995[1964]), 'Leiding en lijdelijkheid in de Nederlandse politiek', reprinted in Daalder, H. (ed.) *Van oude en nieuwe regenten: politiek in Nederland,* Bert Bakker, Amsterdam, pp. 11–39.

Dahl, R. A. (1961), *Who Governs? Democracy and Power in an American City,* New Haven, CT: Yale University Press.

Dahl, R. A. and E. C. Tufte (1973), *Size and Democracy,* Stanford: Stanford University Press.

Darviche, M-S (2000), 'L' action du maire face au public. A propos d' un aménagement urbain du littoral languedocien' , *Pôle Sud,* 13.

Debuyst, F. (1967), *La fonction parlementaire en Belgique: mécanismes d' accès et images,* Brussels: CRISP.

Delcamp, A. (ed.) (1994), *Les collectivités décentralisées de l' Union européenne,* Paris: La Documentation Française.

Denters, B. and P. J. Klok (2005), 'The Netherlands: in search of responsiveness' , in B. Denters and L. E. Rose (eds) *Comparing Local Governance: Trends and Developments,* Basingstoke: Palgrave, pp. 65–82.

Denters, B., van der Kolk, H. Birkenhäger, E. De Jong, H., Loots, M. and Noppe, R. (2000), 'Aan het hoofd der gemeente staat. ... Een onderzoek naar de werking van het formele gemeentelijke bestuursmodel ten behoeve van de staatscommissie Dualisme en lokale democratie', in Staatscommissie dualisme en lokale democratie (eds), *De vernieurwing van de lokale democratie*: Samsom: Alphen aan den Rijn.

Denters, S. A. H. (2000), 'Urban democracies in the Netherlands: social and political change, institutional continuities?' in O. Gabriel, V. Hoffmann-Martinot and H. Savitch (eds), *Urban Democracies*, Opladen: Leske and Budrich, pp. 73–126.

Denters, S. A. H. and H. van der Kolk (1998), 'De gemeenteraad en het raadslid' , in A. F. A. Korsten and P. W. Tops (eds), *Lokaal bestuur in Nederland: Iinleiding in de gemeentekunde*, Samsom, Alphen aan den Rijn, pp. 222–32.

Denters, S. A. H. and P. J. Klok (2003a), 'Rebuilding Roombeek: an institutional analysis of interactive governance in the context of representative democracy', in B. Denters, O. Heffen, J. van Huisman and P. J. Klok (eds), *The Rise of Interactive Governance and Quasi-Markets: A Comparison of the Dutch Experience with the Developments in Four Western Countries*, Dordrecht: Kluwer, pp. 91–110.

—— (2003b), 'A new role for municipal councils in Dutch local democracy?' in N. Kersting and A. Vetter (eds), *Reforming Local Government in Europe: Closing the Gap Between Democracy and Efficiency?* Opladen: Leske and Budrich, pp. 65–84.

Derksen, W. (1980), *Tussen loopbaan en carrière. Het burgemeesterambt in Nederland*, Gravenhage: VUGA Boekerij.

—— (1985), *Macht in de gemeente: Beleidsanalyse als vorm van machtsonderzoek*, Kobra, Amsterdam.

—— (1998), 'De burgemeester' , in A. Korsten and P. Tops (eds), *Lokaal bestuur in Nederland. Inleiding tot de gemeentekunde*, Alphen a/d Rijn: Samson, pp. 197–208.

DETR (1998a), *A Mayor and Assembly for London*, London: Department of the Environment, Transport and the Regions.

—— (1998b), *Modern Local Government: In Touch With the People*, Cmnd 4014, London: The Stationery Office.

—— (1999), *Local Leadership, Local Choice*, London: Department of the Environment, Transport and the Regions.

Deweerdt, M. (1995), 'Overzicht van het Belgisch politiek gebeuren in 1995', *Res Publica*, 37, 3–4, pp. 281–312.

DeWinter, L. (1992), *The Belgian Legislature*, Florence: European University Institute.

DiMaggio, P. J. and W. W. Powell (1991), 'Introduction', in P. J. DiMaggio and W. W. Powell (eds), *The New Institutionalism in Organizational Analysis*, Chicago, IL: The University of Chicago Press.

Duran, P. and J.-C. Thoenig (1996), 'L' État et la gestion publique territoriale', *Revue Française de Science Politique*, 46(4).

Edelenbos, J. and R. Monnikhof (eds) (2001), *Lokale interactieve beleidsvorming: Een vergelijkend onderzoek naar de consequenties van interactieve beleidsvorming voor het functioneren van de lokale democratie*, Lemma Utrecht.

Ejersbo, N., M. B. Hansen and P. E. Mouritzen (1998), 'The Danish local government CEO: from town clerk to city manager', in K. K. Klausen and A. Magnier (eds), *The Anonymous Leader*, Odense: Odense University Press.

Elander, Ingemar and S. Montin (1990), 'Decentralization and Control: Central and Local Government Relations in Sweden', *Policy and Politics*, 18(3), pp. 165–80.

Elcock, H. (2001), *Political Leadership*, Cheltenham: Edward Elgar.

Eulau, H. and K. Prewitt (1973), *Labyrinths of Democracy: Adaptations, Linkages, Representation, and Policies in Urban Politics*, Indianapolis, IN: The Bobbs-Merill Company.

Faber, S. (1967) *Wat verwacht de burger van zijn burgemeester?* Alphen a/d Rijn: Samson.

—— (1974) *Burgemeester en democratie. Verslag en interpretatie van een bestuurskundig onderzoek in Friesland*. Alphen a/d Rijn: Samson.

Falter, R. (2000), 'Coalitie wil burgemeester verkiezen' , *De Standaard*, 20/05/2000.

Ferman, B. (1985), *Governing the Ungovernable City*, Philadelphia, PA: Temple University Press.

Fiers, S. (2001), 'Carrièrepatronen van Belgische parlementsleden in een multi-level omgeving (1979–99)', *Res Publica*, 43(1), pp. 171–91.

Filkin, G., P. Bassam, P. Corrigan, G. Stoker and J. Tizard (1999), *Modernising Local Government*, London: New Local Government Network for Joseph Rowntree Foundation.

Fimreite, A. L. (ed.) (2003), *Styringssystem i storby. Evaluering av styringssystemet i Bergen kommune*, Bergen: Rokkansenteret, Rapport 4.

Flentje, E. H. and W. Counihan (1984), 'Running a Reformed City', *Urban Resources* 2 (Fall) pp. 9–14.

Frederickson, H. G., G. A. Johnson and C. H. Wood (2003), *The Adapted City: Institutional Dynamics and Structural Change*, Armonk, NY: M. E. Sharpe.

Fridolf, M. (1996), *Konkurrensutsättning i Stockholms stad inom äldreomsorgen*, Politiskt-demokratiska aspekter, SOU 1996: 169, bilaga IV, Stockholm: Fritzes.

Gaudin, J.-P. (1985), *Expertise et urbanisme au début du siècle*, Cahiers TTS, 20–21.

Geser, H., F. Höpflinger, A. Ladner, U. Meuli and R. Schaller (1996), *Die Schweizer Gemeinden im Kräftefeld des gesellschaftlichen und politisch-administrativen Wandels*, Schlussbericht NF-Projekt Nr. 12-32586-92, Zürich: Soziologisches Institut der Universität Zürich.

Geser, H., P. Farago, R. Fluder and E. Gräub (1987), *Gemeindepolitik zwischen Milizorganisation und Berufsverwaltung*, Bern, Haupt.

Gidlund, G. and T. Möller (1999), *Demokratins trotjänare. Lokalt partiarbete förr och nu*. SOU 1999: 130, Stockholm: fakta info direkt.

Gidlund, J. (1983), *Kommunal självstyrelse i förvandling*, Stockholm: Liber.

Gilbert, B. (1978), *This City, This Man: The Cookingham Era in Kansas City*, Washington: International City Management Association.

Goldsmith, M. (1995), 'Autonomy and City Limits', in D. Judge, G. Stoker and H. Wollman (eds), *Theories of Urban Politics*, Thousand Oaks, CA: Sage.

—— (2000), 'Representing communities: who and what', in N. Rao (ed.), *Representation and Community In Western Democracies*, Basingstoke: Macmillan.

Government Bill (2001) *Demokrati för det nya seklet*, 02:80.

Granberg, M. and J. Olsson (1999), 'Decentralisering eller centralisering?' in J. Olsson and S. Montin (eds), *Demokrati som experiment. Försöksverksamhet och förnyelse i svenska kommuner*, Örebro: Örebro Universitet, Novemus rapportserie 1999:1.

Greer, A. L. (1974), *The Mayor' s Mandate*, Cambridge, MA: Schenkman.

Gulick, L. (1937), 'Notes on the theory of organization', in L. Gulick and L. Urwick (eds), *Papers on the Science of Administration*, New York: A. M. Kelley.

Gustafsson, A. (1983), *Local Government in Sweden*, Stockholm: The Swedish Institute.

—— (1999), *Kommunal självstyrelse*, Stockholm: SNS Förlag.

Hagen, T. P. (1999), *Storbyenes finanser 1983–1997. Evaluering av det parlamentariske styringssystemet i Oslo kommune. Delprosjekt 3*, Oslo: Norsk Institutt for by- og regionforskning, Notat 105.

Hagen, T. P., T. M. Myrvold, S. Opedal, I. M. Stigen and H. S. Østtveiten (1999), *Parlamentarisme eller formannskapsmodell? Det parlamentariske styringssystemet i Oslo sammenliknet med formannskapsmodellene i Bergen, Trondheim og Stavnager*, Oslo: Norsk Institutt for by-og regionforskning, Rapport nr. 3.

Hagevi, M. (1999), *Kommunala förtroendeuppdrag 1999*, Stockholm: Svenska kommunförbundet.

—— (2000), *Professionalisering och deltagande i den lokala representativa demokratin. En analys av kommunala förtroendeuppdrag 1999*, Göteborg: CEFOS, Göteborgs universitet, CEFOS, Rapport 13.

Hall, P. A. and R. C. R. Taylor (1996), 'Political science and the three new institutionalisms', in *Political Studies*, 44, pp. 936–57.

Hallström, N.-E. (2001), *Bristen på politiker – ett demokratiskt dilemma*, Linköping: Linköpings universitet, Centrum för kommunstrategiska studier, Rapport 2001:1.

Hambleton, R. and D. Sweeting (2004), 'US-style leadership for English local government', *Public Administration Review*, 64, 474–88.

Heinelt, H., E. Kerrouche and B. Egner (2005), 'From government to governance at the local level. Some considerations based on data surveys with mayors and chief executive officers', in H. Wollmann and V. Hoffmann-Martinot (eds), *State and Administrative Modernization in France and Germany*, Wiesbaden: Verlag für Sozialwissenschaften.

Henig, J. R. and W. C. Rich (eds) (2004), *Mayors in the Middle*, Princeton, NJ: Princeton University Press.

Hesse, J. J. and L. J. Sharpe (1991), 'Local government in international perspective: some comparative observations', in J. J. Hesse (ed.), *Local Government and Urban Affairs in International Perspective: Analyses of Twenty Western Industrialised Countries*, Nomos, Baden-Baden, pp. 603–21.

Heywood, A. (2004), *Political Theory: An Introduction*, New York: Palgrave Macmillan.

Hoffmann-Martinot, V. (1988), 'Gestion moderniste à Nîmes', *Annales de la recherche urbaine*, 28.

—— (1999), 'Les grandes villes françaises une démocratie en souffrance', in O. Gabriel et V. Hoffmann-Martinot (eds), *Démocraties urbaines*, Paris: L' Harmattan, pp. 77–123.

Holli, M. G. (1999), *The American Mayor*, University Park, Pennsylvania State University Press.

Holtkamp, L. (2003), 'Parteien in der Kommunalpolitik, Konkordanz- und Konkurrenzdemokratien im BundesLändervergleich', *Polis*, 58, FernUniversität Hagen.

Holtkamp, L., J. Bogumil and L. Kißler (2004), *Kooperative Demokratie*, Ms. Fernuniversität Hagen.

Hunter, F. (1963), *Community Power Structure*, New York: Anchor.

Jacobsen, D. I. (1997), *Administrasjonens makt – om forholdet mellom politikk og administrasjon*, Bergen-Sandviken: Fagbokforlaget.

Jiménez Asenio, R. (2004), 'Política y administración en la reforma del gobierno local, un estudio sobre la forma de gobierno y la alta administración en los "municipios de gran población" ', in T. Font (ed.), *Anuario del Gobierno Local 2003*, Madrid: Marcial Pons.

Johansson, F., L. Nilsson and L. Strömberg (2001), *Kommunal demokrati under fyra decennier*, Malmö: Liber.

John, P. and A. Cole (2000), 'Policy Networks and Local Political Leadership in Britain and France', in G. Stoker (ed.), *The New Politics of British Local Governance*, Basingstoke: Macmillan.

Jones, B. D. (1983), *Governing Urban America*, Boston, MA: Little, Brown and Company Publishers.

Jonsson, L. (2003), *Kommunstyrelseordförande. Kommunledare med politisk förankring*, Nora: Nya Doxa.

Jonsson, L., P. Gustavsson, S.-I. Arnell, Ö. Högberg and R. Jonsson (2002), *Kommunchefers chefskap*, Nora: Nya Doxa.

Jönsson, S., L. Nilsson, S. Rubenowitz and J. Westerståhl (1999), *The Decentralised City: Democracy, Efficiency, Service*, Göteborg: BAS Publisher.

Kammerer, G. M. (1964), 'Role Diversity of City Managers' , *Administrative Science Quarterly*, 84, pp. 21–42.

Kellar, E. (2004), 'Professionalism vs. politics: what are the issues?' *PA Times*, February 2004.

Keller, J. (2001), 'I know where ahwahnago and what ahwannado (I know where I want to go and what I want to do)', *Boston Magazine* (February), p. 96 ff.

Kiss, R. (2002), 'Democracy or community? Australian local government electoral reform', in J. Caulfield and H. O. Larsen (eds), *Local Government at the Millennium*. Opladen: Leske and Budrich.

Kjær, U. (2000), *Kommunalbestyrelsernes sammensætning – rekruttering og repræsentation i dansk kommunalpolitik*, Odense: Odense Universitetsforlag.

Kleinfeld, R. and N. Achim (1996), 'Die Reform der deutschen Gemeindeverfassungen unter besonderer Berücksichtigung der Entwicklung in Nordrhein-Westfalen und in den neuen BundesLändern', in R. Kleinfeld (ed.), *Kommunalpolitik*, Opladen: Leske and Budrich, pp. 73–154.

Klingemann, H. D. and D. Fuchs (eds) (1995), *Citizens and the State*, Oxford: Oxford University Press.

Klok P. J., S. A. H. Denters and M. A. Visser (2002), 'Veranderingen in de Bestuurscultuur', in S. A. H. Denters and I. Pröpper (eds), *Naar een politiek profiel voor de gemeenteraad; Eindrapportage Project duale gemeenten*, Den Haag: VNG Uitgeverij, pp. 53–71.

Knemeyer, F. L. (2001), 'The constitution of local government', in K. König and H. Siedentopf (eds), *Public Administration in Germany*, Baden-Baden: Nomos, pp. 171–82.

Knudsen, T. (1995), *Dansk Statsbygning*, København: Jurist- og Økonomforbundets Forlag.

Kolk, H. van der (1997), *Electorale controle: lokale verkiezingen en responsiviteit van politici*, Enschede: Twente University Press.

Kost, A. and H.-G. Wehling (eds) (2003), *Kommunalpolitik in den deutschen Ländern*, Wiesbaden: Westdeutscher Verlag.

Kotter, J. P. and P. R. Lawrence (1974), *Mayors in Action*, New York: Wiley.

Kozol, J. (1967), *Death at an Early Age*, Boston, MA: Houghton Mifflin.

Kuhlmann, S. (2004), *Lokale Verwaltungsreform in Deutschland und Frankreich: Dezentralisierung, Demokratisierung, Ökonomisierung*, paper for the conference on Stand und Perspektiven der politikwissenschaftlichen Verwaltungsforschung, University Konstanz, 23–25 September.

Kunz, V. and T. Zapf-Schramm (1989), 'Ergebnisse der Haushaltsentscheidungsprozesse in den kreisfreien Städten der Bundesrepublik', in D. Schimanke (ed.), *Stadtdirektor oder Bürgermeister*, Basel: Birkhäuser, pp. 161–89.

Ladner, A. (1991), *Politische Gemeinden, kommunale Parteien und lokale Politik. Eine empirische Untersuchung in den Gemeinden der Schweiz*, Zürich: Seismo.

—— (1999), 'Le esperienze di democrazia diretta della città di Zurigo', *Amministrare*, XXIX. N. 2, La democrazia diretta locale in Svizzera e in California.

Ladner, A. (2002), 'Size and direct democracy at the local level: the case of Switzerland', in *Environment and Planning C: Government and Policy* 20(6), pp. 813–28.

Ladner, A., D. Arn, U. Friederich, R. Steiner and J. Wichtermann (2000), *Gemeindereformen zwischen Handlungsfähigkeit und Legitimation*, Bern: Institut für Politikwissenschaft und Institut für Organisation und Personal.

Larsen, H. O. (1996), 'Le maire norvégien: de l'amateur au professionnel en politique', in V. Hoffmann-Martinot and F. Kjellberg (eds), *Décentraliser en France et en Norvège*, Paris: Pedone.

—— (2002), 'Directly elected mayors: democratic renewal or constitutional confusion?' in J. Caulfield and H. O. Larsen (eds), *Local Government at the Millennium*, Opladen: Budrich and Leske Verlag.

Larsen, H. O. and A. Offerdal (1994), *Demokrati og deltakelse i kommunene*, Oslo: Kommuneforlaget.

Le Bart, C. (1992), *La rhétorique du maire entrepreneur*, Paris: Pédone, N. 13.

—— (2003), *Les Maires. Sociologie d' un rôle*, Villeneuve d' Ascq.

Le Maire, E. and N. Preisler (2000), *Lov om kommunernes styrelse*, København: Jurist- og Økonomforbundets Forlag.

Leach, R. and N. Barnett (1998), 'The new public management and the local government review', in S. Leach (ed.), *Local Government Reorganisation: The Review and its Aftermath* London: Frank Cass.

Leach, S. and C. Copus (2004), 'Scrutiny and the political party group in UK local government: new models of behaviour', *Public Administration*, 82, 331–54.

Leach, S. and D. Wilson (2000), *Local Political Leadership*, Bristol: The Policy Press.

Leach, S. and V. Lowndes (2004), 'Understanding local political leadership: constitutions, contexts and capabilities', *Local Government Studies*, 30(4), pp. 557–75.

Lerman, D. (1990), 'Hampton mayor targets dropouts', *Hampton Times-Herald*, 25 January 1990.

Lidström, A. (1996), *Kommunsystem i Europa*, (Local Government Systems in Europe), Stockholm: Publica.

Lijphart, A. (1979), *Verzuiling, pacificatie en kentering in de Nederlandse politiek*, Amsterdam: De Bussy.

—— (1994), 'Democracies: forms, performance and constitutional engineering', *European Journal of Political Research*, 25, pp. 1–17.

—— (1999), *Patterns of Democracy: Government Forms and Performance in Thirty-Six Countries*, New Haven, London: Yale University Press.

Linder, W. (1994), *Swiss Democracy: Possible Solutions to Conflict in Multicultural Societies*, New York: St. Martin's Press.

Linder, W. and R. Nabholz (1994), *Local Governance and New Democracy*, The Swiss Project, Swiss national report, Bern: Institut für Politikwissenschaft.

Linz, J. J. (1987), *La quiebra de las democracias*, Madrid: Alianza Editorial, Alianza Universidad.

Local Government Act (1991), *SFS 1991: 900 with amendments*, English version: http://www.regeringen.se/sb/d/108/a/39165.

Long, N. E. (1965), 'Politicians for Hire', *Public Administration Review* 25, pp. 115–19.

Longo, F. (1999), *Política i gerencia pública en els governs locals, dins aavv. L'ajuntament gerencial. Reflexions i propostes per gerencialitzar*, Barcelona: Diputació de Barcelona, (col·lecció Perspectiva, 12).

Lorrain, D. (1991), 'De l'administration républicaine au gouvernement urbain', *Sociologie du travail*, 4.

―― (1993), 'Après la décentralisation: L'action publique flexible', *Sociologie du travail*, 3.

Loveridge, R. O. (1971), *City Managers in Legislative Politics*, Indianapolis: Bobbs-Merrill.

Lukes, S. (2005), *Power: A Radical View*, Basingstoke: Macmillan.

Lund, B. H. (1995), *Styringssystemet i Oslo commune. Parlamentarisme og desentralisering*, Oslo: Kommuneforlaget.

Mabileau, A. (1995), 'De la monarchie municipale à la française', *Pouvoirs*, 73.

Maes, R. and M. Boes (eds) (2001), *Proeve van Vlaams gemeentedecreet*, Leuven: Instituut voor Administratief Recht en Instituut voor de Overheid.

Magre, J. (1999), *L'alcalde a Catalunya*, Barcelona: Institut de Ciències Polítiques i Socials.

Maravall, J. M. (1999), 'Accountability and manipulation', in A. Przeworsky, S. C. Stokes and B. Manin (eds), *Democracy, Accountability and Representation*, Cambridge: Cambridge University Press.

March, J. G. (1984), 'How we talk and how we act: administrative theory and administrative life', in T. J. Sergiovanni and J. E. Corbally (eds), *Leadership and Organizational Cultures*, Urbana, IL: University of Illinois Press.

March, J. G. and J. P. Olsen (eds) (1976), *Ambiguity and Choice in Organizations*, Bergen: Universitetsforlaget.

―― (1989), *Rediscovering Institutions: The Organizational Basis of Politics*, New York: The Free Press.

―― (1995), *Democratic Governance*, New York: The Free Press.

Marie, J.-L. (1989), 'La symbolique du changement', in A. Mabileau and C. Sorbets (eds), *Gouverner les villes moyennes*, Paris, Pedone.

Marshall, N., A. Witherby and B. Dollery (1999), 'Management, markets and democracy: Australian local government reform in the 1990s', *Local Government Studies*, (25)3, pp. 34–57.

Maud, J. (1967), Committee on the Management of Local Government, vol. 1, *Report*, London: HMSO.

Meer, F. M. van der and L. J. Roborgh (1993), *Ambtenaren in Nederland: omvang, bureaucratisering en representativiteit van het ambtelijk apparaat*, Samsom H. D., Tjeenk Willink, Alphen aan den Rijn.

Meire, M., H. Waege and F. De Rynck (2002), *Draagvlakanalyse van het nieuw Vlaams gemeentedecreet*, Brussels: Steunpunt Beleidsrelevant Onderzoek.

Mény, Y. (1992), 'La République des fiefs', *Pouvoirs*, 60.

Mills, C. W. (1959), *The Power Elite*, New York: Galaxy.

Montin, S. (1993), *Swedish Local Government in Transition. A matter of rationality and legitimacy*, Örebro: Högskolan i Örebro, Örebro Studies 8, and Göteborg: Göteborgs Universitet, Göteborg Studies in Politics 28.

—— (1998), 'Nytt offentligt ledarskap och politikerrollen', in K. K. Klausen and K. Ståhlberg (eds), *New Public Management i Norden*, Odense: Odense Universitetsforlag.

—— (2000), 'Between fragmentation and co-ordination: the changing role of local government in Sweden', *Public Management* 2(1), pp. 1–23.

—— (2002), *Moderna Kommuner*, Malmö: Liber.

Montin, S. and J. Olsson (1999), 'Fullmäktige experimenterar', in S. Montin and J. Olsson (eds), *Demokrati som experiment. Försöksverksamhet och förnyelse i svenska kommuner*, Örebro: Örebro Universitet, Novemus Rapport 1999: 1.

Montin, S., J. Olsson and H. Pettersson (1996), 'Fullmäktige under förändring? En studie av uppdraget, relationerna och arbetsformerna', in S. Montin (ed.), *Förändringsmodeller och förändringsprocesser i kommuner och landsting. Bilaga V till slutbetänkandet av Kommunala Förnyelsekommittén*, SOU 1996:169, Stockholm.

Montondon, L. (1995), 'Accountability in municipalities: the use of internal auditers and audit committees', *American Review of Public Administration*, 25, pp. 59–69.

Morgan, G. (1986), *Images of Organization*, Newbury Park: Sage.

Mouritzen, P. E. and J. H. Svara (2002), *Leadership at the Apex: Politicians and Administrators in Western Local Governments*, Pittsburgh, PA: University of Pittsburgh Press.

Murphy, R. D. (1971), *Political Entrepreneurs and Urban Poverty*, Lexington, MA: D.C. Heath.

Nalbandian, J. (1994), 'Reflections of a "Pracademic" on the logic of politics and administration', *Public Administration Review*, 54, p. 531.

Neighborhood Office, City of Hampton (1998), *A History of Hampton's Healthy Neighborhoods Initiative*, Hampton, VA, July 1998.

Nelson, K. L. (2002), 'Assessing the CAO position in strong-mayor government', *National Civic Review* 9, pp. 41–54.

Newell, C. (ed.) (2004), *The Effective Local Government Manager*, 3rd ed., Washington: International City Management Association.

Newland, C. A. (1985), 'Council-manager governance: positive alternative to separation of powers', *Public Management*, 67, July, pp. 7–9.

Newton, K. (1974), 'Role orientations and their sources among elected representatives in English local politics', *Journal of Politics*, 36(3) pp. 615–36.

Nichols-Clark, T. and V. Hoffmann-Martinot (1998), *The New Political Culture*, Boulder, CO: Westview Press.

Nisbet, R. and R. G. Perrin (1977), *The Social Bond*, New York: Alfred A. Knopf.

Norris, P. (ed.) (1999), *Critical Citizens: Global Support for Democratic Governance*, Oxford: Oxford University Press.

Offerdal, A. (1989), *Den politiske kommunen* (The Political Municipality), Oslo: Det norske samlaget.

O' Leary, B., B. Grofman and J. Elklit (2003), 'Divisor methods for sequential portfolio allocation in multi-parti executive bodies: evidence from Northern Ireland and Denmark', *American Journal of Political Science*, 49(1), pp. 198–211.

Ostrom, E., R. Gardner and J. Walker (1994), *Rules, games and common-pool resources*, Ann Arbor, MI: University of Michigan Press.

Pavlichev, A. (2004), *The Effects of Internal Characteristics of Municipal Government Agencies and Environmental Factors of Municipalities on the Scope and the Quality of Municipal E-Government Initiatives: Developing an Integrated Approach*, Ph.D. Dissertation, North Carolina State University.

Pedersen, M. N. (1997), 'Når kagen skal deles. Konstitueringens politik', in J. Elklit and R. B. Jensen (eds), *Kommunalvalg*, Odense: Odense Universitetsforlag.

Perrin, B. (1996), 'Coopération intercommunale: état des lieux avant réforme', *La revue du Trésor*, 12.

Peters, G. B. (1999), *Institutional Theory In Political Science: The 'New Institutionalism'*, London: Continuum.

Petersson, O., G. Hernes, S. Holmberg, L. Togeby and L. Wägnerud (2000), *Demokratirådets rapport 2000: Demokrati utan partier?*, Stockholm: SNS Förlag.

Pimlott, B. and N. Rao (2002), *Governing London*, Oxford: Oxford University Press.

Plees, Y. and K. De Leemans (1997), 'Gemeentelijke organisatiemodellen en modelsecretarissen?' *Vlaams Tijdschrift voor Overheidsmanagement*, 2(2), pp. 4–14.

Plotz, D. A. (1992), *Community Problem Solving Case Summaries*, vol. III, Program for Community Problem Solving, Washington, DC.

Poister, T. and G. Steib (1989), 'Management tools in municipal government: trends over the past decade', *Public Administration Review*, 49, pp. 240–48.

Polidano, C. (2001), 'An exocet in a red box: parliamentary accountability and the Sandline affair', *Public Administration*, 79(2), pp. 249–75.

Pollitt, C. (2003), *The Essential Public Manager*, Maidenhead: Open University Press.

Portz, J. (2004), 'Boston: agenda setting and school reform in a mayor-centric system', in Henig and Rich, *Mayors in the Middle*, Princeton, NJ: Princeton University Press, pp. 96–119.

Portz, J., L. Stein and R. Jones (1999), *City Schools and City Politics*, Lawrence: University Press of Kansas.

Pratchett, L. (1999), 'Introduction: defining democratic renewal', *Local Government Studies*, 25(1), pp.1–18.

Pressman, J. L. (1972), 'Preconditions of mayoral leadership', *American Political Science Review*, 66, June, pp. 511–24.

Prewitt, K. (1970), *The Recruitment of Political Leaders*, Indianapolis: Bobbs-Merrill.

Prewitt, K. (1981), *The Recruitment of Political Leaders*, Westport: Greenwood Press.

Przeworski, A., S. C. Stokes and B. Manin (eds) (1999), *Democracy, Accountability and Representation*, Cambridge: Cambridge University Press.

Rae, D. W. (2003), *City: Urbanism and Its End*, New Haven, CT: Yale University Press.

Rao, N. (1993), *Managing Change: Councillors and the New Local Government*, York: Joseph Rowntree Foundation.

—— (1994), *The Making and Un-making of Local Self Government*, Aldershot, Dartmouth.

—— (1998), 'Representation in local politics: a reconsideration and some new evidence', *Political Studies*, 46, pp. 19–35.

—— (2003), 'Options for change: mayors, cabinets or the status quo?', *Local Government Studies*, 29, pp. 1–16.

Rao, N. and K. Young (1999), 'Revitalising local democracy', in R. Jowell, J. Curtis, A. Park and K. Thompson (eds), *British Social Attitudes: The 16th Report*, Aldershot: Ashgate.

Regás, R. (1997) *Pròleg a l'obra de P. Maragall. Los ayuntamientos*. Barcelona: editorial Destino.

Regás, R. (2002), *Los ayuntamientos*, Pròleg a l' obra de P. Maragall, Barcelona: Editorial Destino.

Rich, M. J. (2003), 'Revitalizing urban communities: lessons from Atlanta's Empowerment Zone experience', in B. Holmes (ed.), *The Status of Black Atlanta 2003*, Atlanta: The Southern Center for Studies in Public Policy, Clark Atlanta University, pp. 79–112.

Roberts, N. C. (2002), 'Keeping public officials accountable through dialogue: resolving the accountability paradox', *Public Administration Review*, 626, pp. 58–70.

Røiseland, A. and I. M. Stigen (2003), *Fylkeskommunal parlamentarisme i Nordland. Samspillet politikk-administrasjon*, Oslo: Norsk Institutt for by- og regionforskning, Rapport nr. 15.

Rokkan, S. (1966), 'Norway: numerical democracy and corporate pluralism', in R. A. Dahl (ed.), *Political Oppositions in Western Democracy*, New Haven, CT: Yale University Press, pp. 70–115.

Rondin, J. (1985), *Le sacre des notables*, Paris: Fayard.

Rosanvallon, P. (1998), *Le peuple introuvable, histoire de la représentation démocratique en France*, Paris: Gallimard.

Roubieu, O. (1999), 'Des managers très politique: Les secrétaires généraux des villes', in V. Dubois and D. Dulong (eds), *La question technocratique*, Strasbourg: Presses universitaires de Strasbourg.

Saporta, M. (1998), 'Renaissance report details Atlanta's needs', *Atlanta Journal and Constitution*, 24, March.

Schefold, D. and M. Naumann (1996), *Entwicklungstendenzen der Kommunalverfassungen in Deutschland*, Basel: Birkhäuser.

Schrag, P. (1967), *Village School Downtown*, Boston, MA: Beacon Press.

Schulenburg, K. (1999), *Direktwahl und kommuinalpolitische Führung*, Opladen: Leske and Budrich.

Sellers, J. M. (2002), *Governing from Below*, London: Cambridge University Press.

Serritslew, S. (2003),'Shaping local councillor preferences: party politics, committee structure and social background', *Scandinavian Political Studies*, 3.

Sims, S. J. and R. Vrooman (1998), 'Toward 2007: accountability and change in local government. Steering the course', in R. R. Sims (ed.), *Accountability and Radical Change in Public Organizations*, Westport: Greenwood Publishing Group, Inc.

SOU (2001), Official Government Reports, Att vara med på riktigt – demokratiutveckling i kommuner och landsting, Bilagor till betänkande av kommundemokratikommittén, Stockholm: Fritzes, 2001:48.

Staatscommissie (2000), *Staatscommissie Dualisme en Lokale Democratie. Dualisme en lokale democratie. Rapport van de Staatscommissie Dualisme en lokale democratie*. Alphen aan den Rijn: Samsom.

Stengers, J. (1992), *De Koningen der Belgen. Macht en invloed*, Leuven: Davidsfonds.

Stewart, J. D. (1993), *Supporting the councillor in local government: some ways forward*, Luton: Local Government Management Board.

Stewart, J. D. (1995), 'The internal management of local authorities', in J. Stewart and G. Stoker (eds), *Local Government in the 1990s*, Basingstoke: Palgrave Macmillan.

Stillman, R. J. II (1977), 'The city manager: professional helping hand, or political hired hand?' *Public Administration Review*, 37, November/December, pp. 659–70.

Stoker, G. (1996), 'Introduction. normative theories of local government and democracy', in D. King and G. Stoker (eds), *Rethinking Local Democracy*, Basingstoke: Macmillan.

—— (1999), 'Introduction: the unintended costs and benefits of New Management Reform for British local government', in G. Stoker (ed.), *The New Management of British Local Government*, Basingstoke: Macmillan.

Stoker, G., F. Gains, P. John, N. Rao and A. Harding (2003), *Implementing the 2000 Act with Respect to New Council Constitutions and the Ethical Framework: First Report*, Manchester: IPEG.

Stone, C. N. (1989), *Regime Politics*, Lawrence: University Press of Kansas.

—— (1995), 'Political leadership in urban politics', in D. Judge, G. Stoker and H. Wolman (eds), *Theories of Urban Politics*, London: Sage.

—— (2005), 'Civic Capacity – What, Why, and from Whence?' in S. Fuhrman and M. Lazerson (eds), *The Public Schools*, New York: Oxford University Press, pp. 209–34.

Stone, C. N. and D. Worgs (2004), *Community Building and a Human-Capital Agenda in Hampton, Virginia: A Case Analysis of the Policy Process in a Medium-Size City*, Working Paper, Institute of Public Policy, Washington, DC: George Washington University.

Streib, G. and T. Poister (1990), 'Strategic planning in US cities: patterns of use, perceptions of effectiveness and an assessment of strategic capacity', *American Review of Public Administration*, 20, pp. 29–44.

Strömberg, L. and J. Westerståhl (1984), *The New Swedish Communes*, Göteborg: Department of Political Science, University of Göteborg. Research Reports 1984:1.

Stuurgroep Evaluatie Dualisering Gemeentebestuur (2004), *Aangelegd om in vrijheid samen te werken. Dualisering: bijsturing geboden*, Den Haag: Stuurgroep Evaluatie Dualisering Gemeentebestuur.

Svara, J. H. (1994), *Facilitative Leadership in Local Government*, San Francisco, CA: Jossey-Bass.

—— (1990), *Official Leadership in the City: Patterns of Conflict and Cooperation*, New York: Oxford University Press.

—— (1998), 'The politics-administration dichotomy model as aberration', *Public Administration Review*, 58, January/February, pp. 51–8.

—— (1999a), 'US city managers and administrators in a global perspective', *Municipal Year Book 1999*, Washington: International City Management Association, pp. 25–33.

—— (1999b), 'The shifting boundary between elected officials and city managers in large council-manager cities', *Public Administration Review*, 59, January/February, pp. 44–53.

—— (2001), 'Do we still need model charters? The meaning and relevance of reform in the twenty-first century', *National Civic Review*, 90, Spring, pp. 19–33.

—— (2003), *Two Decades of Continuity and Change in American City Councils*, Washington: National League of Cities.

Svara, J. H. and Associates (1994), *Facilitative Leadership in Local Government: Lessons from Successful Mayors and Chairpersons in the Council-Manager Form*, San Francisco, CA: Jossey-Bass Publishers.

Svenska Kommunförbundet (2000), *Kommunpolitikern – om demokratin*, Stockholm: Svenska Kommunförbundet och Landstingsförbundet.

Swiss Federal Statistical Office (2000a), *Amtliches Gemeindeverzeichnis der Schweiz*, Neuchâtel: SFSO.

Swiss Federal Statistical Office (2000b), *Permanent Resident Population by Municipality in 1998*, Neuchâtel: SFSO.

Thoenig, J.-C. (1996), 'Pouvoirs et contrepouvoirs locaux: rendre la démocratie aux citoyens', in *La décentralisation en France*, Paris: La Découverte.

—— (1999), 'L'action publique locale entre autonomie et coopération', in *Quel avenir pour l' autonomie des collectivités locales?* Paris: Editions de l' Aube.

Thomsen, J. P. F (2000), *Magt og indflydelse*, Århus: Magtudredningen.

Vander Meer, F. M. and Roborgh, L. J. (1993), *Ambtenaren in Nederland: omvang, bureaucratisering en representativiteit van het ambtelijk apparaat*, Samsom H. D.: Tjeenk Willink, Alphen aan den Rijn.

Värna, K. and B. Örnfelt (2003), *Långlivade förvaltningschefer – strategier som verkar utan att synas*, Göteborg: Göteborgs universitet, Förvaltningsskolans rapporter. Rapport 48.

VVSG (2003), *Amendement van de Vereniging van Vlaamse Steden en Gemeenten bij het ontwerp-gemeentedecreet*, Brussels.

Weaver, K. R. and B. A. Rockman (eds) (1993), *Do Institutions Matter? Government Capabilities in the United States and Abroad*, Washington, DC: The Brookings Institution.

Weber, M. (1922 [1971]), *Makt og byråkrati*, Oslo: Gyldendal Norsk Forlag.

Wehling, H. G. (1982), 'Die Süddeutsche Ratsverfassung in Baden-Württemberg uind Bayern', in G. Püttner (ed.), *Handbuch der komunalen Wissenschaft und Praxis*, edn, Vol. 2, Berlin: Sprilnger, pp. 230–40.

Wehling, H. G. (1989), 'Politische Partizipation in der Kommunalpolitik', in *Archiv für Kommunalwissenschaften*, 1989, Hbb. 1, pp. 110–19.

Wehling, H.-G. and H.-J. Siewert (1987), *Der Bürgermeister in Baden-Württemberg*, 2nd edn, Stuttgart ui.a.: Jkohlhammer.

Wheare, Sir K. C. (1955), *Government by Committee: An Essay on the British Constitution*, Oxford, Clarendon Press.

Widdicombe, D. (1986), *Committee of Inquiry into the Conduct of Local Authority Business, Report*, Cmnd 9798, London, HMSO.

Wilson, D. and C. Game (2002), *Local Government in the United Kingdom*, Basingstoke: Palgrave Macmillan.

Wilson, J. Q. (1962), *The Amateur Democrat*, Chicago, IL: University of Chicago Press.

Winkler–Haupt, U. (1989), 'Die Auswirkungen unterschiedlicher kommunaler Führungsorganisationstypen auf den Policy-Output', in D. Schminanke (ed.), *Stadtdirektor oder Bürgermeister*, Basel: Birkhäuser, pp. 143–60.

Wollmann, H. (2000a), 'Local government systems: from historic divergence towards convergence? Great Britain, France and Germany as cases in point', *Government and Policy*, 18, pp. 33–55.

—— (2000b), 'The development and present state of local government in England and Germany – a Comparison', in H. Wollmann and E. Schröter (eds), *Comparing Public Sector Reform in Britain and Germany*, Aldershot: Ashgate, pp. 107–31.

—— (2000c), 'Local government modernization in Germany: between incrementalism and reform waves', *Public Administration*, 78(4), pp. 915–36.

Wollmann, H. (2002a), 'Recent democratic and administrative reforms in Germany's local government: persistence and change', in J. Caulfield and H. O. Larsen (eds), *Local Government at the Millennium*, Opladen: Leske and Budrich, pp. 63–92.

—— (2002b), 'Local government and politics in East Germany', *German Politics*, 11(3), pp. 153–78, reprinted in W. Gellner and J. Robertson (eds) (2003), *The Berlin Republic. German Unification and a Decade of Changes*, London: Frank Cass, pp. 153–8.

—— (2003a), 'Co-ordination in intergovernmental setting', in G. Peters and J. Pierre, *Handbook of Public Administration*, London: Sage, pp. 594–606.

—— (2003b), 'The directly elected (chief executive) mayor and local leadership in German local government in comparative perspective', *Kunnallistieteellinnen Aikakauiskirja*, no. 2, pp. 126–43.

—— (2004), 'Urban leadership in German local politics: the rise, role and performance of the directly elected, chief executive, mayor', *International Journal of Urban and Regional Research*, 28(1), pp. 150–65.

Wolman, H. (1995), 'Local government institutions and democratic governance', in D. Judge, G. Stoker and H. Wolman (eds), *Theories of Urban Politics*, London: Sage.

Worms, J.-P. (1966), 'Le préfet et ses notables', *Sociologie du travail*, 8(3).

Yates, D. (1977), *The Ungovernable City*, Cambridge, MA: MIT Press.

Yee, G. (2003), 'From court street to city hall: governance change in the Boston public schools,' in J. G. Cibulka and W. L. Boyd (eds), *A Race Against Time*, Westport, CT, Praeger, pp. 83–105.

Young, K. (2000), 'Opportunities, constraints and "the Right to Represent" ' , in N. Rao (ed.) *Representation and Community in Western Democracies*, Basingstoke: Macmillan, pp. 194–216.

Young, K. and N. Rao (1994), *Coming to Terms with Change: The Local Government Councillor in 1993*, York: Joseph Rowntree Foundation.

Index